weird but true!

WORLD
2024

Incredible facts, awesome photos,
and weird wonders—
for this year and beyond!

NATIONAL GEOGRAPHIC
WASHINGTON, D.C.

CONTENTS

I'm a great listener!

CONTENTS

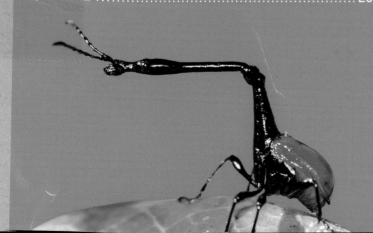

INTRODUCTION

IT'S A WEIRD WORLD OUT THERE ...
and we're here to show you how strange it is!
Our planet is packed with weird and wonderful, strange and peculiar, funny and outrageous sights. In this book, we've brought together some of the weirdest stuff our world has to offer. Prepare to take a remarkable trip to the farthest reaches of every continent. Then dive into the ocean and jet off into space to find out about things that truly are out of this world!

You want weird? You've come to the right place!

FINDING YOUR WAY AROUND

Before you pack your bags for the journey of a lifetime, find out what's **Weird This Year** in Chapter 1. For 2024, we've got the weirdest jobs, inventions, animals, photos, and news the world has to offer. Then travel around the globe one continent at a time. Marvel at **Weird Wonders,** meet unusual animals that are **Oddly Cute,** crunch the numbers in our special features, and find out **What's Weird About This?** Test yourself with quizzes along the way, and find out what your answers reveal about **your personality.** There's so much more weirdness in store, and the only way to find out about it is to turn that page.

Let the adventure begin!

WEIRD in the WORLD

A giant ball, whirling through **SPACE**, covered in **WATER** and a few patches of **LAND** (or continents, as we call them). What a **PECULIAR** place to live!

The **WORLD** has a **LOT** of **ISLANDS**—**HUNDREDS OF THOUSANDS** of them! However, only around **11,000** have people living on them.

If you could **WALK AROUND THE WORLD NONSTOP**, it would take about **A YEAR**.

ARCTIC

NORTH AMERICA

ATLANTIC OCEAN

Equator

SOUTH AMERICA

PACIFIC OCEAN

Jump on the weird wagon!

SOUTHERN

MOST of the world's DINOSAUR FOSSILS have been found in North America, Asia, and South America.

The PACIFIC OCEAN is so big, it takes UP ABOUT A THIRD OF THE PLANET.

Earth is NOT a PERFECT SPHERE: The areas near the EQUATOR BULGE OUTWARD.

Nauru is the world's smallest island country, just four miles (6.5 km) long and two miles (3.2 km) across.

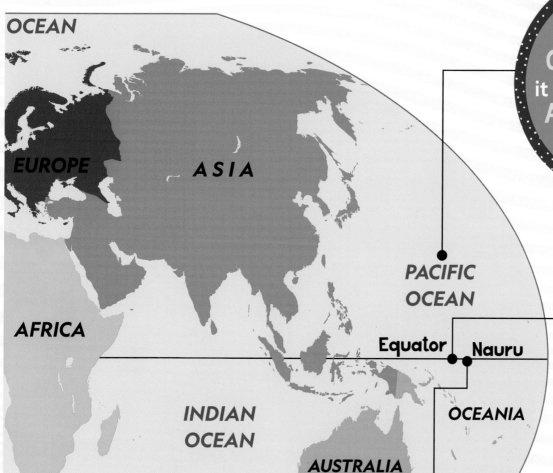

OCEAN

EUROPE

ASIA

AFRICA

PACIFIC OCEAN

Equator   Nauru

OCEANIA

INDIAN OCEAN

AUSTRALIA

OCEAN

ANTARCTICA

WEIRD THIS YEAR

It's a wide world of weird!

If you're on the lookout for the WEIRDEST, strangest, and most bizarre things in the world, you've come to the right place!

13

SAVE THE DATE 2024

These days, there's a special day for almost everything, but some are a little weirder than others! As 2024 goes by, don't forget to celebrate these curious and quirky dates...

JANUARY 3

FESTIVAL OF SLEEP DAY

Sometimes you just don't feel like getting out of bed—so don't! That's the message of Festival of Sleep Day, designed to help everyone make up for any late nights over the winter holiday season.

FEBRUARY 19

INTERNATIONAL TUG-OF-WAR DAY

One of the simplest sports you can imagine, tug-of-war dates back to ancient times. All you need is a rope and a line on the ground. Put a team on each end, and pull!

MARCH 18

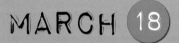

NATIONAL AWKWARD MOMENTS DAY

We've all done it—messaged the wrong person, giggled at something deadly serious, or even passed gas in an elevator. But don't worry. If you're prone to awkward moments, March 18 is your day, so own it!

MAY 9

NATIONAL LOST SOCK MEMORIAL DAY (U.S.A.)

Everyone's experienced having a nice matching pair of socks but ending up with only one. Where do lost socks go? It's a mystery! On this day, take a moment to remember those much missed foot coverings. You could celebrate by making their left-behind partners into cute sock puppets!

APRIL 9

NATIONAL UNICORN DAY

It's no surprise that the one-horned magical creature of myth and legend has its own dedicated day. Celebrate by reading a book about unicorns, making a unicorn cake, or even spending the whole day dressed as a unicorn!

JUNE 27

INTERNATIONAL PINEAPPLE DAY

Hawaii is well known for growing pineapples, but did you know they are originally from South America? In Hawaiian, the pineapple is called *hala kahiki,* which means "foreign fruit." Today, they have their own day on June 27. It's the perfect time to dish up a pineapple-topped pizza!

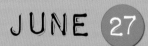

JULY (2)

WORLD UFO DAY

According to UFO fans, on July 2, 1947, a mysterious flying saucer crashed in Roswell, New Mexico, U.S.A. The story has been officially debunked, but its date is the inspiration for World UFO Day, when UFO lovers watch the skies in hopes of spotting an alien flyby.

AUGUST (30)

NATIONAL SLINKY DAY

The Slinky, a toy made from a simple metal or plastic spring that can "walk" down steps, was invented by U.S. Navy engineer Richard James in 1943. He was inspired to create it after seeing a spring fall off a shelf. Since then, millions and millions have been sold. If you have one, this is the day to get it out and play!

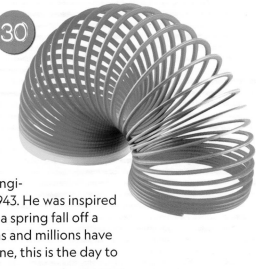

SEPTEMBER (28)

ASK A STUPID QUESTION DAY

There's no such thing as a stupid question, right? Teachers invented this day so that kids could ask anything, even if they're worried it might sound dumb. Why do we have eyebrows? Do dogs know they're dogs? Where did question marks come from? Don't be shy—just ask!

OCTOBER (26)

HOWL AT THE MOON DAY (AND NIGHT!)

This isn't just a day for howling at the moon (though you can if you want to!). It's a day to celebrate and learn about wolves. Did you know that wolves don't actually howl at the moon? They're just calling each other. *Awoooooooo!*

NOVEMBER (19)

WORLD TOILET DAY

Toilets might not seem special, but they have an important job! They wash away waste and help us stay safe from germs, but in some parts of the world, not everyone has access to a toilet. This day reminds us to love our toilets and to campaign for everyone to have them.

DECEMBER (16)

CHOCOLATE-COVERED ANYTHING DAY

The name says it all—to celebrate, all you have to do is dip your favorite foods in melted chocolate! Chocolate-covered strawberries and pretzels are popular treats. You could even try something a little more unusual—like cheese or chips!

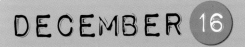

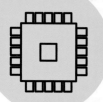

WEIRD FUTURE

What weird inventions, gadgets, and contraptions could be waiting for you in the future? Lots of futuristic tech is already being developed and designed. You don't have to wait until 2054 to take a sneak peak!

Robot Pets

Some robot pets have been around for a while, like the Tamagotchi and Sony's Aibo robot dog. But the robot pets of the future will be different—just as much fun but a lot more lifelike! The Moflin pet, for example, is furry and cuddly, and it can wriggle around and snuggle up to you. It's soft, warm, and makes cute squeaking sounds as it interacts with you. It can also sense its surroundings, so it will learn to recognize you, try to get close to you, and develop its own personality. And it sleeps (while recharging) in its own special pet basket! So what kind of creature is it? It's about the size of a guinea pig, but a Moflin isn't designed to look like any particular type of animal ... it's just a cuddly bundle of fur!

SCIENTISTS HAVE FOUND THAT CUDDLY **ROBOT PETS** CAN REDUCE STRESS AND MAKE PEOPLE FEEL HAPPY AND COMFORTED, JUST LIKE REAL PETS.

Time for cuddles!

Flying Cars

All good sci-fi movies have flying cars, and we've been dreaming about them becoming an everyday reality for decades. So could they be coming at last? Well, flying cars do already exist, and you could be using one soon! The most popular designs are similar to extra-large, people-carrying drones. Drones are lifted off the ground by several small rotors that are attached to a motor. Flying cars like GM's Cadillac VTOL work the same way, with several mini rotors around a small passenger cabin. As long as your destination has a rooftop landing pad, you can zip around the city in minutes! But wait—what if you're not a pilot? Not a problem! These drones will be self-driving and voice-controlled. You just tell your flying car where you want to go, and it does the rest!

FLYING CARS HAVE APPEARED IN MYTHS, LEGENDS, AND STORIES SINCE ANCIENT TIMES. THEY ARE EVEN FEATURED IN INDIAN WRITINGS FROM MORE THAN 3,000 YEARS AGO.

Haptic Suits

Maybe you've already played a game using a virtual reality headset. They let you see and explore a virtual world all around you, but with most VR sets, you can't really feel your environment. That's changing, thanks to haptic suits. Haptic, or touch, technology refers to clothing, gloves, and helmets containing moving parts that can squeeze, shake, or move your body to help you experience the virtual world as completely as possible. Whether you're escaping from an earthquake, getting splatted by an exploding alien, or being chased by a dragon, it will seem almost real!

SURPRISING STATS

The **MOST PUPPIES** ever born in **ONE LITTER** is **24,** to Neapolitan mastiff mom Tia in **2004.**

On average, IT TAKES ABOUT **12 SECONDS** to count to **24.** Try it!

A TESSERACT is a shape with **24 FACES,** or **FLAT SURFACES.** However, it's **FOUR-DIMENSIONAL** and **IMPOSSIBLE** to build in our **3D WORLD.**

In 2012, a truck driver **forgot to shut his back door all the way** and spilled **24 tons** (21.8 t) of sardines onto the road. **Oops!**

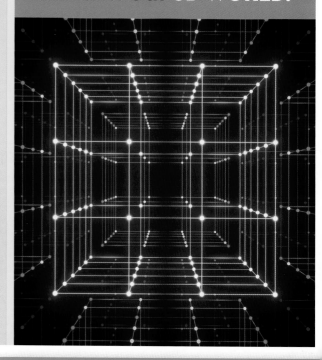

ABOUT THE NUMBER 24

MOVIES RUN AT **24 FRAMES PER SECOND**, WHICH MEANS **EVERY SECOND** IS MADE UP OF **24 FRAMES**, OR IMAGES.

OXANA SEROSHTAN SET A RECORD FOR **TIGHTROPE WALKING IN HIGH HEELS,** BALANCING THE LENGTH OF **24 FEET 7.2 INCHES (7.5 M)** AND BACK AGAIN.

A **SHAPE WITH 24 SIDES** is called an **ICOSITETRAGON.**

Manjit Singh holds the record for **LIFTING THE MOST WEIGHT** with his **EYE SOCKETS: 52.9 POUNDS** (24 kg).

DON'T TRY THESE AT HOME!

BUDIMIR ŠOBAT set the record for the longest time anyone has **HELD THEIR BREATH: 24 MINUTES AND 37 SECONDS.**

WEIRDEST JOBS IN THE WORLD
RUNNERS-UP...

There's more than one way to make a living in 2024, and some of them are extra cool, creative, unusual, and just plain weird. Check out these amazing ways to earn a wage!

Hope the crust isn't soggy!

Pizza Delivery Diver

That's right—DIVER, not driver! That's what you need when you order a pizza while staying in an underwater hotel! Jules' Undersea Lodge in Key Largo, Florida, U.S.A., used to be an underwater science research lab, but it's now used as a very unusual place for guests to stay. To get in, you have to dive 21 feet (6.4 m) down into the depths of a fish-filled lagoon—and once you're inside, it's not very easy to head out for a snack. The lodge does have a kitchen, but if you want a pizza delivery, you can have one. The delivery diver will fetch the pizza, lock it in a watertight box, and take the plunge!

Pet Food Tester

Before a new pet food is given the go-ahead to be sold in stores, someone has to make sure that it tastes OK. If you're a pet food tester, that's you! You have to actually take a (small) mouthful of dog or cat food and inspect it for taste, texture, and smell to make sure it's truly good enough to be placed in front of someone's beloved companion. Luckily, you can spit it out—you don't have to swallow it. Phew! And that's not all there is to this job (so you don't have to chow down on cat food all day long!). You also help come up with recipes for new foods and write information about them for pet owners. Still, some people might prefer to be chocolate or cookie testers instead!

⭐ Bike Fisher

If you're good at catching stuffed toys with a crane claw machine, you could make a great bike fisher in Amsterdam! This city in the Netherlands is famous for its many canals, and it's also one of the world's most cycling-friendly places. Thousands of bikes end up falling into the canals every year. They can block the canals and damage boats. So the city has a team of bike fishers. They use a boat with a giant claw—just like the arcade game, but much bigger! They make their way along the waterways, plunging the claw in to grab whatever they can find and dredging up bikes by the dozen!

THE WORLD'S LONGEST BICYCLE IS 155 FEET 8 INCHES (47.5 M) LONG BUT CAN BE RIDDEN BY JUST ONE PERSON!

⭐ Professional Zombie

Zombies are big business! Zombie-themed movies and TV shows are popular around the world, and some theme parks feature zombie thrill rides. You can even take part in an immersive zombie adventure, where you get chased by zombies and have to escape. All these things need zombie actors. In fact, sometimes hundreds of them are needed for the biggest zombie attacks and crowd scenes. So there are now more than a few people who make a living being a zombie during working hours. There are even zombie schools where you can learn to apply zombie makeup and perfect your wails and grunts and scary, shuffling walk. If you love zombies and horror, it could be the best job ever!

ZOMBIE FANS ARE KNOWN AS "ZOMBOPHILES."

WEIRDEST JOBS IN THE WORLD

And the Winner Is ...

Dog Surf Instructor

WINNER

What's more fun than surfing?

Surfing with your dog! In fact, in addition to jumping on a board with their owners, dogs can be trained to surf on their own boards. They just need a little help to catch the wave, then off they go! At a dog surf training school, instructors combine their surfing skills and dog training expertise, along with treats and rewards, to get water-loving pooches balancing on surfboards and riding the waves in style. While some dogs never get their sea legs, others are naturals—and the top dogs can even compete in surfing contests!

SUPERSTAR DOG SURFER ABBIE GIRL HOLDS THE RECORD FOR FARTHEST DISTANCE SURFED— 351 FEET 8 INCHES (107.2 M)!

WEIRDEST ANIMALS
RUNNERS-UP ...

Scientists have discovered all kinds of creepy, curious, and kooky-looking creatures, and they're still finding more! Meet a few of the strangest animals out there this year ...

Hooded Seal

You may have seen a cartoon seal balancing a ball on its nose. But for this seal, the red ball IS its nose! Hooded seals live in the cold North Atlantic and Arctic Oceans and are famous for their bad temper. The males have not one, but two, inflatable balloons on their heads: a dark, furry one on top of the head and a bright-red inflatable left nostril. They blow them up into bizarre-looking balls to show off to females and to warn other males that they're ready to fight. If that doesn't work, the male shakes his red nose balloon up and down!

Check out this stylish schnoz!

HOODED SEALS CAN USE THEIR INFLATABLE SNOUTS TO MAKE **PINGING** AND WHOOSHING SOUNDS.

Giant Isopod

You're probably familiar with wood lice or pill bugs—those small gray creepy-crawlies that live under stones or dead leaves. Now imagine a pill bug that's 50 times bigger, with sharp claws, munching jaws, and reflective eyes that look like shiny metal! This monster pill bug cousin, which grows up to 20 inches (51 cm) long, is a real creature called the giant isopod. Don't have nightmares—you're not likely to meet one since they live on the deep seafloor, where they mostly hang out waiting for dead animals to drift down from above to provide them with lunch. However, one extra-bold isopod was spotted attacking and snacking on a shark's face! So if you do ever encounter one, treat it with respect.

Orchid Mantis

Clambering through the undergrowth of a Southeast Asian tropical forest, you might be delighted to see this beautiful pink-and-white flower. And then amazed when the flower suddenly grabs a butterfly and eats it! It's actually not a flower at all, but a female orchid mantis with an incredible disguise. Her four back legs have large petal-shaped parts on them, and she can change sections of her body to pink, green, or brown to resemble various kinds of nectar-filled flowers, including orchids. Hungry nectar-loving insects make a beeline for what they think is their next meal, and SNAP! They become lunch themselves!

Asian Sheepshead Wrasse

When you see this fish from behind, it looks like most other fish. But its face is another story! The big bump on its head looks like a giant pink nose, and its wide toothy grin and ginormous chin give it a strange clownlike appearance. (Despite its name, it doesn't look much like a sheep, unless you know some very odd sheep!) These large ocean fish are intelligent and friendly, too. One female sheepshead wrasse, known as Yoriko, made friends with a Japanese diver and came to hang out with him every time he went diving.

WEIRDEST ANIMALS
And the Winner Is ...

WINNER

Honduran White Bat

This could be the cutest bat in the world, as well as one of the weirdest!
Its body is the size of a chicken egg, and it looks like a miniature cuddly toy with its white, fluffy fur and bright yellow ears, nose, and wings. Even cuter, it sleeps in a tent! Honduran white bats are also called the tent-making bats because they chew large leaves along the middle to make them fold down into a tent shape. During the day, they cuddle up together inside their tent to sleep, then fly out at night to feed on juicy figs.

THE HONDURAN WHITE BAT HAS A LITTLE SPIKE ON ITS NOSE, SHAPED LIKE A POINTY LEAF.

THE BAT'S
SKIN IS YELLOW
BECAUSE OF CHEMICALS
IN THE FIGS IT EATS.

It's a
weird BAT
true
world!

27

WEIRDEST PHOTOS
RUNNERS-UP ...

Here's a selection of strange and stunning sights from around the world, caught on camera. But which is the most mind-blowing?

Leaf Sheep

Could any critter be cuter than this little leaf sheep? It has two dot eyes, a pair of sheeplike horns, and what look like leaves all over its back! However, it's not a sheep—or a plant. It's a tiny sea slug that grows only 0.4 inch (1 cm) long. It eats green algae, like a sheep grazing on grass. The parts of the algae that can photosynthesize, or turn sunlight into food, end up in the slug's "leaves," where they keep doing the same job, giving the leaf sheep extra energy. It's one of the few animals that can feed on sunlight like a plant does!

LEAF SHEEP LIVE ONLY UP TO 59 FEET (18 M) BENEATH THE OCEAN'S SURFACE, WHERE SUNLIGHT CAN STILL REACH THEM.

Waves in the Sky

These cool clouds look like waves on a stormy ocean breaking across the sky. Although they're rare, this type of cloud has a name: Kelvin-Helmholtz clouds. They form when two layers of air are blowing along at different speeds: slower air below and faster air above. The faster air above the cloud can drag it up and forward to make wave shapes. Look for them on windy days, especially around sunrise and sunset.

Glowing Termite Towers

This termite mound in the grasslands of Brazil looks as if it's been decorated with string lights! In fact, the light is coming from thousands of click beetle larvae, or babies, that live in little holes in the surface of the mound. They are bioluminescent, meaning that they can glow. On damp nights, they wave their glowing bodies out of their holes to attract prey, which includes flying termites and ants. When the bugs come close enough, they get snapped up!

Tree With a Face

If you were walking through a forest and saw a tree with a face, it might spook you! But look closely—the face doesn't belong to the tree, but to an expertly camouflaged owl. This is the great gray owl, found mainly in the conifer forests of the far north. Its gray-and-brown-speckled feathers blend in perfectly with the rough conifer tree trunks. In fact, only its eyes and face give it away. When it turns its back, it seems to disappear!

WEIRDEST PHOTOS

And the Winner Is ...

Man in the Moon

This incredible photo shows stunt performer and extreme sportsman Andy Lewis slacklining in the dark between two desert towers in Utah, U.S.A—with the ginormous full moon in the background! Setting up the shot took months of planning and lots of luck waiting for the right weather, combined with the full moon in the right position. It was taken from a distance to make the moon appear bigger.

WINNER

FOR MONTHS, PHOTOGRAPHER RENAN OZTURK'S EFFORTS TO CAPTURE THE PERFECT SHOT WERE DELAYED BY POOR TIMING OR CLOUDS.

BY the NUMBERS

A WORLD OF DIFFERENCE!

So many amazing things have happened around you in the past 365 days without you even realizing it. Don't believe us? Check out these numbers. It's amazing what can happen to the world in just one year—and 2024 is no exception!

IN THE YEAR THAT HAS JUST GONE BY, EARTH (ALONG WITH ALL OF US) HAS TRAVELED **584 MILLION MILES** (940 MILLION KM) THROUGH SPACE.

SINCE **ONE YEAR AGO TODAY,** ABOUT **139 MILLION** NEW HUMANS HAVE BEEN **BORN.**

ON AVERAGE, WE EXPERIENCE
4 SOLAR ECLIPSES
IN A YEAR, WHEN THE **MOON** BLOCKS OUT THE **SUN.**
2024, HOWEVER, WILL HAVE ONLY **2.**

IN THE PAST YEAR,
8,760 HOURS
HAVE TICKED BY. THAT'S **525,600** MINUTES,
OR **31,536,000** SECONDS!

AND FOR AT LEAST
ONE-THIRD OF THAT TIME,
YOU HAVE BEEN **FAST ASLEEP.**
THAT'S MORE THAN **121 DAYS,**
OR **FOUR MONTHS,** OF SNOOZING!

WEIRD NEWS
FROM AROUND THE WORLD

**What's the scoop in the wide world of weird?
Check out these curious and hilarious headlines!**

BADGER STRIKES IT RICH

ASTURIAS, SPAIN

Archaeologists in Spain have a European badger to thank for unearthing a horde of Roman coins. The coins were found next to the badger's burrow, where it had probably been rooting around for food after a cold, snowy winter. Instead, the hungry critter dug up the 1,600-year-old loot. Unable to eat the coins, it scattered them around, leading to an exciting find for the experts.

ANCIENT GREEK YEARBOOK

ATHENS, GREECE

When you graduate from school, it's fun to find yourself in the school yearbook ... but did you know that the ancient Greeks did the same thing? When the writing on this 2,000-year-old Athenian stone tablet was finally decoded, it turned out to be a list of names of a class of boys about 18 years old, who had completed a year of training. Sadly, they had to make do without photos!

A WHALE OF A TIME!

ANDØYA, NORWAY

If you love whales, head to this new museum in the north of Norway, opening in 2023. The building itself looks like a whale's back surfacing from the sea, and its windows resemble the baleen, or sieves, in a whale's enormous mouth. You can even climb up on top of it to look for real whales in the ocean nearby!

BIRDS CAN VOTE

CORNWALL, ENGLAND

Jackdaws are already known to be smart, and now scientists have discovered that they can vote! They studied jackdaws to find out how a flock of thousands know when to suddenly take off from a tree all at the same time. Each bird makes a large croaking call when it wants to leave. If the noise from lots of jackdaws doing this is loud enough, it triggers them all to take to the air. Jackdaw-mocracy in action!

EARS OF THE YEAR!

KARACHI, PAKISTAN

When Simba the baby goat was born in Pakistan, he blew everyone away—with his incredible ears! They measured 19 inches (48 cm) long at birth and just kept growing, making Simba an internet sensation. They're so long that teeny Simba trips over them, so proud owner Mohammad Hassan Narejo has given him a little bag he can wear to safely store them. He's also hoping Simba will set a new Guinness World Record for longest-eared goat. No kidding!

LOST WORLD

HUBEI, CHINA

Chinese scientists have discovered something BIG—a massive hole! China's countryside actually has lots of sinkholes: huge holes in the ground that form when the roof of a cave collapses. This new find is more than 630 feet (192 m) deep, and when an adventurous team climbed down inside, they found a pristine ancient forest, caves, and lakes at the bottom. They're planning new studies to see what kinds of unknown plant and animal species might be living there. Watch this space! (Or hole ...)

NAME ACCLAIM

TENNESSEE, U.S.A.

Millipedes aren't known to move very swiftly—and the Swift twisted-claw millipede, or *Nannaria swiftae,* is no exception. So how did it get its name? It was named for music superstar Taylor Swift, because the scientist who discovered it is a big fan! However, it's not the first bug with a name inspired by a singer. There's a fly named for Beyoncé, a treehopper named for Lady Gaga, and a wasp named for Elvis Presley!

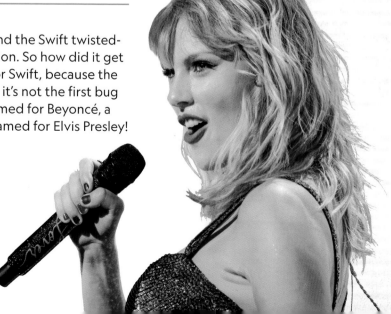

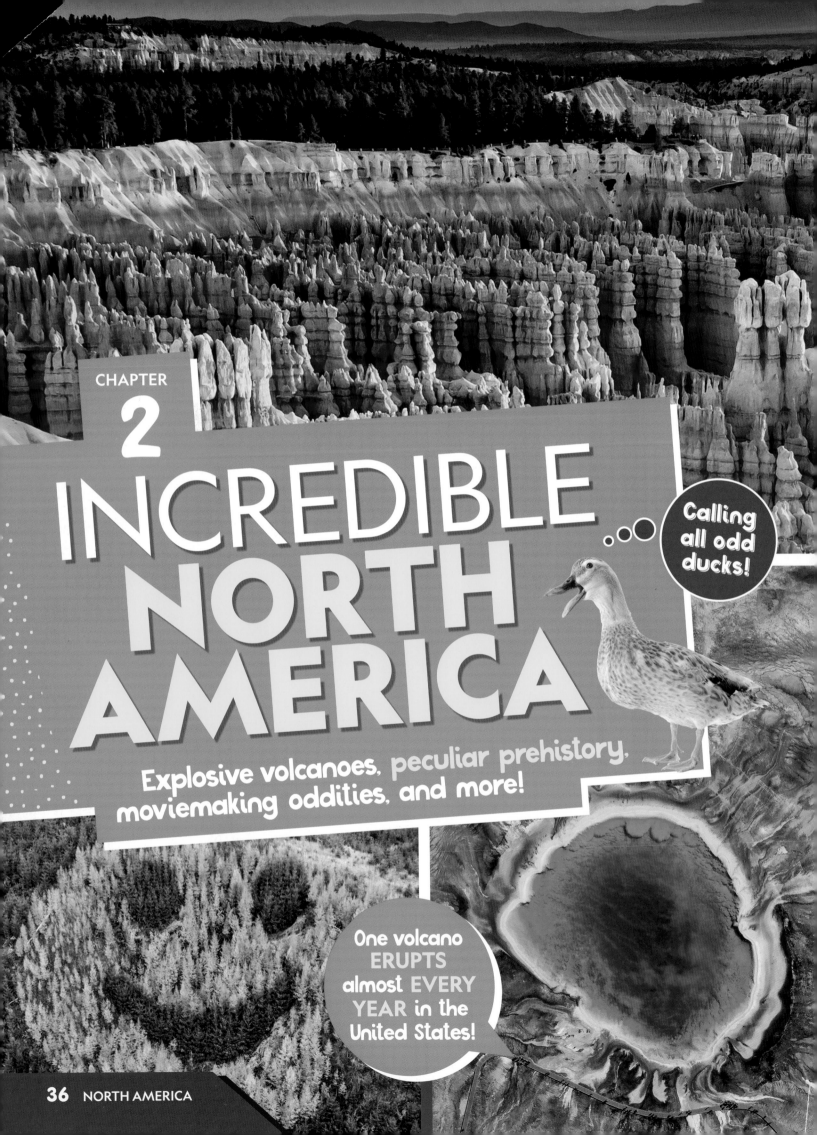

INCREDIBLE NORTH AMERICA

Explosive volcanoes, peculiar prehistory, moviemaking oddities, and more!

Calling all odd ducks!

One volcano **ERUPTS** almost **EVERY YEAR** in the United States!

When this **UNUSUAL SPORT** first began, riders slid on some strange "sleds," including **A TABLE, A MATTRESS, AND EVEN A SMALL FRIDGE!**

In 1972, **SCIENTISTS** making a model of the now extinct *Opabinia* **BURST OUT LAUGHING** once they saw how **WEIRD** it looked!

WORLD'S ONLY
CORN PALA

WEIRD in the WORLD

Whether it's a natural **QUIRK** or manufactured **STRANGENESS**, North America is packed with odd **PLACES, ANIMALS,** and **INVENTIONS.**

The Bay of Fundy has the highest tidal range in the world. From low tide to high tide, the water level can rise by an incredible **52.5 feet (16 m).**

The world's largest **hamburger**—on sale at Mallie's Sports Grill & Bar in Michigan—weighs **1,800 pounds** (816.5 kg) and costs a whopping **$10,000!**

The world's largest single living organism is a fungus in Oregon called the honey mushroom, which measures **3.4 miles** (5.5 km) across.

ATLANTIC OCEAN

Bay of Fundy

Mallie's Sports Grill & Bar

Greenland (Kalaallit Nunaat) (Denmark)

ARCTIC OCEAN

CANADA

Alaska (U.S.)

Oregon

PACIFIC OCEAN

NORTH AMERICA

ASIA
Arctic Ocean
EUROPE
AFRICA
Atlantic Ocean
SOUTH AMERICA
Pacific Ocean

Panama is the only country where you can stand on the same spot and watch the sun rise on the Pacific Ocean and set on the Atlantic Ocean.

THE BAHAMAS
West Indies
CUBA
HAITI
DOMINICAN REPUBLIC
JAMAICA
Caribbean Sea
BELIZE
HONDURAS
NICARAGUA
GUATEMALA
EL SALVADOR
COSTA RICA
PANAMA

Gulf of Mexico

MEXICO

UNITED STATES
San Francisco

The thick, gray mist that sometimes covers San Francisco has a name—Karl the Fog. Karl has a social media account with more than 250,000 followers.

The white baneberry plant found in North America is also known as doll's eyes because of its strange-looking and poisonous fruit.

Here's looking at you, kid!

39

PECULIAR PLACES

Go on—crack a smile!

Smiley Face Forest
Willamina, Oregon, U.S.A.

Drivers traveling on the Oregon Route 18 state highway past Polk County Forest are greeted by a friendly face on the hillside. It's hard to miss this huge smiley, seeing as it has a diameter of 300 feet (91.4 m)—that's almost as big as a soccer field. The forest has been beaming since 2011, when two timber company employees created the face by planting different kinds of trees. The eyes and mouth are Douglas fir trees, and the rest of the face is made from larch. In the fall, the needles on larch trees turn yellow and fall off, which is why that's the best time of year to see this superb smiley. Road-trippers can spot the giant face on the hillside for the next 30 to 50 years, then the fully grown trees will be taken to the sawmill.

IT TOOK LUMBER COMPANY EMPLOYEES A WEEK TO PLAN AND PLANT THE SMILEY FACE.

Pizza Pi
St. Thomas, U.S. Virgin Islands

If you want to attract the waiter's attention at this popular restaurant, do it with a wave! Swimmers at Christmas Cove in St. Thomas can grab a bite during their dip—from a floating pizzeria! Original owners Sasha and Tara Bouis spent two years adding a pizza oven and solar panels to an abandoned boat to create the Pizza Pi. Open every day, a small armada of boats sails up to collect tempting treats from the restaurant's window. The pizzeria also offers a delivery service using a dinghy to distribute food—fast! Customers can munch on a sausage, ham, and bacon pizza or sink their teeth into the Georgia Peacharia, which is topped with mozzarella and peaches!

Lake Kliluk
British Columbia, Canada

Have you ever seen a polka-dotted lake? Travel to the Okanagan Valley in British Columbia, Canada, and you just might. For most of the year, mineral-rich Lake Kliluk—also called Spotted Lake—looks like any other. But during the summer much of the water evaporates, leaving behind yellow, green, and blue polka dots. These dazzling dots get their colors from the minerals left behind, and can vary depending on the type of mineral deposits in a particular spot. Aside from its unusual looks, the lake is also special in another way: It was considered to have special healing powers by the Indigenous people of the Okanagan Nation, who gave the lake its name. Today, the lake is privately owned by the Okanagan Nation Alliance, and is protected for its cultural and ecological significance.

During **World War I,** Lake Kliluk's minerals were collected to make **ammunition.**

Weirdly Cute!
Axolotl Salamander

It might seem strange to "aww" over a slimy, slippery salamander, but axolotls (pronounced ACK-suh-LAH-tuhls) are undeniably cute! Unlike most other salamanders (a type of amphibian), axolotls spend their whole lives in water and are found only in Mexico, in the Xochimilco (pronounced SO-chee-MILL-koh) lake complex. Sadly, axolotls are critically endangered due to pollution, the introduction of invasive fish species, and the demand for axolotls as pets. Nevertheless, axolotls have captured the hearts of many, and scientists are working to save wild axolotls through education efforts and conservation programs.

What's **Weird** About This**?**

Awoooooo!

Sure, this mouse might look like any other—until it throws back its head and lets out a howl! Grasshopper mice, found in prairies and dry areas across North America, communicate over long distances by howling. Their diets are also rather different: Unlike most mice, which tend to eat grains and fruits, grasshopper mice dine on smaller rodents and insects. They've even been known to take on dangerous creatures like scorpions and snakes!

BY the NUMBERS

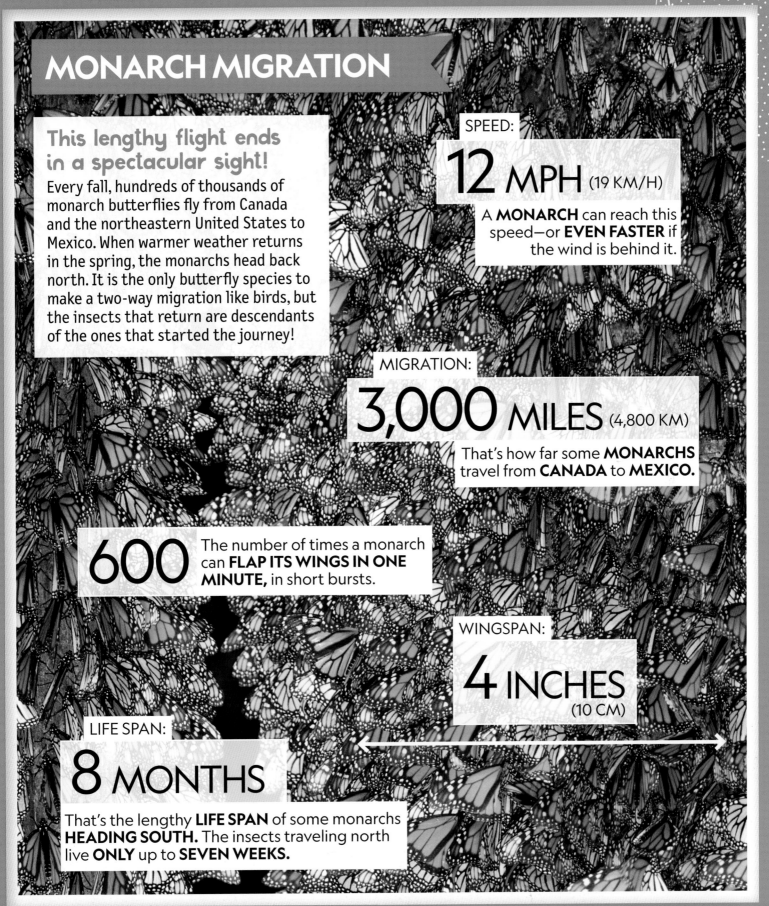

MONARCH MIGRATION

This lengthy flight ends in a spectacular sight!

Every fall, hundreds of thousands of monarch butterflies fly from Canada and the northeastern United States to Mexico. When warmer weather returns in the spring, the monarchs head back north. It is the only butterfly species to make a two-way migration like birds, but the insects that return are descendants of the ones that started the journey!

SPEED:

12 MPH (19 KM/H)

A **MONARCH** can reach this speed—or **EVEN FASTER** if the wind is behind it.

MIGRATION:

3,000 MILES (4,800 KM)

That's how far some **MONARCHS** travel from **CANADA** to **MEXICO.**

600 The number of times a monarch can **FLAP ITS WINGS IN ONE MINUTE,** in short bursts.

WINGSPAN:

4 INCHES (10 CM)

LIFE SPAN:

8 MONTHS

That's the lengthy **LIFE SPAN** of some monarchs **HEADING SOUTH.** The insects traveling north live **ONLY** up to **SEVEN WEEKS.**

BONKERS BUILDINGS

Biomuseo
Panama City, Panama

At the entrance of the Panama Canal, the Biomuseo stands proud in all its colorful glory. The angular building was designed by world-famous architect Frank Gehry. It looks as if the building is rising up from the water. The design reflects the way that Panama began forming millions of years ago as it rose out of the sea, uniting North and South America in the process. This natural history museum is dedicated to Panama's biodiversity and its incredible variety of unique wildlife. Positioned in a 5.9-acre (2.4-ha) botanical park, the building's vivid color attracts clouds of butterflies and moths. Yep, even the bugs are enjoying the vibrant architecture!

THE TEMPERATURE INSIDE THE HOTEL IS ALWAYS BETWEEN 27° AND 41°F (-3° AND 5°C).

Hôtel de Glace
Québec, Canada

Imagine rebuilding a hotel every year. Sounds impossible, right? But that's exactly what happens at Hôtel de Glace. Made entirely from snow and ice, this enchanting crystal palace melts away each spring as temperatures rise, and is then rebuilt in a new form the following winter. A team of between 50 and 100 artists and engineers from all over the world work together to create the new masterpiece, using up to 30,000 tons (27,000 t) of snow and 500 tons (450 t) of ice to build features such as ice sculptures, snow arches, and even an ice slide! Sleeping there isn't as cold as you'd expect thanks to sleeping bags, rugs, and mattresses—some rooms have fireplaces, too.

The World's Only Corn Palace

Mitchell, South Dakota, U.S.A.

Murals are usually made with paint or glass, but one amazing building in South Dakota is adorned with corn instead! Originally constructed in 1892 and rebuilt several times since then, the Corn Palace was designed to celebrate the annual crop-growing season and harvest. Every year, folk artists decorate the walls with an original themed mural. Ancient Egyptian motifs were used in 1911, while space was the 1969 theme—the same year as the first moon landing. The 2022 mural was "Under the Big Top," with circus-themed decor. In the latest murals, university students created designs using 12 shades of naturally colored corn, including brown, red, green, black, and blue!

Welcome to the corniest place on Earth!

Like a **giant** paint-by-numbers kit, the **mural design** is traced onto paper, showing where **each color of corn** should go!

Color-Coded Buildings
Greenland

The colors of Greenland's rainbow villages are part of a secret code! Each building was originally painted depending on its function—green for police and post offices, yellow for hospitals, and so on. Houses were even painted according to the jobs of the people living there. This system was introduced in the 1800s after wooden kit houses had been sent from Scandinavia to Greenland to construct new settlements. The color-coding was meant to help people find their way around before houses were numbered or streets had names. It was also done to make the settlements visible from the sea.

VIBRANT VOLCANOES

Volcano Boarding
Cerro Negro, Nicaragua

I feel the need for speed!

On the slopes of this Central American volcano, what goes up must come down ... fast! When Cerro Negro last erupted, in 1999, boulders tumbled down the western side, while black ash spewed into the air, coating the eastern side. This smooth surface inspired a new activity—volcano boarding! Since 2004, visitors have been renting boards before hiking up a path created by the fallen boulders. The strenuous journey takes an hour in 90°F (32°C) heat, close to craters spewing out stinky sulfur. At the summit, riders put on their jumpsuits and goggles before sitting on their boards and setting off on a rapid five-minute descent. Speeds are measured with a radar gun—a heart-stopping 60 miles an hour (96.6 km/h) is the record. Going that fast has its risks, though, which is why sitting down is safer than standing up for amateurs, and even that is best left to adults. Riders who fall can end up with a jumpsuit full of ash and blistered limbs from the heat!

Río Celeste
Tenorio Volcano National Park, Costa Rica

Surrounded by lush Costa Rican forests, this vibrant river seems to appear out of the blue. And that's fitting, because the Río Celeste is very, very blue. Along the incredible neon turquoise waterway, visitors will find a spectacular waterfall and many hot springs. The main attraction, though, is the Río Celeste's amazing color, which is completely natural. This ultra-blue waterway begins where two colorless rivers meet. Buena Vista River contains a large amount of aluminum and silicon. Sour Creek is highly acidic because it flows near a volcano and is rich in sulfur. When these two rivers join together, their minerals interact and create a vivid blue color. Sightseers should avoid the rainy season, though—sediment carried by heavy rain can turn the water a dull brown!

A local legend claims that **Río Celeste** is so blue because God was **painting the sky**—and dipped the brush in the river!

Craters of the Moon
Idaho, U.S.A.

It's like taking a trip to outer space, without ever leaving Earth! The unusual terrain of Idaho's Craters of the Moon National Monument & Preserve covers 753,000 acres (3,050 sq km)—nearly four times the area of New York City. About 2,000 years ago, magma forced its way up through cracks in the ground. The surface of flowing lava was cooled by the air, creating caves and tunnels made with walls of hardened lava. However, volcanic rock is delicate and breaks easily, so the roofs of lava caves often collapse, revealing passages that were once hidden away! Craters of the Moon is also home to groups of impressive-looking spatter cones. They're formed when the force of an eruption decreases and lava builds up around the vent, forming small, steep-sided structures—a little souvenir of the volcano's immense power.

Yellowstone Supervolcano
Yellowstone National Park, Wyoming, U.S.A.

If a volcano sounds dangerous, then a supervolcano should definitely be avoided, right? Well, not really! The word is used to describe volcanoes that have produced massive eruptions, but that doesn't mean that they erupt frequently. One of the world's most famous supervolcanoes is in Yellowstone National Park. It has had at least three major eruptions in the past. The last was a lengthy 640,000 years ago and may have released more than 240 cubic miles (1,000 cubic km) of material into the sky. Yellowstone's magma reservoir is buried underground, but hot springs on the surface bubble up from the boiling chambers below. With their glorious rainbow colors, these springs are a stunning sight. And it's all thanks to bacteria: As the water spreads out, it cools from the center, creating rings decreasing in temperature. Each ring is home to different types of bacteria. These tiny organisms react in different ways to the sunlight and give the springs their vibrant colors!

COOL CAVES

Stalacpipe Organ
Luray Caverns, Virginia, U.S.A.

These caverns in Virginia are part of a working musical instrument known as the Great Stalacpipe Organ. When the organ is played, rubber mallets tap the stalactites that hang naturally from the cavern ceilings, which make different sounds depending on their size! A scientist and mathematician named Leland W. Sprinkle built the instrument over three years in the 1950s, and it is now a popular tourist stop. It can even be played by an organist for wedding ceremonies.

Covering 3.5 acres (1.4 ha), this is the largest musical instrument in the world.

Ra Paulette's Caves
New Mexico, U.S.A.

This may look like a palace, but it's actually a hand-carved desert cave. And it's all the work of American sculptor Ra Paulette. Found in the desert north of Santa Fe, it's just one of his sandstone masterpieces, transporting visitors to another world. To build them, Paulette tunneled into the soft cliffs by digging and chiseling. Some of his epic templelike creations are 40 feet (12 m) tall—that's as high as a four-story building—with intricate textures and patterns. Each cave is unique, and includes features such as skylights, special spots for candles, and columns. So peaceful are these spaces that some have been used as spiritual retreats for meditation and healing.

It's crystal clear that this cave is weird!

SCIENTISTS ESTIMATE THE CAVES' LARGEST CRYSTAL HAS BEEN GROWING FOR OVER 500,000 YEARS.

Naica Crystal Caves
Chihuahuan Desert, Mexico

These 36-foot (11-m)-long beauties are among the largest natural crystals ever to be discovered. Each one weighs up to 55 tons (49 t), which is about as heavy as nine adult male African elephants. In 2000, a team of miners found the gigantic gypsum crystals 1,000 feet (300 m) beneath Naica Mountain in Mexico, inside a cave now known as the Cave of Crystals. Over thousands of years, a mineral called selenite formed these colossal crystals, thanks to the optimum conditions found within the cave. Immersed in hot, mineral-rich water, the crystals grew and grew to the breathtaking size they are today.

HORSETAIL FALL'S FIREFALL

Yosemite National Park, California, U.S.A.

WEIRD WONDERS

See the optical illusion that turns water into fire!

This narrow waterfall tumbles a dizzying **2,000 FEET** (610 M) down El Capitan's rocks.

This incredible sight is becoming one of Yosemite National Park's most popular attractions. For 11 and a half months of the year, a small waterfall on the side of the 3,000-foot (910-m) rock formation known as El Capitan goes mostly unnoticed. But then, in the last two weeks of February, if the conditions are just right—meaning a clear sky and the presence of enough snow to make the waterfall flow—the setting sun lights up the water so the fall glows bright orange, as if it's on fire. The amazing sight has come to be known as a "firefall," and attracts photographers and visitors from all around the world.

No wonder this site is so flame-ous!

MADCAP MUSEUMS

Neon Museum
Las Vegas, Nevada, U.S.A.

Las Vegas is famed for the vibrant signs that line the Strip, but what happens when those signs are no longer wanted? Many of them end up in the Neon Boneyard. It might sound like a Scooby-Doo location, but it's actually one of the outdoor areas at the Neon Museum. This museum, established in 1996, is dedicated to preserving these sparkling signs from recent history. The boneyard, which is packed with huge light installations from the 1930s to the present day, is best wandered at night, when the restored signs can be seen in their full glory.

The Troll Hole Museum
Alliance, Ohio, U.S.A.

Trolls—magical, cave-dwelling creatures with mops of wild hair—may come from Scandinavian folklore, but thousands of these cute, furry little figures have found their way to the small town of Alliance, Ohio. As of 2018, the Troll Hole Museum was home to a record-breaking 8,130 troll dolls, and the collection has been growing ever since. Today, troll dolls and related memorabilia of all shapes, sizes, and colors fill 14 rooms to the rafters. Here, you can learn everything there is to know about the origins of these fabulous furballs, and meet a host of troll-ified musicians, celebrities, and athletes in a variety of wacky settings, from a pop concert to a pro-football hall of fame.

The Peculiarium

Portland, Oregon, U.S.A.

Described by its owners as an "art gallery dedicated to learning and terror," even the origin story of the FreakyButTrue Peculiarium is a little strange. Supposedly (but who knows if it's true), the adventurer Conrad Talmadge Elwood traveled the world collecting strange and mysterious exhibits! Today, visitors can enjoy a whole host of weird—and not-so-true—wonders, including a dog with three eyes, a haunted dollhouse, Bigfoot, and an alien autopsy scene where you can become the patient! Its collection of creepy life-size mannequins includes Krampus, famous from folktales where he punishes naughty children at Christmas! He was supposed to be a temporary festive exhibit but was so popular with visitors, he's now a permanent resident. Although Krampus is not real, a jokey sign says, "Unattended children will be fed to Krampus!"

Who are you calling peculiar?

Desserts at the Peculiarium café are topped with edible crickets and scorpion pieces!

Gopher Hole Museum

Torrington, Alberta, Canada

If you want to find out what stuffed gophers look like dressed in full costume, then this is the museum for you. Meet the gophers of Torrington, Alberta! The taxidermy has been posed in different mini scenes with beautifully painted backdrops. There are dozens of gophers, all displayed in weird and wonderful costumes in order to show the daily life and history of the town. The creatures wear all kinds of different outfits, complete with props.

53

weird but true!

THE ORIGINAL

HOLLYWOOD

SIGN, in CALIFORNIA, U.S.A., read **HOLLYWOODLAND.**

The Hollywood Walk of Fame doesn't just honor human celebrities—

BUGS BUNNY, SHREK, AND GODZILLA all have stars.

Foley artists create sound effects for movies. The sounds of hatching **VELOCIRAPTORS** in *Jurassic Park* were really **ICE-CREAM CONES BREAKING.**

AN OVERTURNED **POULTRY TRUCK** IN 1969 MIGHT BE THE REASON THERE IS A **COLONY OF FERAL CHICKENS** LIVING BY THE HOLLYWOOD FREEWAY.

The lights on top of the **CAPITOL RECORDS TOWER** spell out "Hollywood" in **MORSE CODE.**

HOLLYWOOD!

Hollywood is the INSPIRATION for other film industries, including **BOLLYWOOD** in **INDIA** and **HOGAWOOD** in **JAPAN.**

MAKING *PIRATES OF THE CARIBBEAN: ON STRANGER TIDES* **COST A MASSIVE** **$397 MILLION.**

The classic Christmas film ☀ *IT'S A WONDERFUL LIFE* was filmed in the **SUMMER—** ☀ during a **HEAT WAVE.**

Director James Cameron said his **MAIN REASON** for making the film *TITANIC* was to dive to the **WRECK OF THE REAL SHIP.**

An actor's **scream** from a **1951 film** has been used as a **sound effect** in more than **400 FILMS** and TV shows, including *Toy Story* and *Raiders of the Lost Ark.*

AHHHHH!

What's **Weird** About This**?**

Having a bad hair day? Head to Canada's Yukon and you might win a prize! Every winter, people compete to create the most unusual hairdos in the hot springs. Competitors submerge their heads underwater and then, when they emerge, sculpt their hair into strange shapes! After a few minutes in the cold air, which should be below minus 4°F (-20°C), any wet hair, which also includes beards, eyebrows, and eyelashes, will freeze. At that point, contestants ring a bell to be photographed. What are the judges looking for? They want to see plenty of white frost and ice—plus lots of imagination! There are several prizes, including best group photo and most creative hairstyle. Interest has spread internationally, with competitors traveling from Asia and Australia to take part. The prizes have grown, too, with winners receiving $2,000—and free soaks in the hot springs!

BY the NUMBERS

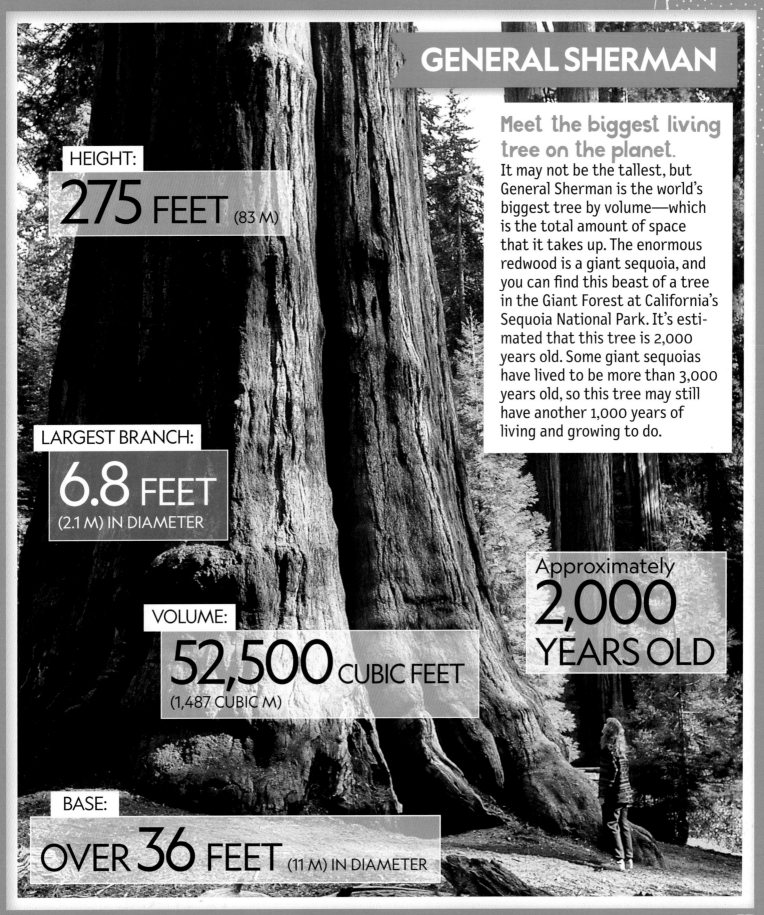

GENERAL SHERMAN

HEIGHT:
275 FEET (83 M)

LARGEST BRANCH:
6.8 FEET
(2.1 M) IN DIAMETER

VOLUME:
52,500 CUBIC FEET
(1,487 CUBIC M)

BASE:
OVER **36** FEET (11 M) IN DIAMETER

Meet the biggest living tree on the planet.
It may not be the tallest, but General Sherman is the world's biggest tree by volume—which is the total amount of space that it takes up. The enormous redwood is a giant sequoia, and you can find this beast of a tree in the Giant Forest at California's Sequoia National Park. It's estimated that this tree is 2,000 years old. Some giant sequoias have lived to be more than 3,000 years old, so this tree may still have another 1,000 years of living and growing to do.

Approximately
2,000
YEARS OLD

WEIRD DAYS OUT

Bug Carousel
Bronx, New York, U.S.A.

This bug-themed carousel at the Bronx Zoo puts a unique spin on the traditional fairground horse. You can ride on anything from a praying mantis to a grasshopper! Of course, a carousel wouldn't be complete without cheerful fairground music, would it? The Bug Carousel goes one step further—with tunes composed using real insect sounds. Each colorful critter has been carved from basswood and beautifully painted in accurate detail, meaning visitors can learn while they enjoy the ride.

The **Bug Carousel** features **64 different types** of insects.

Underwater Music Festival
Key West, Florida, U.S.A.

Diving gear is essential at this music festival on Looe Key in the Florida Keys—it happens 20 feet (6 m) below the water's surface! Underwater speakers pump out an ocean-themed playlist, including songs like "Yellow Submarine" by the Beatles and "Fins" by Jimmy Buffett, while the band members mime along with instruments created by a local artist. Music fans can dive down to enjoy the tunes as they explore the reef, while those who prefer dry land can enjoy the underwater beats from the radio. The festival is a ton of fun, but it's got a serious message. It aims to remind people about the importance of preserving the coral reef.

Cow Chip Throw
Prairie du Sac, Wisconsin, U.S.A.

Forget throwing a javelin or a discus, at the Wisconsin State Cow Chip Throw, contestants lob cow chips (aka cow dung)! The festival continues a tradition that started in the 1970s. The idea is pretty simple: Adult competitors start with two chips (children compete with one chip each) and see who can throw it farthest. Oh, and gloves are banned! That's right, you've really got to go for it. If they so choose, players are allowed to lick their fingers before picking up their dung. Why? Word has it that this technique helps with that all-important grip!

THE RULES STATE THAT AN INDIVIDUAL COW CHIP MUST BE A MINIMUM OF SIX INCHES (15 CM) IN DIAMETER.

Radish Sculpting
Oaxaca, Mexico

Pumpkins are carved at Halloween, so why not radishes at Christmas? Noche de Rábanos means Night of the Radishes, and it's when the red-skinned veg is carved into everything from intricate figurines to miniature churches. Radish carving is a pre-Christmas tradition in Oaxaca, Mexico. It was started by local farmers who would display their carved radishes as a way to showcase their produce at the market. Customers loved the displays, and many bought them to decorate their table at Christmas. In 1897, December 23 was officially made Noche de Rábanos, and it is still celebrated with a radish-carving competition.

PERSONALITY QUIZ

North America is home to **some weird and wonderful** beaches, but which would be your dream destination? Time to find out ...

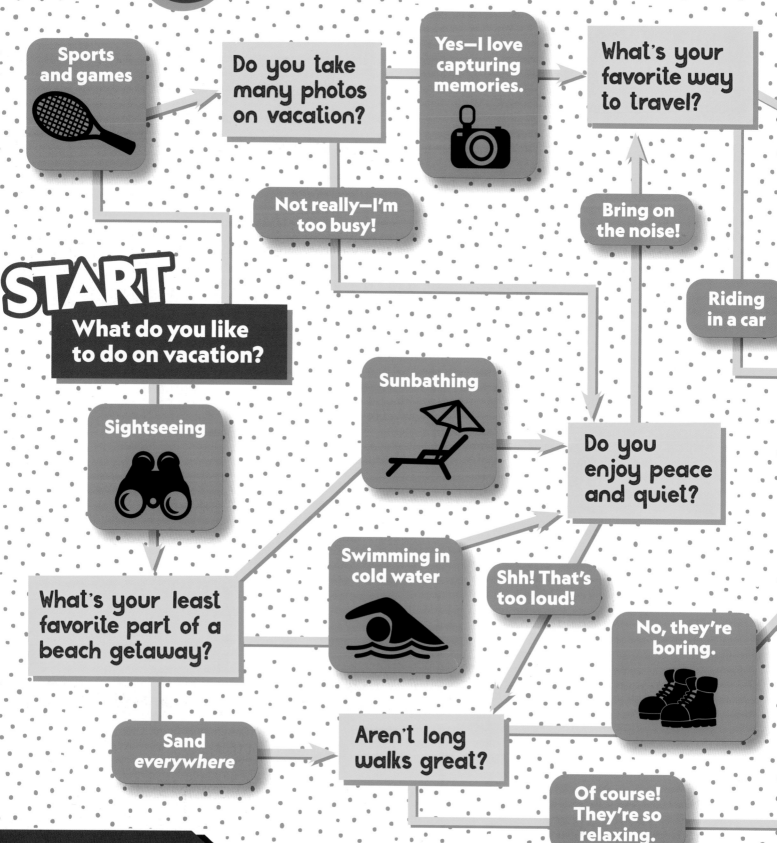

Sports and games

Do you take many photos on vacation?

Yes—I love capturing memories.

What's your favorite way to travel?

Not really—I'm too busy!

Bring on the noise!

Riding in a car

START
What do you like to do on vacation?

Sightseeing

Sunbathing

Do you enjoy peace and quiet?

What's your least favorite part of a beach getaway?

Swimming in cold water

Shh! That's too loud!

No, they're boring.

Sand everywhere

Aren't long walks great?

Of course! They're so relaxing.

Safari park

Music festival

Which day out sounds like the most fun?

Cruising on a boat.

Mainly black or white

What does your swimsuit look like?

Bright and colorful

Yes, just tell me how many towers!

Can you build an impressive sandcastle?

No, I'm too busy playing in the waves.

Pig Beach, Big Major Cay, Bahamas

No people live on Big Major Cay, but it is home to around 20 pigs and piglets. Villagers from nearby islands travel by boat to feed them, and the smart swine swim out to be the first in line! The pigs are happy to share their beach with tourists—provided that sightseers don't get in the way of their next meal!

Basin Head Provincial Park, Prince Edward Island, Canada

You're probably familiar with the sound of waves lapping against the shore, but here you can listen to the beach, too! It is nick-named the "Singing Sands" because it makes a high-pitched sound when stepped on! The air between the grains of sand has to escape, and the noise emits from the escaping air and particles rubbing together.

Papakōlea Beach, Hawaii, U.S.A.

At the beach, the sea is blue and the sand is white, right? Not here—the sand at Papakōlea is green! That's because it contains the mineral olivine, created by thousands of years of lava flows. It does require a short hike to reach the beach, but it's worth it because Papakōlea is one of only four green-sand beaches in the world!

Glass Beach, California, U.S.A.

With breathtaking blues and pretty pinks, it looks like a huge blanket of shiny jewels has been draped over the coast! For decades, locals used to throw their trash—from broken bottles to battered bowls—into the sea. Over the years, the tide has smoothed this litter into gorgeous sea glass.

FREAKY FOSSILS

Giant Ants
Wyoming, U.S.A.

Paleontologist Bruce Archibald didn't have to do much digging to make an impressive fossil discovery—it was sitting in a drawer at the Denver Museum of Nature and Science! As soon as he saw it, Dr. Archibald realized it was the first full-bodied fossil of the giant ant in North America. At two inches (5 cm) long, this impressive insect was the same size as a modern-day hummingbird! The same giant ants have also been found in Europe. Scientists aren't sure whether they migrated east or west, but either way would have meant crossing the Arctic region. That would normally be too cold for the insects, but during the Eocene epoch, between 56 and 34 million years ago, there were short periods when the temperature shot up, which is probably when the ants made their long journey over land bridges.

Modern-day *Dorylus* **ants in Africa can grow to be two inches (5 cm) long!**

I've got my eyes on you!

Opabinia
British Columbia, Canada

What has a long trunk, a backward-facing mouth, and five eyes? This might sound like a joke, but it's an accurate description of a marine animal that lived 508 million years ago in the Cambrian period! *Opabinia* belonged to the arthropod group, which have hard exoskeletons but no backbone, and was about the size of a mouse. But it's that absurd-looking head that makes this extinct creature so memorable. Its long proboscis ended in a claw that would carry particles of food from the seafloor to its mouth. *Opabinia* probably didn't have any teeth, so it could only have eaten small, soft fragments. You might think this bizarre creature is unique, but in 2022, another pre-historic marine animal, *Utaurora comosa*, was identified as belong-ing to the same family. It had five eyes, too!

Dueling Dinosaurs
Hell Creek, Montana, U.S.A.

Finding one fossilized dinosaur isn't easy, so finding two together is a paleontologist's jackpot. This incredible fossil was discovered in 2006 by three ranchers. After a two-week excavation, an almost complete 28-foot (8.5-m)-long *Triceratops* skeleton was revealed ... along with the claw of a carnivorous theropod! More digging uncovered the second dinosaur skeleton—a 22-foot (6.7-m)-long juvenile *Tyrannosaurus rex*! The fossils became known as the Dueling Dinosaurs because their positions suggest that they may have been fighting. There's even a *T. rex* tooth embedded in the *Triceratops*!

Dinosaur Footprints
Holyoke, Massachusetts, U.S.A.

You can't walk with dinosaurs, but you can certainly follow in their footsteps! More than 800 prehistoric tracks can be seen in the sandstone at Dinosaur Footprints in Holyoke. In the early Jurassic period, the region was filled with lakes and swamps. It was an ideal location for dinosaurs to drink and feed—and leave footprints on the mudflats. No bones have been found at the site, so it's not possible to identify each exact type of dinosaur. Instead, the fossilized footprints have been given their own species names! One set of tracks is called *Eubrontes*— they look very similar to the prints that the predator *Dilophosaurus* would have left. Holyoke also contains smaller prints that came from a dinosaur called *Grallator* that walked on two legs.

Quirky CREATURES!

Orange-Spotted Tiger Clearwing
Mexico

Butterflies are beautiful to look at, but this winged wonder has a remarkable chrysalis stage, too—its pupa is silver or gold! The metallic-looking outside of the chrysalis is made of chitin, which is found in the external skeletons of some insects and crustaceans. It always provides body armor, but sometimes it also has a shiny appearance. This eye-catching look helps protect the insect: The pupa's gleaming surface reflects nearby plants, providing camouflage. Plus, predators can be scared off when they see their own reflections!

Crab Invasion
Bay of Pigs, Cuba

Every spring, red-black-and-yellow crabs swarm Cuba's Bay of Pigs for weeks at a time. The pincered creatures take over the town as they travel from the forests to the sea. This happens during mating season. The migration causes chaos for local traffic! It's not a walk in the park for the crabs, either, which face obstacles including swimming pools and cars.

Motyxia Millipedes
Sequoia National Park, California, U.S.A.

There are more than 12,000 species of millipedes, but only a few glow in the dark—and, bizarrely, they all live in California! *Motyxia* millipedes hide underground during the day but emerge lit up at night. This acts as a warning to predators. Millipedes in the *Motyxia* genus secrete poisonous cyanide, and their glow reminds animals that have attempted to attack one to stay away!

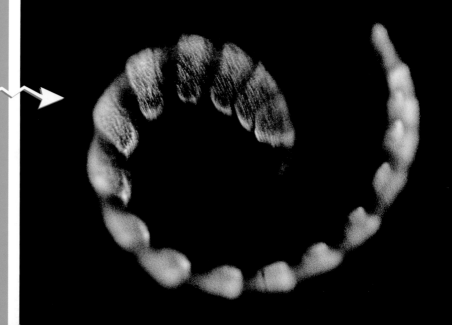

Star-Nosed Mole
North America

Star-nosed moles have a burst of tiny tentacles on their nostrils. These are always moving to help them figure out their surroundings and find prey. The moles' tentacles help make them the world's fastest eaters—they can find and devour a meal in less than a quarter of a second!

Solenodon
Dominican Republic and Haiti

The name "solenodon" might sound like something from prehistoric times, and sure enough, this small shrewlike creature's ancestry can actually be traced back 76 million years—to the time of dinosaurs! It has venomous saliva, which it injects into its prey, such as spiders and insects. Solenodons don't do well in a chase, though. They're clumsy animals because of their poor vision and awkward way of walking. If frightened, they can trip or even fall head over heels!

Rhinoceros Beetle
Central America

It doesn't take a genius to figure out why this critter is called a rhinoceros beetle! It's also known as the Hercules beetle, after the mythological hero who was famed for his strength—and not without reason! This beetle is the strongest insect in the world relative to its body size.

Peabody Hotel Ducks
Memphis, Tennessee, U.S.A.

In the 1930s, the general manager of the Peabody thought it would be a fun joke to put some ducks in the hotel's lobby fountain. The guests loved the idea, and ducks have had their own penthouse there ever since! Every morning, the ducks march down a red carpet for a six-hour swim in the marble fountain. Then it's back upstairs to their own glass-walled room—complete with a fountain and mini model of the hotel—which cost a hefty $200,000 to build!

Let's go for a dip!

65

HUMAN-MADE MASTERPIECES

Dr. Seuss House
Talkeetna, Alaska, U.S.A.

Over 20 years ago, a man in Alaska built a log cabin. Nothing strange about that—but he didn't stop with just one cabin. He kept on building upward, cabin upon cabin ... upon cabin! The mega-cabin now has between 14 and 17 floors, some of which are only accessible by ladder, and the entire structure reaches 185 feet (56 m) into the sky. It has been nicknamed the "Dr. Seuss House" after the children's author and cartoonist—it looks like it has come right out of one of his books! This towering construction can't get any higher into the sky because 200 feet (61 m) is officially federal airspace.

From the top of the Dr. Seuss House, you can see for 300 miles (480 km)!

"The Moss Lady"
Victoria, Canada

This mega "Moss Lady" lies tucked under a soft blanket of moss, with living plants sprouting like hair from the top of her head. Snoozing peacefully, she measures 35 feet (10 m) long—that's about as long as a school bus. The sculpture is made from a combination of boulders, wire, cement, and pipes. It was built in 2015 by an artist named Dale Doebert, who was inspired by a similar sculpture at the Lost Gardens of Heligan in Cornwall, England.

Leaves me alone. I want to sleep!

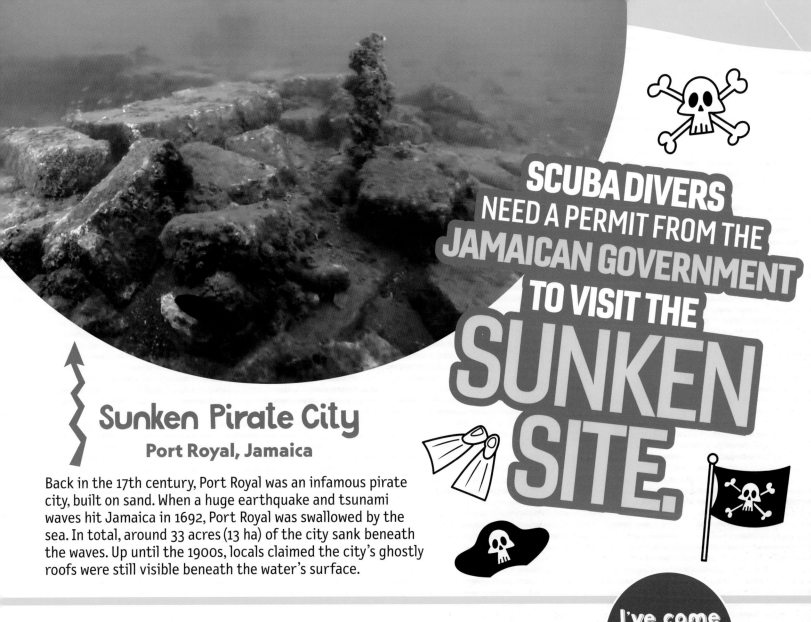

Sunken Pirate City

Port Royal, Jamaica

Back in the 17th century, Port Royal was an infamous pirate city, built on sand. When a huge earthquake and tsunami waves hit Jamaica in 1692, Port Royal was swallowed by the sea. In total, around 33 acres (13 ha) of the city sank beneath the waves. Up until the 1900s, locals claimed the city's ghostly roofs were still visible beneath the water's surface.

The Golden Mean

Oakland, California, U.S.A.

Do you follow your dreams? Kyrsten Mate did! She woke up one morning with visions of a giant snail car and told her husband, Jon Sarriugarte, that they had to build it! Sarriugarte is a blacksmith, and he set to work finding a car to transform. He bought a 1966 VW bug for $200, removed the body, and steam cleaned what was left. Steel tubing was used for the base of the shell and doors. The vehicle's name refers to the "golden ratio"—a mathematical principle that is represented in the spirals of the giant shell. Sarriugarte is no stranger to art cars, and enjoys installing fire effects in them. The Golden Mean is no different: It shoots flames from its feelers! It also glows in the dark, and its lights can pulse in time to the car's sound system. And thanks to engine enhancements, the Golden Mean doesn't move at a snail's pace!

I've come out of my shell.

ROCKY WONDERS

Stone Spheres
Diquís Valley, Costa Rica

These boulders may decorate the gardens of many modern Costa Rican homes, but their history dates back centuries. Nobody knows why the mysterious stone spheres, or Diquís Spheres, were made. They were discovered by workers clearing land in the Diquís Valley back in the 1930s, and they vary in size from ones you can hold in your hand to examples that are eight feet (2.5 m) in diameter. It is thought that ancient makers would chip away at them, using stone tools to create their almost perfect spherical shape.

One of the best known hoodoos at **Bryce Canyon** is named **"Thor's Hammer"** for its distinctive shape.

Bryce Canyon
Utah, U.S.A.

Say howdy to hoodoos at this hoodoo hot spot! Hoodoos are massive rock spires that exist on every continent in the world. Bryce Canyon is home to the world's largest concentration of them. From the top, you can look down in wonder at the mysterious red rock formations. As the sun moves during the day, different patterns and shapes form on the hoodoos, and visitors say they can see unusual figures and faces! A variety of trails take hikers into the canyon, bringing them up close to these breathtakingly beautiful rocks. They might look like they were created by magic, but the bizarre spindly structures have natural origins. For more than half the year, Bryce Canyon can be both above and below water's freezing point in a single day. Snow falls on the rocks, melts, and the water trickles into cracks in the rocks. When the temperature falls again, the water turns into ice and expands, breaking the rocks apart!

Hidden Beach
Marieta Islands, Mexico

Playa del Amor, or Hidden Beach, sits beneath a crater on one of Mexico's uninhabited Marieta Islands. To get there, visitors must either swim or kayak. With its white sand, sparkling water, and hidden location, this secret beach is picture perfect! While the islands formed as a result of volcanic activity, the craters are thought to be damage caused by military testing. The good news is that today the island is swarming with marine life. The area is now protected as a national park and UNESCO reserve.

Fly Geyser
Nevada Desert, Nevada, U.S.A.

This rainbow-colored wonder in the middle of the Nevada desert is human-made—albeit by mistake! So how did this beautiful accident occur? It all started around 100 years ago when residents were looking for water for their crops. They drilled a well and found 200°F (93°C) boiling water—much too hot for what they wanted—so it was abandoned. Decades later, a geyser (or hot spring) formed at the spot. Then, in 1964, an energy company built another well nearby. But the water wasn't hot enough for what they needed. This well was abandoned, and the hot water burst out to form a second geyser—Fly Geyser. It "stole" the water pressure from the original geyser, and it can fire boiling water five feet (1.5 m) into the air! Fly Geyser is always growing as the minerals from the water solidify into weird shapes.

FLY GEYSER'S **VIVID COLORS** ARE DUE TO THE **ALGAE** COVERING IT.

QUIZ WHIZ

Some answers are weird but true— and others are too weird to be true! Can you separate the facts from the fakes?

1 What is this venomous creature called?
a. Solenodon
b. Elephant mole
c. Haitian star shrew
d. Mexican moonrat

2 What did the famous Hollywood Sign originally say?
a. Hollywoodland
b. Jollywood
c. Tinsel Town
d. Woodland Films

3 Which two fossils combine to make the Dueling Dinosaurs?
a. *Allosaurus* and *Diplodocus*
b. *Velociraptor* and *Iguanodon*
c. *Spinosaurus* and *Stegosaurus*
d. *Tyrannosaurus rex* and *Triceratops*

Where can the largest musical instrument in the world be found?

a. In the Corn Palace in South Dakota, U.S.A.

b. In a geyser at Yellowstone National Park, Wyoming, U.S.A.

c. In underground caverns in Virginia, U.S.A.

d. Suspended in the trees of Vancouver Forest, Canada

 What is a hoodoo?

a. A sheep-wolf hybrid

b. A strong North Atlantic wind

c. A huge rock spire

d. A tree that grows upside down

 What extreme sport takes place at Cerro Negro, Nicaragua?

a. Earthquake karting

b. Volcano boarding

c. Avalanche tobogganing

d. Cliff base jumping

 Which species of butterfly makes a two-way migration?

a. Orange-spotted tiger clearwing

b. Homing marsh admiral

c. Striped boomerang

d. Monarch

 Which huge emoji-style design appears in a forest in Oregon, U.S.A.?

a. Thumbs up

b. Red heart

c. Smiley face

d. Laughing cat

Answers: 1. a, 2. a, 3. d, 4. c, 5. c, 6. b, 7. d, 8. c.

71

3

SPECTACULAR SOUTH AMERICA

This continent is full of freaky frogs, bizarre buildings, kooky cars, and more!

These facts are ribbit-ing!

Sally Lightfoot crabs HELP CLEAN MARINE IGUANAS by feasting on their DEAD SKIN AND PARASITES.

BUNNY HARVESTMEN have been on Earth for 400 MILLION YEARS, since even before the dinosaurs!

Each of these superpowered telescopes weighs an INCREDIBLE 474 TONS (430 t)!

73

WEIRD in the WORLD

SPECTACULAR

South America is stuffed full of **SPECTACULAR** sights, from **STRANGE-COLORED LAKES** to **ZEBRAS** directing **TRAFFIC** to breathtaking **BUILDINGS.**

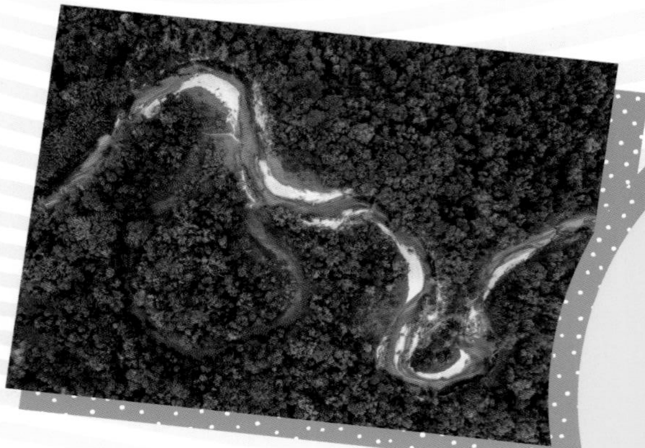

In 2011, Brazilian scientists discovered a new river called the Hamza about 2.5 miles (4 km) underground, beneath the Amazon River!

Celendín, Peru, is famous for making wide-brimmed straw hats, and there's even a huge hat with benches underneath at the entrance to the town!

NORTH AMERICA

AFRICA

Atlantic Ocean

SOUTH AMERICA

Pacific Ocean

Southern Ocean

ANTARCTICA

Caribbean Sea

COLOMBIA

VENEZUELA

GUYANA

SURINAME

French Guiana (France)

ATLANTIC OCEAN

ECUADOR

Galápagos Islands (Ecuador)

Celendín

PACIFIC OCEAN

PERU

A m a z o n   r a i n f o r e s t

Amazon River

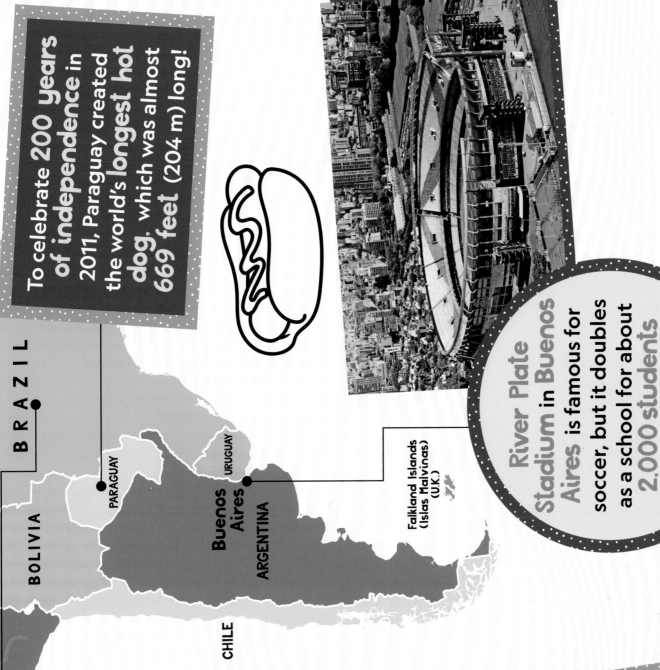

To celebrate 200 years of independence in 2011, Paraguay created the world's longest hot dog, which was almost 669 feet (204 m) long!

BRAZIL

PARAGUAY

BOLIVIA

URUGUAY

Buenos Aires

ARGENTINA

CHILE

Falkland Islands (Islas Malvinas) (U.K.)

River Plate Stadium in Buenos Aires is famous for soccer, but it doubles as a school for about 2,000 students from preschool to university level!

Almost half of the total human population of South America lives in Brazil.

It's believed that the bald uakari's bright red, bald face may attract mates, because sick animals usually have pale faces!

PECULIAR PLACES

Colonia Tovar
Aragua, Venezuela

The town of Colonia Tovar looks like it belongs in Germany. The houses have white walls with dark wooden beams. The restaurants serve bratwurst sausages, apple strudel, and Black Forest cake. But Colonia Tovar isn't actually in Germany—it's west of Caracas, Venezuela! In 1842, a group of settlers left southern Germany to make the long journey to create a home in South America. Originally they stayed isolated from their new neighbors, but now the residents of Colonia Tovar speak Spanish, and the town is a popular destination for weekend visitors from nearby Caracas.

Lençóis Maranhenses National Park
Maranhão, Brazil

Is it a mirage? A computer-generated movie set? Neither. Lençóis Maranhenses National Park is a surreal but natural mix of rolling sand dunes and stunning blue-green freshwater lagoons that stretch as far as the eye can see. The park covers 380,000 acres (1,538 sq km)—almost the size of London, England. Its name means "bedsheets" in Portuguese. You can see why—the dunes look like endless white sheets waving in the wind. Scattered among the dunes are hundreds of temporary lakes that fill up during the rainy season (between January and June). The water can't drain away through the impermeable rock below, so the lagoons remain full for many months. Visitors can even take a dip in the beautiful clear water.

The park is home to the **wolf fish,** which survives the dry season by **burrowing** into the **mud** and going into a deep sleep!

Caño Cristales
Meta, Colombia

In a remote region of the Serranía de la Macarena, a mountain range in Colombia, an hour's trek into the wilderness, there's a rainbow-colored river that appears for only a few months each year, sometime between June and December. The Caño Cristales, meaning "crystal channel," includes a variety of vibrant colors, especially a bright pinkish red. That might sound like something out of a sci-fi movie, or perhaps the result of a worrying pollution problem—but it's actually neither. It's completely natural. When the combination of the water level and the warm sunshine is just right, a riverweed that grows in the water blooms bright red. Along with the yellow sand, green mossy rocks, turquoise water, and dark river depths, it creates a breathtaking display known to locals as the "liquid rainbow."

OLIVEIRA'S STORE HAS HOT-DOG -FLAVORED ICE CREAM.

Heladería Coromoto
Merida, Venezuela

Would you like to try beef or garlic ice cream? You can taste these, and a whole lot more, at Heladería Coromoto, a world-famous and extremely weird ice-cream parlor in Venezuela. Ice-cream maker Manuel da Silva Oliveira started the store after perfecting his skills in other ice-cream companies. He began with normal flavors like vanilla and chocolate, but wanted to create something different. After inventing a recipe for avocado ice cream, he caught the bug for creating ever wackier flavors. On any particular day, you can choose from around 60 different types of ice cream, but Oliveira has created 860 of them altogether. Some are based on popular Venezuelan foods, such as pabellón criollo (beef with rice and black beans), mushroom, and chili flavors!

EYE-CATCHING ODDITIES

Cuyaba Dwarf Frog
Brazil, Bolivia, and Paraguay

Bottoms up! That's the Cuyaba dwarf frog's approach when it is under threat. Instead of facing off against an opponent or making a run for it, this unusual amphibian turns around and presents its backside! That might sound sort of odd, but this little two-inch (5-cm)-long frog has two black glands with outer white rings on its rear end. When the frog feels threatened, it puffs up its body and lifts itself up, making the glands look like big eyes! If that doesn't scare away its predators, the glands give the frog another defense tactic: They squirt poison!

EDUARDO'S SON LUCA WAS SO IMPRESSED WITH CASA BOLA THAT HE BUILT HIS OWN GLOBE-SHAPED HOUSE!

Casa Bola
São Paulo, Brazil

Eduardo Longo had a ball while working on Casa Bola—or at least, he built one! Longo designed the house as part of a project to build apartment buildings made up of dozens of spherical houses. He started work on Casa Bola in 1974 and spent five years building it himself, despite not having any construction experience. The housing project was never developed further, but this amazing building became Longo's home. Its four levels contain three bedrooms, a dining room, a living room, bathrooms, and a kitchen. Furniture had to be specially created because standard designs would not fit against the curved walls! Much of the interior is white, giving it a futuristic feel, but there is more color on the outside, including a curved yellow slide that can be used to exit the house!

Vinicunca
Andes Mountains, Peru

It's not hard to see why Vinicunca is also known as Rainbow Mountain. This incredible striped peak might look too bizarre to be real, but it's all natural. Vinicunca is made up of 14 different minerals, which create various hues. The red layer, for example, comes from clay, while the yellow band gets its color from sulfur. Until 2015, this weird wonder was totally hidden—completely covered in snow! When that melted, the stripes were revealed. Visitors need to be in good shape because a steep walk is required to reach Vinicunca—but with such a stunning sight as the destination, it's worth it.

What's the mata mata with taking it slow?

Mata Mata Turtle
Ecuador, Venezuela, and Brazil

What's the "mata" with this odd-looking reptile? With its wide, flat neck and triangular head, it looks kind of like it has been squished! But that's just how the mata mata turtle usually looks. It lives in water but isn't a strong swimmer, so prefers to stand in shallow depths, poking its long snout above the surface like a snorkel to breathe. The mata mata has poor eyesight, but it can hear well and has fleshy flaps along its neck, which detect when prey is nearby. The turtle's ridged shell looks like a piece of tree bark—handy camouflage for when it waits motionless for unsuspecting fish and shrimp. When they get close enough, it opens its mouth wide, creating a vacuum to swallow its meal. The mata mata's mouth can't chew, though, so it swallows fish whole!

Mata matas can weigh up to **38 pounds (17 kg)**—about the weight of a **four-year-old child!**

WEIRD WONDERS

This salt lake covers over

4,086 SQUARE MILES
(10,582 sq km)

on a plateau high up in the Andes.

Can you figure out what's happening in this photo? At first glance, this person seems to be riding their bike in the sky, or perhaps cycling on water. In fact, they are crossing the breathtaking Salar de Uyuni in Bolivia. It's the world's biggest salt flat—a vast, white, almost totally flat expanse of salt, 80 miles (130 km) wide, left behind after an ancient lake dried up. In the rainy season, from January to April, it's covered in a shallow layer of still water, transforming it into the biggest mirror anywhere on Earth.

SALAR DE UYUNI

Uyuni, Bolivia

But where's the pepper?

WEIRD VACATION DESTINATIONS

Skylodge Pods
Cusco, Peru

If you're scared of heights, look away! To get to this hotel, you have to trek up a 1,300-foot (400-m)-high mountainside and inch your way along a *via ferrata*—a climbing path with metal ladders and cables bolted to the rock to cling on to. When you finally reach your room, it's a see-through metal-and-plexiglass pod fixed to the side of a cliff! The Skylodge Adventure Suites, as they're called, dangle above Peru's Sacred Valley, close to the ancient Inca ruins of Machu Picchu. Each lodge contains a dining area, bathroom, and beds. Of course, the view is fantastic, both down to the valley floor and up to the night sky. Whether you'll be able to relax enough to fall asleep is another matter!

Hotel Unique
São Paulo, Brazil

This trendy hotel is well-named: It's not every day you see a building that looks like it's ready to set off to sea! While some people see a boat in the hotel's shape and porthole-like windows, others think it looks more like a slice of watermelon. Whatever you see, the Unique's unusual bowl-shaped design means the floors get wider the higher up in the hotel you go. That means the roof is pretty big—and for good reason! There you'll find a red-tiled rooftop pool with an underwater sound system that pumps nightly tunes from a DJ. No wonder the Unique is making waves in São Paulo!

All hands on deck!

Supersize Swimming Pool
Algarrobo, Chile

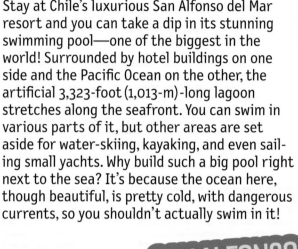

Stay at Chile's luxurious San Alfonso del Mar resort and you can take a dip in its stunning swimming pool—one of the biggest in the world! Surrounded by hotel buildings on one side and the Pacific Ocean on the other, the artificial 3,323-foot (1,013-m)-long lagoon stretches along the seafront. You can swim in various parts of it, but other areas are set aside for water-skiing, kayaking, and even sailing small yachts. Why build such a big pool right next to the sea? It's because the ocean here, though beautiful, is pretty cold, with dangerous currents, so you shouldn't actually swim in it!

SAN ALFONSO DEL MAR'S **SUPERSIZE POOL** TAKES UP MORE SPACE THAN **60 OLYMPIC-SIZE SWIMMING POOLS!**

Montaña Mágica Lodge
Neltume, Chile

Imagine staying inside a miniature magic mountain, covered in rainforest plants, with a real waterfall cascading past your window! Head to the Montaña Mágica Lodge in Chile, and you can! Although it looks like something conjured up by a wizard, the lodge is actually a building made of stone and wood, not a real mountain. It's in a nature reserve, surrounded by rainforest where you can spot amazing wild animals, such as the 13-inch (33-cm)-tall pudu, the world's smallest deer, as well as birds, butterflies, condors, and cougars. To get into the lodge, you have to cross a rope bridge from a treetop walkway.

BY the NUMBERS

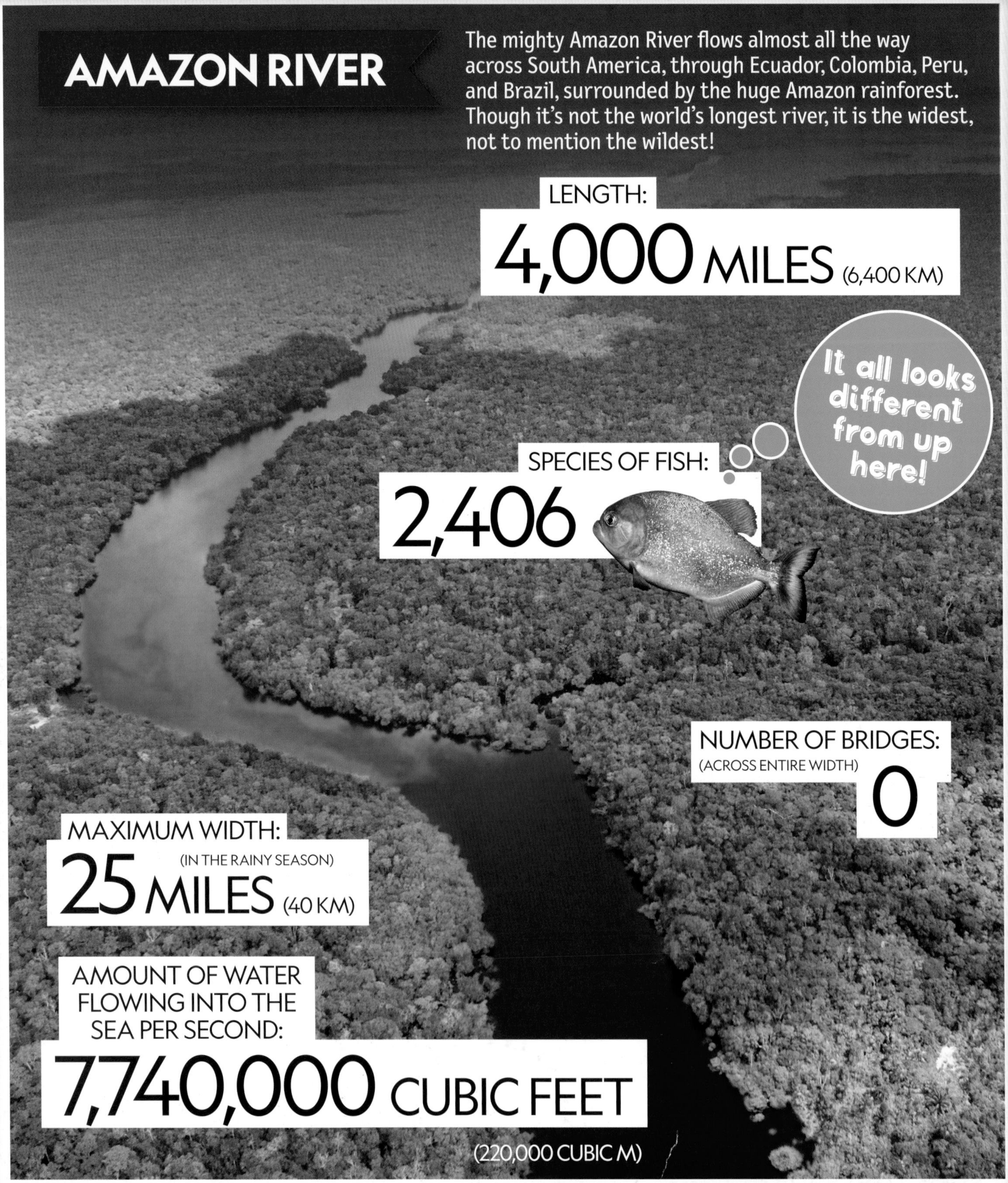

AMAZON RIVER

The mighty Amazon River flows almost all the way across South America, through Ecuador, Colombia, Peru, and Brazil, surrounded by the huge Amazon rainforest. Though it's not the world's longest river, it is the widest, not to mention the wildest!

LENGTH:
4,000 MILES (6,400 KM)

SPECIES OF FISH:
2,406

It all looks different from up here!

NUMBER OF BRIDGES:
(ACROSS ENTIRE WIDTH)
0

MAXIMUM WIDTH:
(IN THE RAINY SEASON)
25 MILES (40 KM)

AMOUNT OF WATER FLOWING INTO THE SEA PER SECOND:
7,740,000 CUBIC FEET
(220,000 CUBIC M)

What's **Weird** About This?

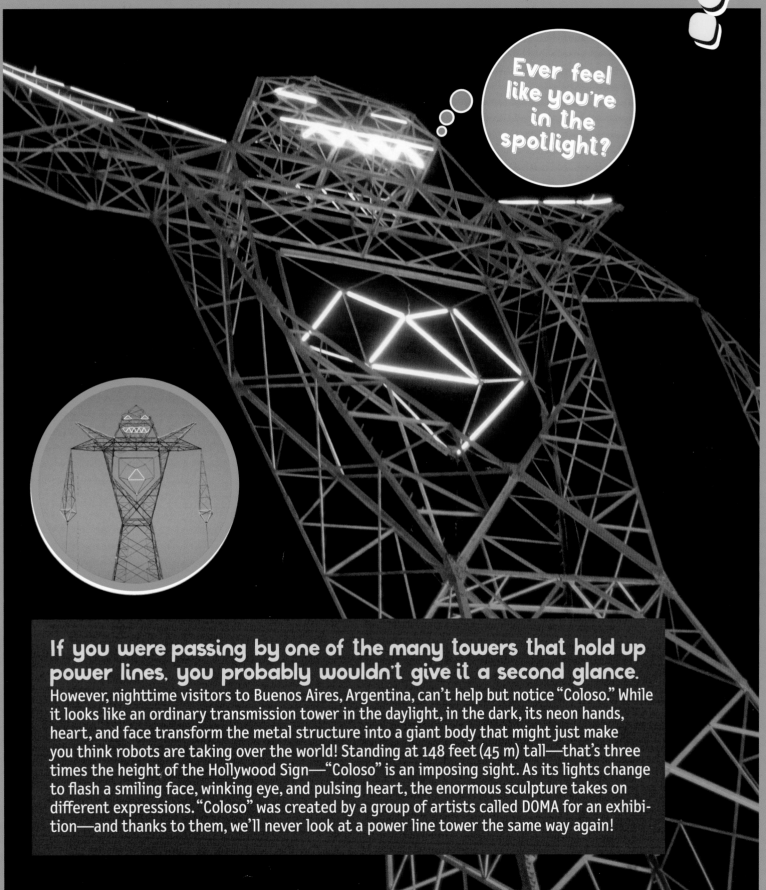

Ever feel like you're in the spotlight?

If you were passing by one of the many towers that hold up power lines, you probably wouldn't give it a second glance. However, nighttime visitors to Buenos Aires, Argentina, can't help but notice "Coloso." While it looks like an ordinary transmission tower in the daylight, in the dark, its neon hands, heart, and face transform the metal structure into a giant body that might just make you think robots are taking over the world! Standing at 148 feet (45 m) tall—that's three times the height of the Hollywood Sign—"Coloso" is an imposing sight. As its lights change to flash a smiling face, winking eye, and pulsing heart, the enormous sculpture takes on different expressions. "Coloso" was created by a group of artists called DOMA for an exhibition—and thanks to them, we'll never look at a power line tower the same way again!

DRY AS A BONE

Where Rain Never Falls

Atacama Desert, Chile

If you're going for a trek in the Atacama Desert, don't forget a water bottle! This beautiful mountainous desert in northern Chile is the world's driest place, apart from Antarctica, where it doesn't rain much and it's too cold for ice to melt! In total, the Atacama receives about half an inch (15 mm) of rain per year. But there are places in the middle where not a single drop has ever been recorded. These areas are so dry that there are no plants, not even cacti—just red, gray, and golden rocks, carved into shapes by the wind. Moviemakers often come here to film scenes set on the moon!

The VLT's **huge telescopes** can spot items smaller than a DVD as far away as the **International Space Station.**

Very Large Telescope

Arica, Chile

The aptly named Very Large Telescope, or VLT, is exactly what it sounds like: a telescope with out-of-this-world proportions. It's responsible for many incredible discoveries, including finding R136a1, one of the biggest stars known to humans. (When R136a1 formed, it had a mass 320 times bigger than our sun!) The VLT gets its power from eight telescopes that can work together as one, or separately. Four of them are huge: They have massive mirrors, each 27 feet (8.2 m) across—about the length of a bus! The VLT was built in the Atacama because it's a perfect location for stargazing, due to the combination of high altitude, low humidity, and lack of light pollution.

Mano del Desierto
Antofagasta, Chile

Close to the Pan-American Highway—which stretches from the southern tip of South America all the way to Alaska, U.S.A.—there's a ginormous hand reaching up out of the ground. It's the "Mano del Desierto," or "Hand of the Desert," a 36-foot (11-m)-tall sculpture located outside of Antofagasta, Chile. It's a breathtaking sight for those who stop to take a look up close. Though it's built from iron and concrete, it resembles the desert rocks, making it seem to be a living part of the Atacama itself. It's the "handiwork" of Chilean sculptor Mario Irarrázabal.

Talk to the hand!

THE GIANT "MANO DEL DESIERTO" IS TWICE THE HEIGHT OF A GIRAFFE.

Weirdly Cute! Viscacha

What is this chilled-out, chubby, yet slightly grumpy-looking creature? It appears to be a cross between a rabbit and a squirrel, with its big ears and long, bushy tail. It's actually a viscacha, a cat-size animal often spotted in the less dry parts of the Atacama, where there are a few desert plants to eat. Viscachas make their homes under and in between desert rocks. During the day, they relax on top of the rocks to catch some rays. At night, when the desert temperature can drop to almost freezing, their thick fur keeps them warm.

RIDICULOUS RIDES!

Joseso
Argentina

If good things really do come in small packages, then the Joseso must be one of the best cars ever built. In the 1950s, when resources were scarce after World War II, small vehicles were very popular with motorists in Europe. This inspired Argentine businessman José María Rodríguez to design his own microcar. The cute little Joseso looked like a toy vehicle scaled up for human use! Its 520-CC engine, which allowed a top speed of about 40 miles an hour (65 km/h), was at the back of the car, with the back seat pushed to one side to make room for it. There was no room for a trunk, but the back seat could fold down to carry luggage. Unfortunately for Rodríguez, the promised support from the government didn't happen—and only 200 cars were built between 1959 and 1960. A few still survive today, occasionally turning heads at classic car shows.

La Garrucha Cable Car
Jardín, Colombia

Wait a minute—is that a floating shed? Not quite! Look closer and you'll see cables holding it up. That's because La Garrucha is a cable car, and it transports passengers over a steep gorge! The town of Jardín is located next to a ravine, and one of the quickest ways to get across it is in La Garrucha. The car is suspended in the air by two steel cables, and a truck engine powers it back and forth every 30 minutes. With the ground hundreds of feet below, some travelers may prefer not to look down. At the top of the valley, a café and amazing views greet those brave enough to make the journey. And for anyone who can't face the return trip, there are other ways to cross the gorge, including a sturdier-looking suspension bridge!

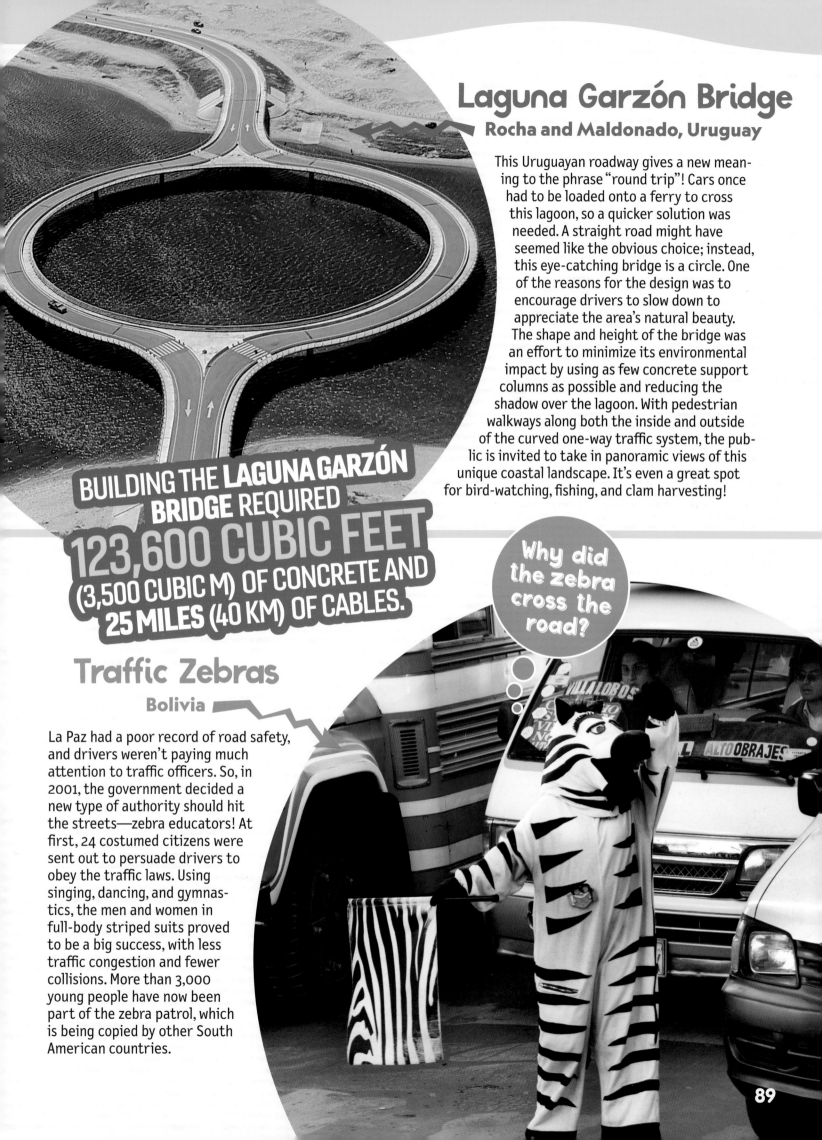

Laguna Garzón Bridge
Rocha and Maldonado, Uruguay

This Uruguayan roadway gives a new meaning to the phrase "round trip"! Cars once had to be loaded onto a ferry to cross this lagoon, so a quicker solution was needed. A straight road might have seemed like the obvious choice; instead, this eye-catching bridge is a circle. One of the reasons for the design was to encourage drivers to slow down to appreciate the area's natural beauty. The shape and height of the bridge was an effort to minimize its environmental impact by using as few concrete support columns as possible and reducing the shadow over the lagoon. With pedestrian walkways along both the inside and outside of the curved one-way traffic system, the public is invited to take in panoramic views of this unique coastal landscape. It's even a great spot for bird-watching, fishing, and clam harvesting!

BUILDING THE **LAGUNA GARZÓN BRIDGE** REQUIRED **123,600 CUBIC FEET** (3,500 CUBIC M) OF CONCRETE AND **25 MILES** (40 KM) OF CABLES.

Why did the zebra cross the road?

Traffic Zebras
Bolivia

La Paz had a poor record of road safety, and drivers weren't paying much attention to traffic officers. So, in 2001, the government decided a new type of authority should hit the streets—zebra educators! At first, 24 costumed citizens were sent out to persuade drivers to obey the traffic laws. Using singing, dancing, and gymnastics, the men and women in full-body striped suits proved to be a big success, with less traffic congestion and fewer collisions. More than 3,000 young people have now been part of the zebra patrol, which is being copied by other South American countries.

Bizarre BUGS!

... and spiders!

Goliath Birdeater

When you hear that an animal has the name "birdeater," you might imagine a snake, crocodile, or wild cat. But the goliath birdeater is none of these. It's actually the world's biggest, heaviest spider. It can grow to the size of a dinner plate, and with its powerful legs and large fangs, it really does sometimes catch birds to drag back to its burrow for its next meal. More often, though, it preys on insects, worms, frogs, lizards, and mice.

Peanuthead Bug

The name says it all! This large Amazon rainforest bug has a head that looks like a giant unshelled peanut. However, scientists think it frightens predators away because to them, it resembles a lizard's head. This makes the bug look like a bigger and more dangerous animal than it really is. If that doesn't work, it spreads its wings, revealing an even bigger decoy—a set of scary fake eyes!

Glasswing Butterfly

These incredible insects look almost too delicate to be real, but glasswing butterflies' colorless wings actually help them survive. See-through wings are perfect for blending into surrounding plants, keeping the insects safe from hungry predators. Camouflage isn't their only survival skill, either. They can carry as much as 40 times their own weight and fly fast—up to eight miles an hour (13 km/h). If one is caught, the glasswing butterfly has enough poison to kill a predator!

Of course I'm a real spider!

Decoy Spider

This sneaky spider, discovered in a remote part of Peru, has a genius way of scaring off its enemies. The arachnid is tiny, only about 0.2 inch (5 mm) long, and is in danger of being eaten by other spiders, large bugs, frogs, and lizards. So it uses dead flies, bits of leaf, and skin it has shed to build a much bigger fake spider in the middle of its web! By moving around on the web, it can even make its creation twitch and shake, so hungry predators will think it's alive and steer clear.

Panda Ant

Is it an ant? Is it a tiny six-legged panda? Nope! Guess again. The panda ant is actually a type of wasp from Chile and Argentina, which was given the name "panda ant" for obvious reasons! Its black-and-white patterns, which only the females have, act as a warning to predators. The wasp also has a horribly painful sting, earning it another nickname, "cow killer"—though the sting isn't actually bad enough to kill a cow. Phew!

Bunny Harvestman

What do you get if you cross a rabbit with a spider? Well, the bizarre bunny harvestman might just be the result! In reality, it's neither of those things—this eight-legged wonder belongs to an order of animals called Opiliones, or "daddy longlegs," rather than true spiders. The two yellow spots look like eyes, adding to the illusion, but the arachnid's real eyes are farther down its abdomen!

Leaf-Mimic Katydid

These impressive creatures take the art of camouflage very seriously! As the name suggests, the katydid's body looks like a green leaf. To blend in, these fake leaves look decayed or speckled, and some even have a translucent section resembling a hole! Amazingly, no two leaf-mimic katydids look the same. This makes it very tricky for a potential predator to spot its prey!

PERSONALITY QUIZ

Which South American festival should you visit?

Write down your answers for each question, **and see which letter you** picked the most often.

1 Which of these animals is your favorite?
a. Turtle
b. Butterfly
c. Horse

2 What kind of music do you prefer to listen to?
a. Electronic music
b. Pop
c. Country and western

3 It's Saturday! What are you up to?
a. Going to the beach
b. Touring a historic house and gardens
c. Hiking in the woods

4 It's snack time. What are you having?
a. Ice cream
b. Salad
c. Roast beef sandwich

5. Which of these would you most likely wear to a party?

a. Tie-dyed T-shirt and shorts
b. Any bright colors!
c. Button-down shirt and blue jeans

6. Which of these is your best subject in school?

a. P.E.
b. Biology
c. History

7. What's your favorite thing about going on vacation?

a. Meeting new people
b. Seeing the sights
c. Checking out the wildlife

Mostly A's
You're off to ...
Paraty Mud Block, Brazil.
Smear yourself in sticky mud—and party at Paraty! In 1986, teenagers played in the mud on the beach until their family and friends couldn't recognize them! Now, adults, children, and animals get coated in black sludge annually and take part in an afternoon parade.

Mostly B's
You're off to ...
Medellín Flower Festival, Colombia.
Why not be one of the thousands of tourists who visit Medellín every August for 10 days of flower fun? The *silleteros* parade is a highlight—with more than 500 growers arranging floral displays on wooden carriers to take around the streets.

Mostly C's
You're off to ...
San Antonio de Areco Gaucho Festival, Argentina.
Time to find out if you can cut it as a cowboy or cowgirl! This festival of gauchos was first celebrated in 1939 and includes rodeos and a massive bonfire. And when you've worked up an appetite, head for the big barbecue area!

GROOVY GALÁPAGOS

Marine Iguana

The Galápagos Islands are home to the world's only water-loving lizards. Marine iguanas evolved from land iguanas around 4.5 million years ago. And although they spend most of their time out of the water, they do head to the ocean to feed. Their blunt snouts are perfect for nibbling algae from rocks, and their long, sharp claws stop them from being washed away. The marine iguana's flat tail is also perfect for swimming. All that ocean dining does create one problem, though—a lot of salt is consumed, too. Luckily, marine iguanas have a special method for dealing with the unwanted sodium chloride: They have developed nasal glands that expel it by sneezing.

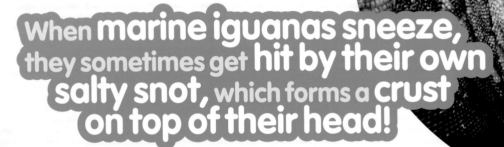

When **marine iguanas sneeze,** they sometimes get **hit by their own salty snot,** which forms a **crust on top of their head!**

Sally Lightfoot Crab

This cool crustacean is easy to identify ... and almost impossible to catch! Baby Sally Lightfoot crabs are dark brown or black, which helps them hide on the black rocks formed from lava that is found on the Galápagos Islands. The crabs molt their shells as they age—and on each newer shell, their red spots get larger until the original black color is completely gone. They no longer need camouflage because they are so agile, able to run in any direction and climb up vertical slopes using the tips of their pointed legs. They are so light on their feet, these extraordinary creatures can skitter across the surface of water! Legend has it that they are named after a Caribbean dancer—and Sally Lightfoot crabs certainly have all the right moves!

Magnificent Frigatebird

Ahoy there, mateys! There be piracy problems in the Pacific! But ain't no gold nor pearls being stolen—'tis fish. Magnificent frigatebirds are nicknamed "pirate birds" because they steal food from other species—even if it has already been eaten! They chase other birds, grab their tail feathers, and shake them violently. The poor victim releases the fish or squid it's holding in its beak or even vomits up recently digested food, which the pirate bird then steals!

THE MALE BIRD'S RED THROAT POUCH, CALLED A GULAR SAC, HELPS IT ATTRACT A MATE AND TAKES 20 MINUTES TO FULLY INFLATE!

Slowly but surely!

Galápagos Tortoise

Jeanne Calment, the oldest known human, lived to be an amazing 122 years old, but humans aren't likely to overtake Galápagos tortoises anytime soon. The oldest on record lived to be 176! Tortoise Harriet was taken from the Galápagos Islands by British naturalist Charles Darwin in 1835 and arrived in Australia in 1842. She lived at the Brisbane Botanical Gardens for more than 100 years. In 2005, Harriet's 175th birthday was celebrated, with cards from around the world and her favorite red hibiscus flowers to munch on!

WEIRD WONDERS

This natural wonder's scenic pillars and high ceilings have earned it the nickname "marble cathedral" by locals. The region was covered by glaciers up until 10,000 years ago, when they retreated, forming General Carrera Lake. Over thousands of years, lake water eroded the nearby cliffs' marble stone, creating striking caves. Unfortunately, this erosion means that this amazing phenomenon will one day collapse. Visitors travel by boat to explore the stunning interior but experience something new each time because the caves' appearance keeps changing. Sunlight reflects off the deep turquoise water, and the amount of light entering the caves and the level of the water change dramatically depending on the weather and season, creating different tones and hues on the walls.

INCREDIBLE HEAT AND PRESSURE

are needed to turn rock into marble.

MARBLE CAVES

General Carrera Lake, Chile

PERPLEXING PLANTS

Yareta Plant

Andes Mountains

Go trekking high in the Andes mountains and you might see something that looks like a giant green booger stuck to the rocks! This strange, alien-like blob is actually a yareta, a tough mountain plant. It grows a thick mass of stems, topped by thousands of tiny leaves and flowers that form a dense, solid mat. It may look soft and kind of slimy, but the yareta is actually firm like wood. You can even sit down on one and it won't get squashed! Growing like this helps the yareta to hold in water and warmth, and stops it from getting blown away by the icy mountain winds. Yaretas grow very slowly, and some are believed to be up to 3,000 years old!

The **yarenta plant** can grow to **20 feet** (6 m) across—the size of a **large car.**

"Floralis Genérica"

Buenos Aires, Argentina

There's definitely something strange about this flower—it's made of metal, it's 75 feet (23 m) tall, and each of its six huge stainless-steel petals is 43 feet (13 m) long. It's a flower the size of a seven-story apartment block! You can see it in the middle of the busy city of Buenos Aires, the capital of Argentina. In 2002, Argentine architect Eduardo Catalano designed and paid for the spectacular sculpture as a gift to his city. It stands in a park in the middle of a circular pool that reflects it like a mirror. Every night at sunset, it slowly closes its petals, and a red light glows from inside. In the morning, at 8 a.m., it opens again for the day.

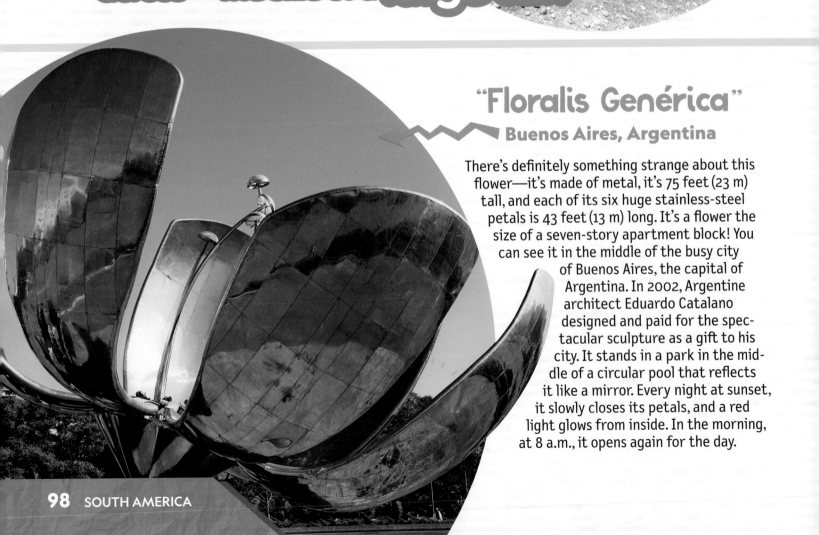

Shy Plant
Tropical South America

Can a plant be shy? The *Mimosa pudica*, also called the shy plant or touch-me-not plant, has an amazing ability. If you touch it, or just brush past it, the leaves suddenly droop and fold up. This makes it harder for some animals, such as caterpillars, to eat it. Plants aren't known for their speedy moves, so how does the mimosa do this? It has special water-filled cells at the base of each leaf. Touching the leaf makes the cells empty out their water and become floppy, like a deflated balloon—and the leaf collapses. But these plants are smart, too! Scientists have tried playing harmless tricks on mimosas, like sprinkling them with water. At first, they close up, but after the trick is repeated a few times, they learn that there's no danger and stop reacting!

Where's my lipstick?

Hot Lips Plant
Colombia, Costa Rica, and Ecuador

Pucker up! These lips look like they're about to plant a kiss ... but they're a plant! *Palicourea elata*, also known as hot lips, grows in Central and South American rainforests. It's a double deception: Those scarlet smackers aren't the flowers, either—they're leaves that open up to let the real white flowers poke through. The leaves' color and shape attract birds and butterflies, which pollinate the plant. Humans are fond of them, too. The Indigenous peoples of the Amazon use the plant to treat a range of illnesses.

STRANGE STRUCTURES

Sacsayhuamán
Cusco, Peru

Take a close look at these walls. They were built around 600 years ago, near the city of Cusco, Peru, by the Inca people. They're made of solid stone blocks, some up to 28 feet (8.5 m) high—and there's no mortar or cement used. Instead, the blocks were all cut to fit together exactly. Although many are oddly shaped, they fit so perfectly that you can't even slide a piece of paper between them. They were also carved into rounded shapes, making them look a little like giant pieces of bubble gum that have been squished together. The Inca built three huge zigzagging walls like this to defend the hilltop fort of Sacsayhuamán.

These ancient walls are so well constructed that they've survived centuries of earthquakes.

Plastic Bottle House
Puerto Iguazú, Argentina

Thrown-away plastic bottles are a big problem in many parts of the world. But there is an ingenious way to get rid of them: Turn them into houses! This house in Argentina was built from thousands of plastic bottles stacked up inside sturdy frames to make the walls. The homeowner has made sofas and beds from old bottles, too, and there's even a curtain made of strung-together bottle tops! This particular house is open to the public for tours, but many more bottle houses are being built as normal, everyday dwellings.

Casa Terracota

Villa de Leyva, Colombia

You might drink out of a ceramic mug or put flowers in a ceramic vase, but you probably wouldn't imagine something as big as a house could be made out of pottery! Architect Octavio Mendoza Morales didn't want to use ordinary bricks for his house because he thought this traditional material would be too limiting and rigid for how he wanted the building to be constructed and used. So he chose clay instead, which he fired and hardened in the sun to create a ceramic house. The architect began building the house in 1999 and completed the main structure in 2016, but he says he will continue to work on it for the rest of his life. Inside, Casa Terracota has vibrant tile mosaics embellishing the sloping walls. All the furniture is made from clay, too!

Amazon Tall Tower Observatory

Amazon Rainforest, Brazil

Want to take a trip up the tallest tower in South America? Then head to the jungle! Oh, and you'll have to be a scientist, a technician, or a visiting journalist to be allowed up. This skyscraping structure isn't a modern office building in a big city, but a special science research base, deep in the Amazon rainforest. Named the Amazon Tall Tower Observatory (ATTO), it was built in 2015 and rises 1,066 feet (325 m) into the sky. Yet it's only 10 feet (3 m) from side to side! It takes an hour to climb to the top. On the way up, there are platforms where scientists can work, as well as a deck right at the summit. The tower is also covered with high-tech sensors for measuring pollution, temperature, humidity, and climate change above the rainforest.

LUCKILY FOR THE EXPERTS WHO WORK ON THE AMAZON'S OBSERVATORY TOWER, THERE'S AN ELEVATOR!

Going up?

KOOKY COLORS!

The Colors of Guatapé
Colombia

Welcome to Guatapé, the world's most colorful town! Though it may resemble a dream world or a film set for a fantasy movie, this is a real place in Colombia, where people live and work—and spend a lot of time painting their houses. The tradition started around 100 years ago, when people put 3D-tiled and painted panels around the base of the buildings. Gradually, they began painting the rest of the buildings in bright colors, too—and now every street is a rainbow of patterns and pictures, and the town has become a tourist attraction. The locals take great pride in their colorful homes, and are often seen out on the streets cleaning and retouching their paintwork.

Paint the town all the colors of the rainbow!

THE **MURALS** ON THE **BUILDINGS** TRADITIONALLY TELL THE **HISTORY OF THE FAMILY OR BUSINESS** THAT OWNS THEM.

Laguna Verde
Altiplano, Bolivia

At Laguna Verde, you can look, but don't touch! This stunning salt lake is a glorious green, although the color can vary due to sediment being stirred up by strong winds. Visitors on different days might experience a bright turquoise or a pale aquamarine. The color is due to large quantities of minerals—such as sulfur, calcium, lead, and the poisonous chemical arsenic—in the water, which make the lake a terrible spot for a swim! The local flamingos have figured this out and won't feed from Laguna Verde.

Laguna Verde is about **40 miles** (64 km) south of **Laguna Colorada**—a **red lake!**

Weirdly Cute!

Golden Poison Frog

At an average length of one inch (2.5 cm)—about the same as a paper clip—this Colombian amphibian might seem cute and colorful. But it's best not to get too close: It's one of the most poisonous animals on the planet! One tiny frog could have enough venom to kill 10 adults. The local Emberá people smear the frogs' poison on the tips of their blowgun darts for hunting animals. That's why this strangely adorable yet deadly animal is also known as the golden dart frog. The lethal toxins are present in the creatures' skin secretions, and the bright color warns potential predators that this is a snack they don't want to attack!

TOTALLY WILD FACTS ABOUT

weird but true!

The peculiar-looking **POTOO BIRD** can **disguise itself** as a **tree stump**—but only when it **closes** its **BULGING, BRIGHT YELLOW EYES.**

MALE RIVER DOLPHINS, or **BOTOS,** found in the Amazon's waterways are often an **UNUSUAL PINK COLOR ...** and according to local folklore, they can shape-shift into **HANDSOME HUMAN MEN!**

THE GLASS FROG HAS **TRANSPARENT SKIN, WHICH MEANS YOU CAN SEE ITS BONES AND ORGANS AND WATCH ITS HEART BEATING!**

The **common basilisk lizard** can **ESCAPE FROM DANGER** by spreading out its toes and running across water.

Catch me if you can!

AMAZONIAN ANIMALS

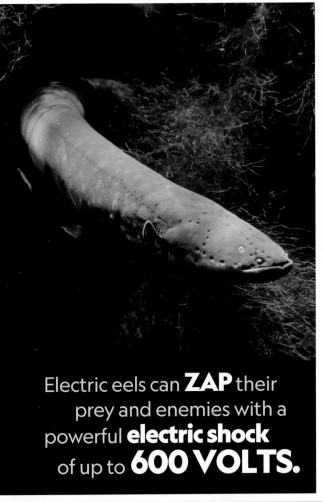

Electric eels can **ZAP** their prey and enemies with a powerful **electric shock** of up to **600 VOLTS.**

The chicken-size **hoatzin** has a **HUGE STOMACH** where its **food** stays until it **rots** and ferments—making the hoatzin famous for its **TERRIBLE, STINKY SMELL.**

KINKAJOUS RAID **BEES' NESTS** FOR **HONEY.**

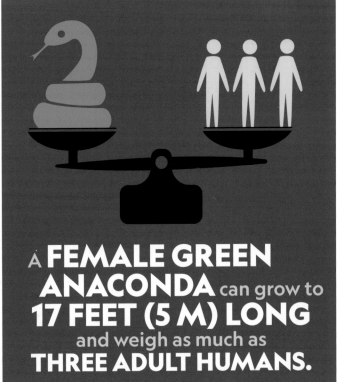

A **FEMALE GREEN ANACONDA** can grow to **17 FEET (5 M) LONG** and weigh as much as **THREE ADULT HUMANS.**

QUIZ WHIZ

You've taken an **amazingly weird** tour of South America, but how many freaky facts can you remember? Time to find out!

1 How does the Cuyaba dwarf frog protect itself?

a. It does a dance to intimidate predators.

b. It puffs up its poisonous glands to squirt poison.

c. It bites anything that approaches it.

d. It burrows itself into the ground.

2 Why is Laguna Verde green?

a. It is an optical illusion caused by the sun and ice.

b. It contains high levels of minerals.

c. Locals painted the rocks on the bottom of the lake.

d. It's full of bright green algae.

3 What is Chile's VLT?

a. Volcanic Lava Territory

b. Vampire Leech Termite

c. Visible Light Tornado

d. Very Large Telescope

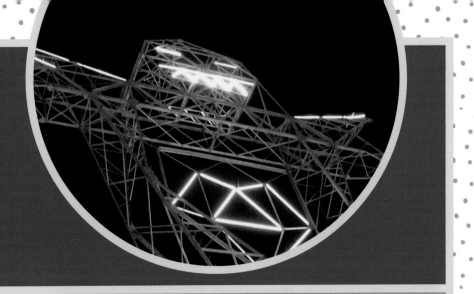

4 What is the name of this art project in Buenos Aires?

a. Coloso
b. Volticon
c. Galvano
d. Ronald

5 What's odd about the Venezuelan town of Colonia Tovar?

a. It's underground.
b. It looks like a German town.
c. The mayor is a manatee.
d. It has four festivals every week.

6 What did architect Octavio Mendoza Morales use to build a house in Colombia?

a. Pasta
b. Plants
c. Plastic
d. Pottery

7 Which of these is the only true fact about the Joseso car?

a. Its engine is clockwork.
b. It has a top speed of 70 miles an hour (113 km/h).
c. Only 200 of the cars were built.
d. It was the first new car of the 1940s.

8 Why does a marine iguana sometimes have a crust on its head?

a. It's salt from the marine iguana's powerful sneezes.
b. It grows it to protect its head from predators.
c. It rubs against clay to keep its hair dry when swimming.
d. It uses sand particles as protection against sunburn.

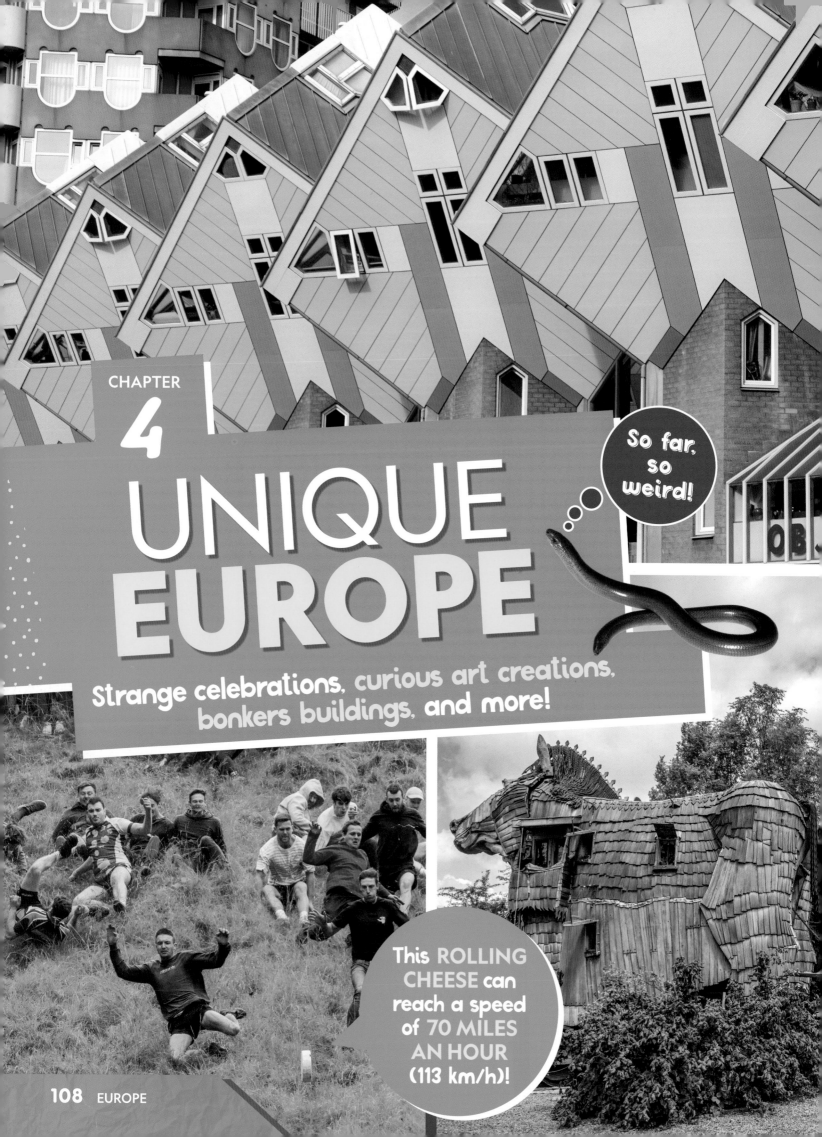

4

UNIQUE EUROPE

So far, so weird!

Strange celebrations, curious art creations, bonkers buildings, and more!

This ROLLING CHEESE can reach a speed of 70 MILES AN HOUR (113 km/h)!

This sculpture of a shark DIVING HEADFIRST into a roof is 25 FEET (7.6 m) long!

FIORENZA

WEIRD in the WORLD

WILLKOMMEN, BIENVENUE, and WELCOME TO EUROPE!

Instead of **roads**, the Dutch village of **Giethoorn** has **mostly canals**, and you have to **get around by boat!**

In remote Mývatn, Iceland, passersby can take a free **hot outdoor shower** in **water from a volcanic hot spring.**

Mývatn
ICELAND

How weird!

The Horniman Museum in London, England, is famed for its **overstuffed** walrus—they didn't know what it should look like, so the walrus is **way too big!**

NORWAY

SWEDEN

UNITED KINGDOM

IRELAND (ÉIRE)

North Sea

DENMARK

Baltic Sea

RUSSIA

London

Giethoorn

NETHERLANDS

GERMANY

POLAND

BELGIUM

LUXEMBOURG

CZECHIA (CZECH REP.)

SLOVAKIA

ATLANTIC OCEAN

LIECHTENSTEIN

AUSTRIA

Bay of Biscay

FRANCE

SWITZ.

HUNGARY

Geneva

SLOVENIA

CROATIA

ITALY

PORTUGAL

ANDORRA

MONACO

SAN MARINO

BOSNIA & HERZEGOVINA

SPAIN

MONTENEGRO

KOSOVO

VATICAN CITY

ALBANIA

Mediterranean Sea

MALTA

NORTH AMERICA

Arctic Ocean

ASIA

Atlantic Ocean

EUROPE

AFRICA

It may be the SECOND SMALLEST of the world's continents, but it's big on STRANGE PLACES, EVENTS, and ANIMALS.

In the **German language**, you can create compound words, and this is **one of the longest**: *Donaudampfschifffahrt-selektrizitätenhauptbetriebswerkbauunterbeamtengesellschaft.*

(It means "Society for Sub-Civil Servants of the Danube Steamshipping Electrical Services Main Depot Building.")

RUSSIA

Barents Sea

FINLAND

ESTONIA

LATVIA

LITHUANIA

BELARUS

KAZAKHSTAN

UKRAINE

MOLDOVA

Palace of the Parliament

ROMANIA

SERBIA

BULGARIA

NORTH MACEDONIA

TÜRKİYE (TURKEY)

GREECE

CYPRUS

GEORGIA

AZERBAIJAN

Caspian Sea

Black Sea

With **1.5 billion pounds** (680 million kg) of steel and bronze, the **Palace of the Parliament** in Romania is said to be the **heaviest** building in the world.

Near Geneva, Switzerland, the **muddy** Arve River joins the **crystal-clear** Rhône—and the **two rivers** flow along side by side!

111

NATURALLY BIZARRE

Northern Lights
Tromsø, Norway

Who needs fireworks when you can watch the northern lights? Luckily, this spectacular nighttime display isn't exclusive to just one country. They can be seen in Canada, Greenland, Sweden, and lots of other places in the Northern Hemisphere. One of the best locations to witness the stunning light show is near Tromsø, Norway. It has perfect viewing conditions—with long, dark nights between September and March and little light pollution. Also called the aurora borealis, the spectacular colors are created when tiny particles called electrons come from the sun and mix with gases in Earth's atmosphere, making them glow. And you can never be certain what you're about to see.

Legend claims that there is a golden cave under Krupaj Spring guarded by a water spirit called Tartor.

Krupaj Spring
Milanovac, Serbia

Visiting Krupaj Spring feels like stepping into a fairy tale. But first you have to find this vibrant, tucked-away turquoise lake. Between an old water mill and a hill is a small, easy-to-miss passageway. Take the narrow path through lush forest, past ponds full of fish, and you'll reach the stunning spring. After all that walking, you might be tempted to dive in. But with the water a chilly 50°F (10°C), you might want to think again! Still, there are mysteries to be explored under the rippling surface. Scuba divers have discovered a dizzying maze of underwater canals and have given the tunnels nicknames, such as "the Slide" and "the Stomach." It's no wonder that this fairy-tale spring has inspired myths and stories.

Take a seat and enjoy the view.

Green Lake

Tragöss, Austria

In a mountain village in Austria, you'll find the perfectly clear, small yet beautiful Green Lake, bordered by a pretty park with flowering trees, benches, and a wooden bridge. Well, that's what you'll find if you go during the winter! In the spring, as ice on the surrounding mountains starts to melt, extra water flows into the lake, and it gets much deeper. So deep, in fact, that the trees, pathways, benches, and bridge all end up underwater. Scuba divers used to be able to explore the magical world of the park submerged in the clear blue-green water. However, since 2016, diving there has been banned to protect the lake and prevent pollution.

Stone Mushrooms

Beli Plast, Bulgaria

These massive rocks are commonly known as the Stone Mushrooms—and they certainly wouldn't look out of place on a giant's dinner plate! They stand around eight feet (2.4 m) tall—the height of a soccer goal. They look like they've been carved, but that's not right. A local legend even claims that these bizarre rock formations are the severed heads of four sisters—and that's wrong, too! Their magnificent shapes were actually created naturally. The rocks were once mostly covered by water, which wore them down by erosion over thousands of years to create the thinner stalks. When the water dried up, the sun and wind continued shaping them.

WEIRD SHAPES

Shrinking Sphere
Tartu, Estonia

If you've seen a shape like this before, it was probably brightly colored, made of plastic, and bought from a toy store. It's a Hoberman sphere, a kind of ball that can fold and shrink down to a much smaller shape. Engineer and artist Chuck Hoberman invented it in 1992, and it went on to become a popular toy. But there are also much bigger Hoberman spheres in museums and science centers around the world—and this one, in the AHHAA Science Centre in Tartu, Estonia, is the biggest of them all. It's made of aircraft aluminum and is suspended in midair, where it constantly shrinks and grows. At its full size, it's 19 feet (5.9 m) across—as big as a large classroom!

Human Street Sculpture
Vienna, Austria

You've probably seen plenty of stone and metal statues of people in city centers, but what about art made up of actual people? This is part of a real-life living, moving artwork created by Austrian artist Willi Dorner called "Bodies in Urban Spaces." To perform the show, a team of dancers, dressed in easy-to-spot, brightly colored sweats, leads the audience through the city streets. Every so often, they suddenly arrange themselves into human patterns, shapes, or surprising positions, sometimes cramming themselves into doorways or onto window ledges, at other times using steps, walls, benches, or even other artworks as part of the performance. It's been performed in Vienna and other cities in Austria and across Europe—with each new location offering new arrangement options!

At Home in a Cube!
Rotterdam, Netherlands

Imagine living inside a giant yellow tilted cube perched on top of a concrete stalk. Well, in Rotterdam, you can do just that! These unique homes were designed in the 1970s by famous Dutch architect Piet Blom. Although they're geometric, Blom based the design on a tree. The narrow "trunks" leave plenty of space on the ground, while the cubes on top touch each other like trees in a forest, allowing those inside to bask in the sunshine. One house is open to the public and another is a hotel, so anyone can go and see what they're like inside. Don't worry—the floors aren't tilted, too! They're flat, but the walls, ceilings, and windows are all at different angles.

THE CUBE HOUSES FORM A BRIDGE TO CROSS ONE OF THE BUSIEST ROADS INTO THE CITY!

SURREAL SPORTS

Calcio Storico

Florence, Italy

Italians are famous for their love of soccer, which they call *calcio*, or "kick." And once a year, in the city of Florence, they play soccer as it used to be played—an old-fashioned version dating back at least 500 years, called *calcio storico*, or "historic soccer." The rules are very different—in fact, they're almost nonexistent! Pretty much everything you can't do in modern soccer, you CAN do in calcio storico! Each team has 27 players, dressed in medieval jester-style outfits. To get the ball into the net, they can use any body part. They're allowed to wrestle, grab, and elbow their opponents, trip each other up, and even have mass brawls. And the prize for the winners? Traditionally, it's a cow—but these days, they get a free dinner instead.

Strike while the iron's wet!

Extreme Ironing
United Kingdom

Is it a sport, a stunt, or just a joke? No one is sure, but extreme ironing is very popular—and one of the most surreal activities you can imagine. All you have to do is iron something on an ironing board in a ridiculously unlikely or challenging location. It could be a mountaintop, a roof, a rock face, up a tree, while waterskiing, or in countless other silly situations. Extreme ironing is said to date from 1980, inspired by a British man who took his ironing board camping with him. It gradually took off, and now it's spread to other countries and branched out into several different categories, including bungee ironing, high-altitude ironing, and underwater ironing (don't worry, the electricity isn't turned on!). There's even an Extreme Ironing World Championship.

Pumpkin Paddling

Ludwigsburg, Germany

If you love pumpkins—like really, *really* love pumpkins—you need to go to the Ludwigsburg Pumpkin Festival. Held every fall on the grounds of the fabulous Ludwigsburg Palace in southwestern Germany, it lasts more than a month and features over 450,000 pumpkins in hundreds of varieties and sizes. There are biggest pumpkin contests, pumpkin carving contests, pumpkin sculptures, pumpkin-based food stalls, and of course, the pumpkin regatta! Racers paddle their way across the palace lake sitting inside huge hollowed-out pumpkins, which float perfectly (although they are hard to steer). Anyone can take part in the race. Then, at the end of the festival, everyone joins in to smash up the pumpkins.

Bossaball

Spain

BOINGGG!!! Few sports are as lively as bossaball. If you haven't heard of it, that might be because it's pretty new. The sport was invented in Spain in 2004, inspired by the music and martial arts styles of Brazil, and its name means "styleball" in Portuguese. It's similar to volleyball, but it's played while bouncing on a giant inflatable court, with a built-in trampoline on each side of the net. Each four-person team has one player on the trampoline who can bounce right up above the net to score points. The fancier the moves they make in midair, the more points they score. Meanwhile, the referee is also a DJ who plays high-energy Latin music to bounce along to!

Dead WEIRD!

The Catacombs
Paris, France

Deep underneath the busy Parisian streets lie the remains of more than six million people. In the 18th century, the cemeteries couldn't cope with the number of corpses, so they were moved to tunnels beneath the city. Some of the bones were simply stacked up, but others were arranged in patterns and designs. Several hundred thousand visitors line up each year to walk just over a mile (1.6 km) through the bone-lined passageway. The complete network of tunnels, however, covers around 186 miles (300 km)!

Kaplica Czaszek
Czermna, Poland

This chapel's walls and ceiling are covered with the skulls and bones of more than 3,000 people! It was created between 1776 and 1794 by a local priest. He put everything into the decoration—his skull even became part of the altar after he died! The crypt under the chapel contains another 21,000 skeletons.

St. Michan's Mummies
Dublin, Ireland

St. Michan's Church was built on former swampland and some think methane gas rising up from the soggy ground is the reason the bodies are mummified. Notable residents include one corpse nicknamed the "Crusader," after the religious wars known as the Crusades. He was a tall man for the time, at 6.5 feet (2 m). His legs were broken and folded underneath, probably so he could be squashed into the coffin!

Hampton Court Palace
Molesey, England

Once home to King Henry VIII, it's not surprising that at least two of the royal's six wives are said to haunt Hampton Court. Some claim the ghost of Jane Seymour—Henry's third wife—carries a candle near the room where she died. Catherine Howard—Henry's fifth wife, who was beheaded for treason—is said to run through the Haunted Gallery screaming for mercy!

Sedlec Ossuary
Sedlec, Czechia (Czech Republic)

In 1870, woodcarver Frantisek Rindt was hired for an unusual and gruesome task. When a local abbot brought soil from Jerusalem to the church at Sedlec, it became a popular place to be buried. The ossuary, a room under the church, soon filled up with the remains of tens of thousands of people. Rindt was hired to decorate the chapel with the bones. First, he bleached them to make them all the same color. Then he carved them to create some astonishing structures, including a family crest and a chandelier!

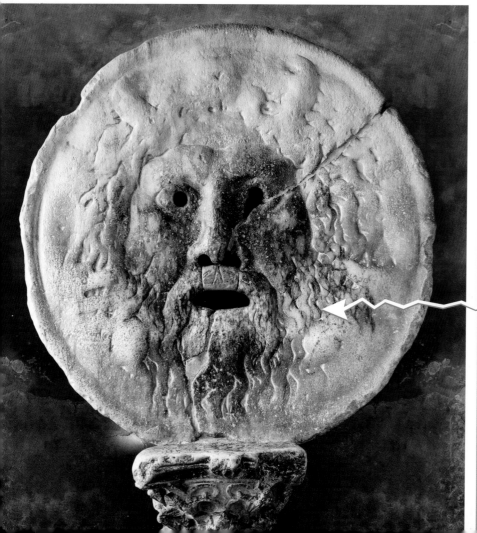

Bocca della Verità
Rome, Italy

An ancient legend claims that if you tell a lie when you stick your hand into this stone face's mouth, it will be bitten off! Some think that hundreds of years ago, the hands of lying lawbreakers were placed in the large stone disc and severed as a punishment.

PECULIAR PLANTS

Poison Garden
Alnwick, England

What could be more relaxing than a walk through a plant-filled garden? Pretty much anything when all the vegetation in it could kill you! Behind these garden gates are around 100 plants you won't find at your local florist shop. In the collection, there's giant hogweed, which can burn your skin and give you blisters that last for up to seven years! Another plant to avoid is *Aconitum,* also known as wolfsbane. It may have pretty blue flowers, but it also has poisonous roots, poisonous stems, and poisonous leaves. And its berries? Yes, you guessed it ... poisonous. The gardeners who work here often have to wear protective suits, gloves, and visors. Visitors are told not to smell, touch, or taste the plants.

Each year people are said to faint from breathing in the garden's toxic fumes!

Crooked Forest
Gryfino, Poland

If you go into these woods, you're in for a big surprise— you'll find around 400 pine trees with the same bizarre bend at the bottom of their trunks. No one knows what caused the trees to grow this way. One idea is that a heavy snowfall might have flattened the saplings, which then grew upward when the snow melted. A popular suggestion is that the crooked trees were created on purpose in the 1930s by foresters who wanted curved wood for shipbuilding or furniture-making, but the outbreak of World War II interrupted their plans and the trees were left to grow upward again. Others believe the trees were flattened during the war by German tanks, when the local town, Gryfino, was destroyed.

What's **Weird** About This **?**

The dragon arum goes by many names: the dragonwort, the Indian turnip—and the stink lily! That last name might describe this peculiar plant the best, because what really makes it unusual is its odious odor. To attract flies for pollination, it gives off a disgusting rotten-meat smell. Thankfully, the stench only lasts for about 24 hours each year! Found in Greece, the striking dragon arum has large purple leaves surrounding a dark purple column, called a spadix. It can grow to a height of more than 39 inches (1 m), so it's easy to spot—and avoid.

EYE-CATCHING ODDITIES!

"Idiom"
Prague, Czechia (Czech Republic)

Reading a book can transport you to a different place. And if you look inside the tower of books outside Prague Municipal Library, it really seems like they can send you on a long, magical journey! This impressive art installation is called "Idiom," or the "Column of Knowledge." Created by Slovakian artist Matej Krén, it's an impressive 17-foot (5.2-m)-high tower that climbs from the floor to the ceiling. A 10-foot (3-m)-tall tear-shaped opening on one side allows visitors to peer inside and enjoy an amazing view. Carefully positioned mirrors at the top and the bottom make it appear as if the colorful tunnel stretches on forever—in both directions. Each year some books are replaced to keep the tower in perfect condition. You may have been lost in a book before, but here you can experience what it feels like to be lost in thousands of them!

"IDIOM" IS CONSTRUCTED FROM AROUND 8,000 BOOKS!

Crooked House
Sopot, Poland

Would you walk inside a building that looks like it's about to fall down? Poland's Krzywy Domek, which translates to "Crooked House," looks like it's straight out of a cartoon! And that's not far from the truth. The architects who designed the building were inspired by the drawings of Per Dahlberg and Jan Marcin Szancer, who illustrated more than 200 books, including fairy tales. Built in 2004, the warped walls and glass are totally safe. Even though it might look like a bit of a squeeze from the outside, there's plenty of room inside. The Crooked House is part of a shopping center and covers 43,000 square feet (4,000 sq m), which is similar to the area inside a standard outdoor running track.

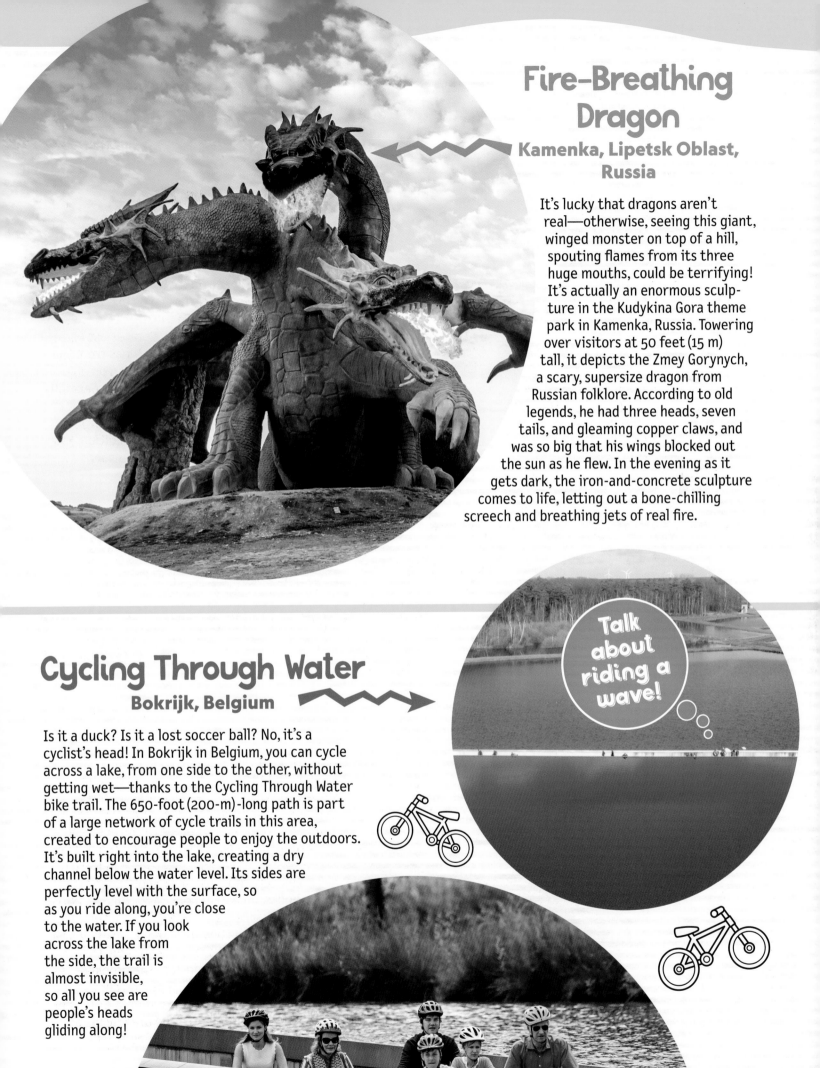

Fire-Breathing Dragon
Kamenka, Lipetsk Oblast, Russia

It's lucky that dragons aren't real—otherwise, seeing this giant, winged monster on top of a hill, spouting flames from its three huge mouths, could be terrifying! It's actually an enormous sculpture in the Kudykina Gora theme park in Kamenka, Russia. Towering over visitors at 50 feet (15 m) tall, it depicts the Zmey Gorynych, a scary, supersize dragon from Russian folklore. According to old legends, he had three heads, seven tails, and gleaming copper claws, and was so big that his wings blocked out the sun as he flew. In the evening as it gets dark, the iron-and-concrete sculpture comes to life, letting out a bone-chilling screech and breathing jets of real fire.

Cycling Through Water
Bokrijk, Belgium

Is it a duck? Is it a lost soccer ball? No, it's a cyclist's head! In Bokrijk in Belgium, you can cycle across a lake, from one side to the other, without getting wet—thanks to the Cycling Through Water bike trail. The 650-foot (200-m)-long path is part of a large network of cycle trails in this area, created to encourage people to enjoy the outdoors. It's built right into the lake, creating a dry channel below the water level. Its sides are perfectly level with the surface, so as you ride along, you're close to the water. If you look across the lake from the side, the trail is almost invisible, so all you see are people's heads gliding along!

Talk about riding a wave!

123

FASCINATING FACTS ABOUT

weird but true!

Every **JANUARY,** the people of Shetland, **SCOTLAND,** celebrate the event **Up Helly Aa** by **SETTING FIRE TO** a reproduction of **A VIKING SHIP.**

In one Spanish village, **MEN JUMP OVER ALL THE BABIES** born in the past year! The tradition is said to free them from evil.

DON'T TRY THESE AT HOME!

The town of Mohács, Hungary, holds a **SIX-DAY CARNIVAL** where men dress up in **DEVIL MASKS** and **SHEEP COSTUMES** **TO SCARE AWAY THE WINTER.**

ON **NOVEMBER 5,** IN THE TOWN OF **OTTERY ST. MARY,** ENGLAND, VILLAGERS CARRY **BARRELS OF BURNING TAR** THROUGH THE STREETS **ON THEIR BACKS.**

WEIRD YEARLY EVENTS

Every spring, **CONTESTANTS IN GLOUCESTERSHIRE,** England, participate in an event in which they **RACE DOWN A HILL TRYING TO CATCH A ROUND CHEESE.**

In Mataelpino, Spain, locals have **REPLACED BULL-RUNNING** with *boloencierro,* or "ball-running," in which they **CHASE A 10-FOOT** (3-m)-wide **BALL THROUGH THE STREETS.**

In 1993, **A POWER OUTAGE** disrupted **NEW YEAR'S EVE CELEBRATIONS** in Bérchules, Spain—so they **POSTPONED** their party **UNTIL AUGUST. (THE TRADITION STUCK!)**

ANIMAL ANTICS

Kindergarten Wolfartsweier

Wolfartsweier, Germany ➤

If you grow up in the village of Wolfartsweier, Germany, you get to go to kindergarten inside a giant cat! Built in 2011, this cool kitty was created by a team that included the famous children's book author and illustrator Tomi Ungerer, and it's designed with fun in mind. The cat's mouth is the front door, and its big round eyes are upstairs windows. The front paws contain play areas, and at the back of the building, kids can slide down the cat's tail! This kindergarten is definitely a cat, but buildings like this, in the shape of animals or other objects, are actually known as "ducks." Whether a building looks like a cat, an elephant, a shoe, or a basket—it's a duck!

I'm no one-trick pony!

La Balade des Gnomes

Durbuy, Belgium

Here's another great European "duck": a hotel in the shape of a horse! Not just any horse, but the famous Trojan Horse of Greek mythology. In the legend, the Greek army hid inside a giant wooden horse on wheels to sneak into the enemy city of Troy. The horse is just one of several guest rooms and cabins at La Balade des Gnomes hotel in Belgium, all with a mythological or adventure theme. (The others include a moon room, a desert island, and a troll's den.) If you stay in the horse, you'll be a lot more comfortable than the ancient Greek soldiers were—it has a TV lounge, three cozy beds, a wooden jacuzzi, and a coffee machine!

Duck House

Brighton, England

Do you need a rubber duck? How about hundreds of them? In Brighton, England, there's a shop that sells more than 400 different varieties of rubber ducks to keep you company in the bathtub. At Duck House, you can find a superhero duck, a Star Trek duck, a guitar-playing rock star duck, a queen duck with a crown, or even a spooky ghost, vampire, or zombie duck! Whatever your interest or hobby, favorite sport or TV show, there's a duck for you!

Weirdly Cute!

Slowworm

Few creatures can be more confusing than this bizarre burrowing beast! The slowworm is also called the deaf adder or the blind-worm. But it's not blind, it's not deaf, it's not really that slow, and it's not even a worm! It's not a snake, either, although it kind of looks like one. In fact, it's a type of legless lizard. Like other lizards, it can blink (snakes can't—they have no eyelids!), and when in danger, it can shed its tail. The tail keeps on wriggling, distracting its predator while the rest of the slowworm makes its getaway. If that doesn't work, slowworms can also produce an extra-stinky poop to put predators off! Despite this, gardeners love them because they gobble up pests like slugs and snails. And just look at that adorable face!

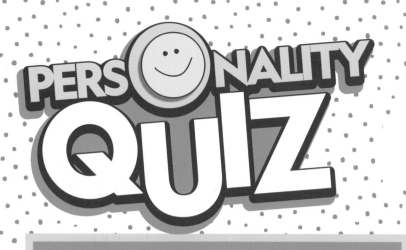

PERSONALITY QUIZ

Which unique European animal are you?

Write down your answers for each question **and see which letter you** picked the most often.

1 **What are you like at parties?**

a. I'm usually on the lookout for food.
b. I'm always the best dressed.
c. I hang out in a big group with my pals.
d. I don't like parties!

2 **What would you rather eat?**

a. A burger
b. Candy
c. Leafy greens
d. Popcorn shrimp

3 **How would you describe your look?**

a. Stylish yet relaxed
b. Maximum glam!
c. Just got out of bed
d. Unique and mysterious

4 **You're off on a day trip in the great outdoors. Which would you choose?**

a. A mountain hike
b. A picnic in a flower-filled meadow
c. A trek through a wild forest
d. An adventurous caving trip

5 **Which of these is your dream vacation home?**

a. A little stone cottage
b. A sunny villa
c. A nice grassy campsite
d. A secret bunker

6 What role would you have in a fairy-tale play?

a. The wise wizard
b. The magical fairy
c. The hairy giant
d. The dragon

7 Choose a color.

a. Gold
b. Red
c. Brown
d. Black

8 What's your ideal weather?

a. Bright and frosty
b. Hot and sunny
c. Cool and cloudy—I don't want to overheat.
d. Dark, dreary, and damp

Mostly A's

You are ... an Iberian lynx! You're one wild, rare, and beautiful cool cat, and you'd love the high life up in the snowy and rocky mountains of Spain. You may look cute on the outside, but you're actually a fast, sharp-witted hunter.

Mostly B's

You are ... a six-spot burnet moth! When it comes to looking good, you take the crown. You're not afraid to show off a bit, and you love to soak up the sun, like this stylish moth that's active during the day.

Mostly C's

You are ... a European bison! Just like this animal, which makes its home in remote forests, you like to live off the beaten path. You're a friendly beast and love to hang out with your herd.

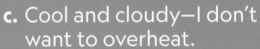

Mostly D's

You are ... an olm! You're a mysterious lone wolf, just like this aquatic salamander that makes its home in the underground rivers of southern Europe.

ANNUAL ABSURDITIES!

Caga Tió
Catalonia

There are lots of Christmas customs: singing festive songs, leaving out cookies for Santa, feeding the log that poops out sweets … Wait, what? The log that poops out sweets? That's right! Caga Tió is a hollow log with a happy face at one end—and it "poops" out sweets from the other! In the weeks before Christmas in Catalonia, children cover their festive friend with a blanket and feed him bread and orange peel. On Christmas Eve, Caga Tió delivers small presents. As encouragement, children whack it with a stick and sing a song, ordering the log to poop out gifts of sweets, nuts, and small toys!

Caga Tió means "poop log"!

Air Guitar World Championships
Oulu, Finland

If you have no great musical skill but love to put on a performance, this could be the perfect event for you. Every year, competitors from around the world head to Oulu to pluck, strum, and get their groove on to their favorite tracks. It's open to all ages and you don't need any special equipment—just enthusiasm. The organizers think that if everyone in the world played air guitar at once, all bad things would vanish and it could lead to world peace. Now that's gotta be worth a try!

What's **Weird** About This **?**

Keep the noise down!

Once a year, fireworks light up the night sky on the Greek island of Chios. But it's not to entertain the local people—this is rocket-powered rivalry! For hundreds of years, an annual battle has taken place in the town of Vrontados. The targets are two churches on separate hills around 1,300 feet (400 m) apart. Bizarrely, no one seems to know why this colorful contest began! Local legend claims that until 1889 cannons were used, but after they were banned, homemade rockets took their place. Each year, up to 80,000 fireworks are fired between the two churches. The aim is to hit the opposing church's bell tower, although it's hard to see in all the chaos when that happens.

FLOWER FIELDS

The Netherlands

WEIRD WONDERS

Wake up and smell the flowers with this human-made colorful wonder.

More than

HALF THE WORLD'S FRESH CUT FLOWERS

come from the Netherlands.

A definite case of flower power!

Can you tell what these stunning multicolored stripes are made of? Maybe they're part of a vibrant carpet or a traditional woven fabric? Nope! Take a closer look, and you'll see that this is an aerial photograph. It shows the fabulous flower fields of the Netherlands, where flowers such as tulips, daffodils, and hyacinths are important crops. Tourists flock to see the fields in bloom in April and May before the flowers are cut and sent off around the world.

DISHING THE DIRT!

Stay in a Sewer!
Ottensheim, Austria

How would you like to spend the night in a sewer pipe? It sounds damp, dirty, and stinky ... and like a rat might nibble your toes while you snooze! But don't worry—with these sewer bedrooms, it's a totally different story. At Dasparkhotel in Ottensheim, Austria, each room is made from a section of seven-foot (2-m)-wide concrete sewer pipe, standing in a park. They're safe and cozy, and each one comes with a comfortable bed, a skylight, a lamp, and even a power socket so you can charge your phone! They're also eco-friendly since they're made from reused discarded pipes, and cheap—in fact, each guest decides how much to pay for the night. Sleep tight!

World Bog Snorkelling Championships
Llanwrtyd Wells, Wales

Participants in this bizarre competition are ready to make a splash! The course is a water-filled trench carved through marshy bogland. Wearing a snorkel, mask, and flippers, the contestants attempt to cover 360 feet (110 m) as speedily as possible—relying solely on flipper power! Neil Rutter has proven to be the snorkeler to beat recently, taking home the title in 2017, 2018, and 2019 and setting a world record of 1 minute 18.82 seconds on the way. Of course, many people compete for fun and plunge into the dirty water wearing costumes. Dinosaurs, pea pods, and sharks have all been seen battling the bog!

LLANWRTYD WELLS HOLDS A **BIKE BOG SNORKELING** COMPETITION WHERE YOU CAN RIDE ALONG **THE COURSE ON A CUSTOMIZED BICYCLE!**

GREEN EVENT

Mud! Glorious mud!

Swamp Soccer
Finland

Any soccer players who complain about a damp field or a few drops of rain might want to pass on swamp soccer. This physically demanding sport is played on muddy bogs and players can find themselves buried up to their waists in sludge! The game originated in Finland in 1998 when 13 teams competed in the first tournament. In the 2019 World Championships, around 200 teams battled it out. Matches usually last just 24 minutes because charging through the mud is so exhausting. That might explain why goals aren't that common, too. Anyone who pays the entry fee can play in the world championships, but all players have one thing in common—they don't mind a good mud bath!

Treasure Seekers
Staffordshire, England

Getting muddy is fun, right? Getting muddy because you've found buried treasure is even better! In 2009, a metal detectorist named Terry Herbert was searching a farmer's field when his detector beeped. At that point he had no idea what he had discovered. It was the largest ever find of Anglo-Saxon gold and silver—that means the items are around 1,500 years old. Over 4,000 pieces of jewelry and other objects were uncovered by the end of the year.

The hoard was valued at a staggering £3.28 million ($4.6 million)!

IMPROBABLE ITALY

International Highline Meeting Festival
The Dolomites, Italy

Most festival-goers sleep in a tent or maybe a camper van. But not at the International Highline Meeting Festival! This meetup, held every year in Italy's Dolomites mountain range, is for fans of highlining—an adventure sport that involves walking along a slack, bouncy tightrope strung between two cliffs or mountaintops. After a busy day of rope-walking—and enjoying festival food and music—the attendees head for bed and snuggle up in tiny hammocks suspended below a highline, dangling hundreds of feet above the ground. Just in case anyone has a nightmare or starts sleepwalking, each person has a safety line attached to the rope as well. Not the easiest setup if you need a midnight bathroom run!

Feva Restaurant
Veneto, Italy

Bored of the same old menu options? In that case, the Feva restaurant in Veneto, in northern Italy, will be like a breath of fresh air. The chefs there have come up with a very light snack, known as *aria fritta*, or "fried air." It's made of very thin layers of tapioca (made from cassava, a potato-like plant), which are deep-fried and dried, forming a puffy ball that looks like a tiny cloud. It's then filled with ozone, a type of oxygen gas, and sprayed with flavorings before being served on a bed of fluffy cotton candy. When you bite into one, it's said to be like breathing fresh Italian mountain air. Delicious! Luckily for the restaurant's customers, it's just an appetizer, and they can get something more filling to follow.

BY the NUMBERS

GARGANTUAN GAMES

The Colosseum was built between A.D. 72 and 80 in ancient Rome. Big enough to easily fit a soccer field inside, this amazing arena hosted some unusual events, which were free to watch, including gladiator contests, animal hunts, and prisoner executions. The Colosseum was sometimes even filled with water for mock naval battles!

36 TRAPDOORS IN THE ARENA WERE USED FOR SPECIAL EFFECTS, INCLUDING AMAZING SCENERY AND EXOTIC ANIMALS SUDDENLY APPEARING!

MORE THAN **6 MILLION** TOURISTS VISIT THE REMAINS EVERY YEAR.

164 FEET (50 M) HIGH—THAT'S ABOUT THE HEIGHT OF A MODERN 12-STORY BUILDING.

620 FEET (189 M) LONG

AND **513 FEET** (156 M) WIDE (THIS MAKES IT THE LARGEST AMPHITHEATER IN THE WORLD!)

50,000 SPECTATORS COULD FIT IN THE ARENA.

Going UNDER!

I'm getting tunnel vision!

Piusa Sand Caves
Piusa, Estonia

For almost 50 years, Piusa was home to a huge quarry. But when the workers left the 13.7-mile (22-km) network of caves and corridors, new residents moved in—bats! Between October and May, more than 3,000 of the flying mammals come to Piusa Sand Caves to hibernate. That makes the caves the biggest wintering colony of bats in Eastern Europe. The caves are now protected, but you'd have to be batty to want to disturb these creatures!

Olms
Italy, Slovenia, and Croatia

These salamanders were first identified in 1689, when locals thought they were baby dragons! Olms have spent so long in dark caves that they're almost blind. Instead, they rely on their smell and hearing to catch prey. But they can survive for years without eating!

Large Hadron Collider
Meyrin, Switzerland

There are a lot of big science projects taking place at CERN (the European Council for Nuclear Research). And you don't get much bigger than the Large Hadron Collider, which makes tiny particles travel at extremely accelerated speeds. It's a vast underground ring of magnets—16.8 miles (27 km) in circumference. That's the "large" part—and it's a collider because it smashes particles together up to one billion times every second! Ultimately, it will help scientists learn what the universe was like when it was created in the big bang.

British Museum Tube Station
London, England

Announcements in London's metro system tell travelers to "mind the gap" between the train and the platform. But should some stations warn people to mind the spirits instead? Farringdon Station is said to have a "Screaming Specter," and it's claimed an "Elderly Angel" calls Aldgate Station home. Abandoned stations provide perfect haunting spots, too. The British Museum Station, open between 1900 and 1933, is supposed to be home to the ghost of either the Egyptian pharaoh Amun-Re, or his daughter—depending on who you ask. Legend says the ghost screams so loudly that the sound carries through the tunnels to other stations!

I miss my mummy!

Fingal's Cave
Isle of Staffa, Scotland

The translation of this cave's original Gaelic name is the "Cave of Melody." The echoes of waves inside the huge, arched hollow inspired 19th-century composer Felix Mendelssohn to write *Fingal's Cave Overture*. Writers, poets, and artists have also visited the cave to be inspired.

Syri i Kaltër
Albania

When you gaze into this water, are you looking at it ... or is it looking at you? Syri i Kaltër translates to "Blue Eye," and this beautiful pool lives up to its name. The dark waters in the center look like a pupil surrounded by a turquoise-and-green iris. No one knows exactly how deep it is. Divers have swam down 164 feet (50 m), but still couldn't see the bottom!

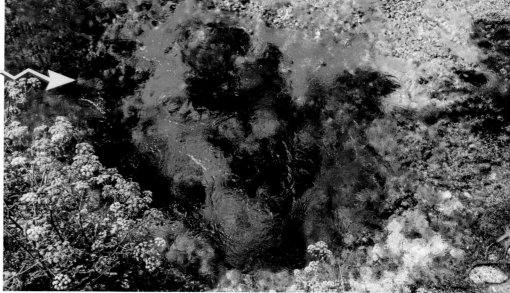

Škocjan Caves
Matavun, Slovenia

The Škocjan Caves make up one of the largest known underground canyons on Earth. The caves were inhabited from around 10,000 years ago, through the Stone and Bronze Ages, and the remains of an Iron Age temple have been discovered there, too. The caves are now home to a remarkable collection of plants and animals. The total length of all the cave passageways is around 3.7 miles (6 km), and visitors can marvel at the numerous pools and huge stalagmites within.

139

BIZARRE BUILDINGS

Seed Stash
Svalbard, Norway

This solitary concrete structure jutting out of the icy wilderness may look like a super-villain's hideaway, but it's a lot more important than that! It's the Svalbard Seed Vault, where seeds from all over the world are stored to keep all the species and varieties of plants and crops safe. If any of them are wiped out by disasters or climate change, we can use the stored seeds to get them back. The vault contains over a million different types of seeds. If you're wondering how they fit them in such a small space, don't worry: This is just the doorway! The vault itself is down a tunnel, deep inside a mountain on the remote Arctic island of Svalbard, to protect it from disasters, wars, weather, and attack.

The Pan House
Zagaré, Lithuania

If you ever need to borrow a pan in Lithuania, a man named Edmundas Vaiciulis has quite a collection! The only problem is they are attached to his house. Vaiciulis prefers to do things his own way and doesn't always follow the rules. He only lasted one week in his first ever job because his boss didn't like his hairstyle or his footwear, and he refused to change either! When he bought half of a house, he wanted to rebuild all of it, but the owners of the other half were happy with the building as it was. Unable to renovate, Vaiciulis decorated the exterior with pots, pans, and old machinery parts instead. The Pan House, as it's known, is now one of the most photographed homes in Zagaré.

Kunsthofpassage
Dresden, Germany

If you've ever said it's too rainy to go outside, you probably don't live in Dresden! A sudden downpour is the ideal weather to take a trip to the Kunsthofpassage. Here you'll find five small, themed courtyards created by local artists, sculptors, and designers. In the Courtyard of Elements, the front of one building is covered with funnels, pipes, and gutters, which look like bizarre musical instruments. And that's exactly what they are! When the rain begins, so does the soggy symphony. The drops loudly pitter-patter off the metalwork and flow through the pipes, splattering on the paving slabs in the yard below. Local residents must need earplugs on a rainy night!

One courtyard features images of wild monkeys and giraffes on its walls.

Fish Out of Water
Headington, Oxford, England

Strolling around the leafy Oxford suburb of Headington, you might be surprised to find an enormous shark statue plunging into the roof of one of the houses. The 25-foot-long (7.6-m) fiberglass shark, called the Headington Shark, was commissioned in 1986 by the then owner of the house as a political statement. While neighbors were at first fairly unhappy about the, um, unusual decor, most now agree it's pretty fin-tastic.

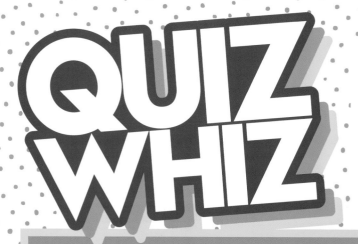

QUIZ WHIZ

It's hard to keep track of all this weirdness! See how much you can remember with this quiz. Grab a piece of paper and write down your answers.

1 What natural object inspired Rotterdam's cube houses?
a. A rock
b. A seashell
c. A tree
d. A wave

2 Which of these is NOT a real contest?
a. The High-Altitude Hammock Race
b. The Extreme Ironing World Championships
c. The Ludwigsburg Pumpkin Regatta
d. World Bog Snorkelling Championships

3 What unusual feature has been built in a lake in Belgium?
a. A garage
b. A cycle path
c. A chicken coop
d. A laundromat

4 Which of these was invented by a restaurant in Italy?

a. Fried water
b. Fried fire
c. Fried air
d. Fried mud

5 Which animal can be found sticking out of a roof in Oxford, England?

a. A horse
b. A dragon
c. A giraffe
d. A shark

6 What can you find hidden away in a vault in Svalbard, Norway?

a. Old books
b. Rubber ducks
c. Seeds
d. Very large telescopes

8 In a competition in Gloucestershire, England, contestants try to catch ...

a. A bull
b. A round cheese
c. A toy car
d. A person dressed as a zebra

7 What's the name for a building that looks like an object?

a. A duck
b. A goose
c. A swan
d. A woodpecker

Answers: 1. c, 2. a, 3. b, 4. c, 5. d, 6. c, 7. a, 8. b

143

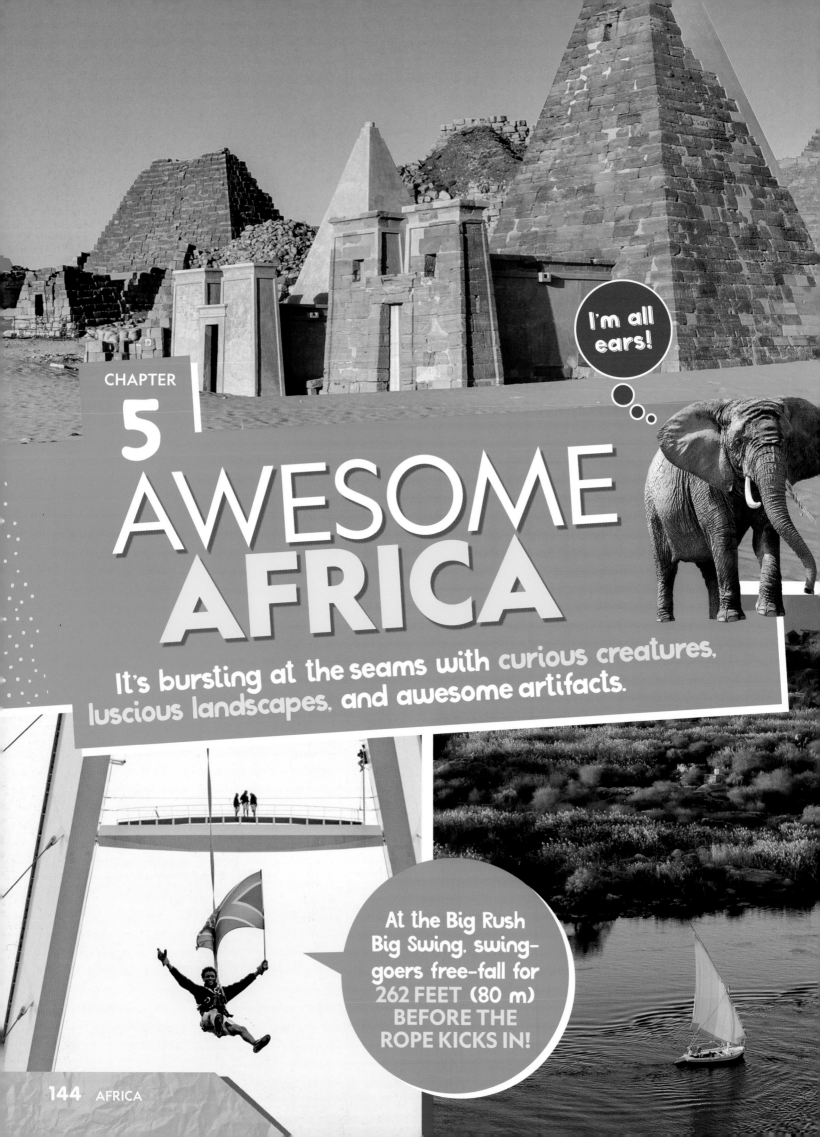

I'm all ears!

5 AWESOME AFRICA

It's bursting at the seams with curious creatures, luscious landscapes, and awesome artifacts.

At the Big Rush Big Swing, swing-goers free-fall for **262 FEET (80 m) BEFORE THE ROPE KICKS IN!**

This BRIGHTLY COLORED building is inspired by TRADITIONAL GHANAIAN TEXTILE PATTERNS!

As many as 100 SOCIABLE WEAVER FAMILIES can live in a nest at ONE TIME.

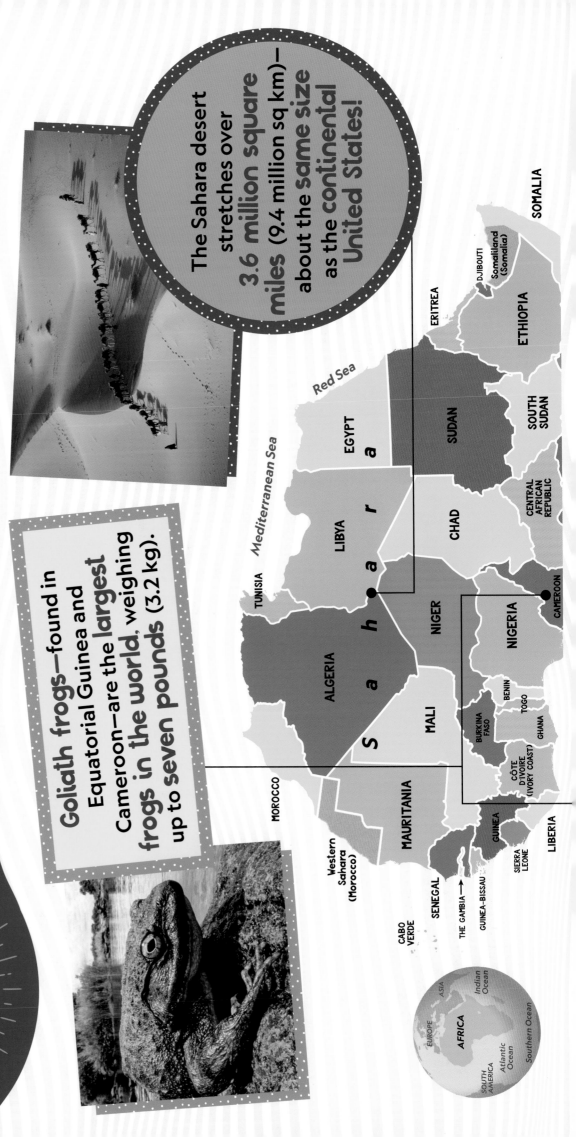

WEIRD in the WORLD

Explore an **INCREDIBLE CONTINENT** full of **STRANGE SIGHTS, AWESOME CELEBRATIONS,** and **FASCINATING ANIMALS.**

The Sahara desert stretches over 3.6 million square miles (9.4 million sq km)—about the same size as the continental United States!

Goliath frogs—found in Equatorial Guinea and Cameroon—are the largest frogs in the world, weighing up to seven pounds (3.2 kg).

Mediterranean Sea

Red Sea

TUNISIA

MOROCCO

Western Sahara (Morocco)

ALGERIA

LIBYA

EGYPT

S a h a r a

MAURITANIA

MALI

NIGER

CHAD

SUDAN

ERITREA

DJIBOUTI

Somaliland (Somalia)

SOMALIA

ETHIOPIA

SOUTH SUDAN

CENTRAL AFRICAN REPUBLIC

CABO VERDE

SENEGAL

THE GAMBIA →

GUINEA-BISSAU

GUINEA

SIERRA LEONE

LIBERIA

CÔTE D'IVOIRE (IVORY COAST)

BURKINA FASO

GHANA

TOGO

BENIN

NIGERIA

CAMEROON

SOUTH AMERICA

EUROPE

ASIA

AFRICA

Atlantic Ocean

Indian Ocean

Southern Ocean

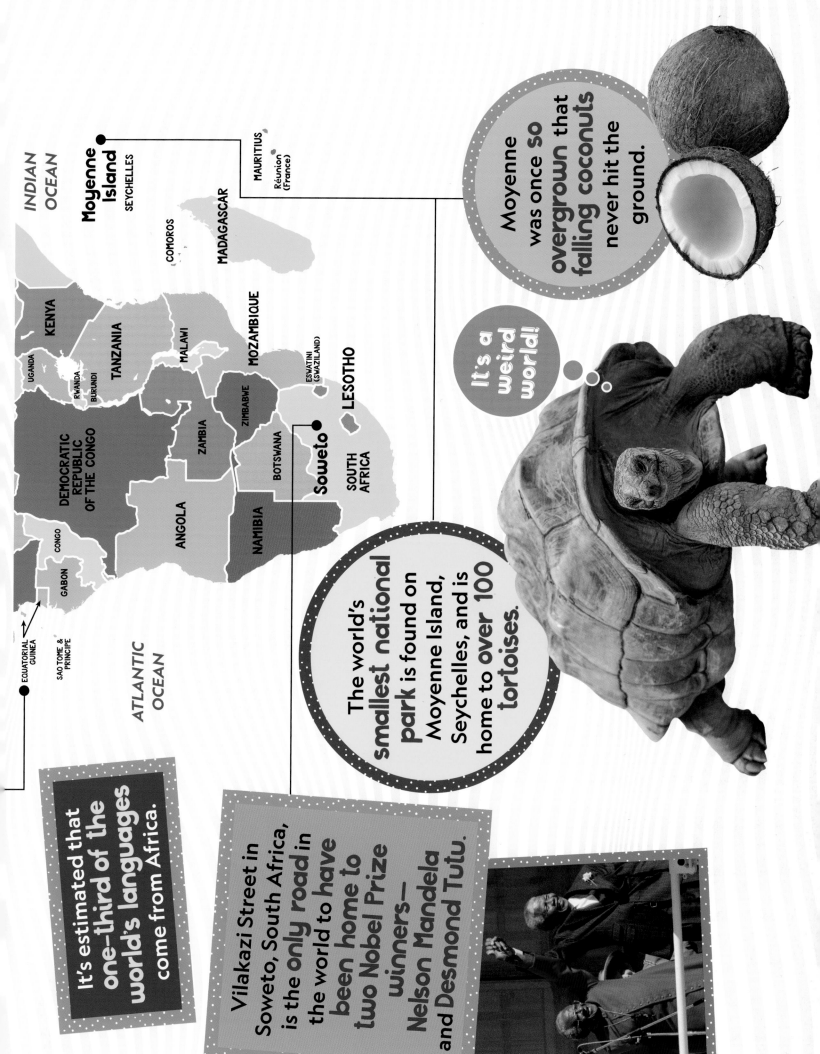

INDIAN OCEAN

Moyenne Island
SEYCHELLES

MAURITIUS

Réunion (France)

MADAGASCAR

COMOROS

KENYA

UGANDA

RWANDA

BURUNDI

TANZANIA

MALAWI

DEMOCRATIC REPUBLIC OF THE CONGO

MOZAMBIQUE

ZIMBABWE

ESWATINI (SWAZILAND)

ZAMBIA

CONGO

GABON

EQUATORIAL GUINEA

SAO TOME & PRINCIPE

ANGOLA

NAMIBIA

BOTSWANA

Soweto

SOUTH AFRICA

LESOTHO

ATLANTIC OCEAN

Moyenne was once so overgrown that falling coconuts never hit the ground.

It's a weird world!

The world's smallest national park is found on Moyenne Island, Seychelles, and is home to over 100 tortoises.

It's estimated that one-third of the world's languages come from Africa.

Vilakazi Street in Soweto, South Africa, is the only road in the world to have been home to two Nobel Prize winners—Nelson Mandela and Desmond Tutu.

BIZARRE VEHICLES

Traffic Robots
Kinshasa, Democratic Republic of the Congo

You might think you've been transported into a futuristic movie set when driving around Kinshasa! Gigantic aluminum robots fitted with cameras on their shoulders and eyes can be found towering high above the bustling traffic. Designed to tackle serious traffic incidents, the robots' cameras broadcast a live feed to the central police command to help control the road's busy flow. With around nine million residents in the capital city, car accidents were frequent and have now greatly decreased. These solar-powered, revolutionary road officers have red and green lights on their hands to signal oncoming traffic. They can even talk or sing to motorists and pedestrians below!

Shipwreck Lodge
Skeleton Coast National Park, Namibia

This beautiful location, complete with rolling sand dunes and waves crashing in the distance, looks idyllic, but the Skeleton Coast in Namibia has a darker side. When the dry air of the desert meets the cold water of the Atlantic, it causes dense fog that can disorient sailors and cause their ships to run aground. Although this is no longer such a regular occurrence, the many wrecks along this coastline were the inspiration behind the design of these isolated lodges. They provide a unique experience for those wanting to bask in the eerie tranquility of the Skeleton Coast.

Microlight Flights
Victoria Falls, Zambia

This breathtaking experience is not for the faint of heart. Daredevils can get the feeling of being "kissed by an angel" as they glide through a mist of water droplets above the colossal Victoria Falls. Swooping over this part of the Zambezi River in a microlight, or lightweight plane, will definitely make you feel small—the water in Victoria Falls drops an incredible 360 feet (110 m). If you can cope with feelings of vertigo, the views are said to be unparalleled, and you may even catch a glimpse of some roaming wildlife on your journey.

VICTORIA FALLS IS CLASSIFIED AS THE WORLD'S LARGEST SHEET OF FALLING WATER.

I'm off to a flying start!

Macrobat
South Africa

Meet the Macrobat! Currently just a concept, this revolutionary design is set to transform personal air travel. Phractyl, a South African start-up company, has shared its vision for an all-electric birdlike aircraft that could tilt its wings, squat down, and even take off and land almost vertically. Currently designed as a one-seater, the plane could be piloted on board or remotely. It has many planned purposes, including as a taxi or to deliver medical supplies. The craft has a maximum travel range of 93 miles (150 km) and would be built to carry a 330-pound (150-kg) load. A prototype is under construction, and it sounds like a soaring success!

Curious CREATURES

Hairy Frog

Frogs are not hairy. But the hairy frog is—kind of! During the breeding season, the male frog grows strange tassel-like parts along his sides. They are actually made of skin, and they're thought to help the frog take in extra oxygen when he's underwater guarding his eggs. However, that's not even the weirdest thing about hairy frogs! They also have bones in their feet that can turn into claws. If the frog is in danger, its toe bones snap, then stick out through its skin, ready to fight off predators. This has earned it the nickname "the Wolverine frog"!

Satanic Leaf-Tailed Gecko

This small tree lizard from the island of Madagascar is a master of camouflage. It's not just its tail that looks like an old, dead leaf—so does every other part of its body! Its brilliant disguise helps it to hide from predators, and also to creep up on prey without being seen. To add to the effect, the gecko can flatten itself against a tree trunk. So far, so leafy, but why is it called "satanic"? It's because it has bright red eyes and two little horns, which give it a devilish look.

South African Springhare

It looks like some kind of "kanga-rabbit," with its long springy back legs that let it leap up high. However, this awesome animal is a springhare. Measuring just up to one foot (45 cm) in length, this kooky burrowing creature is only slightly larger than an aardvark's tongue! Yet these miniature hoppers can leap more than six feet (2 m). Their curious qualities don't stop there, though—they also glow fluorescent pink and orange under UV light.

Ground Pangolin

This creature might look like it's half reptile and half pine cone, but it's actually a strange, scaly mammal called a pangolin! Pangolins use their impressive scales—which make up about 20 percent of the animal's body weight—as defense against predators. When a hungry animal gets close, the pangolin curls up into a tight ball, and its scales act like tough armor. Pangolins can even close their ears and nostrils to protect themselves from attacks!

Aardvark

This long-nosed super-sniffer is quite the character. With such a prominent snout, it's no surprise that its name translates from Afrikaans as "earth pig." Aardvarks may look strange, but their bodies are perfectly adapted to their sub-Saharan homes. Their incredibly powerful claws mean they can easily burrow and dig up termite mounds—where their favorite food lives. Their thick skin protects them from insect bites, and their long ears disperse heat, helping them to survive in warmer climates. Aardvark sightings are rare because they are nocturnal, spend a lot of time underground, and are solitary animals.

Feasting on termites isn't "aard" with this snout!

Shoebill

You can probably guess how this bird got its name! One of Africa's strangest-looking creatures, the shoebill has a huge beak that looks like a shoe. Or maybe a whale, seeing as it's also known as the whale-headed stork (though it's not considered a stork anymore). It's a huge, fish-eating waterbird, standing up to five feet (1.5 m) tall! You might not expect a bird like this to have a beautiful singing voice—and you'd be right. Instead, the shoebill makes a clattering noise with its beak, or a strange mooing sound like a cow.

RECORD BREAKERS

Twin Town
Igbo-Ora, Nigeria

In most parts of the world, twins are unusual, but in Igbo-Ora, Nigeria, they're everywhere! This small town has the highest rate of twin births in the world. At least one person in 10 here is a twin. What's more, it's traditional to name twins Taiwo and Kehinde, meaning "first-born" and "second-born"—so a lot of Igbo-Ora's twins have the same names! Some locals say the high twin rate is due to their diet, which includes a lot of okra leaves and yams, but no one is really sure. Since 2018, the town has even held a Festival of Twins, attended by twins from far and wide.

Loudest Insect
Sub-Saharan Africa

What's that noise that sounds like a high-pitched chain saw at top speed? If you're in Africa, it might just be an insect: the shrill thorntree cicada. The males vibrate drumlike parts on their bodies to attract females, generating an ear-busting racket that's been measured at 106.7 decibels, making this mild-mannered bug the loudest insect in the world. So you might wonder, how does the cicada itself stand the noise? Its ears are on its sides, with special flaps to cover them up so it doesn't deafen itself. Genius!

The noise made by the thorntree cicada is as loud as a rock concert!

The Big Rush Big Swing

Moses Mabhida Stadium, Durban, South Africa

Brave enough to take a seat? The Big Rush Big Swing sits 348 feet (106 m) above this World Cup soccer arena. As it swings (at a height taller than the Statue of Liberty!), it completes a massive 722-foot (220-m) arc under the stadium's colossal roof. Thrill-seekers of all ages can enjoy the ride: There is no age limit—riders as young as eight have taken a swing, as well as some 75-year-olds! If you're in no hurry to experience the "big rush" yourself, there is a viewing gallery in the stadium where you can watch friends and family take the plunge.

Most Vuvuzelas

Nelson Mandela Stadium, Port Elizabeth, South Africa

South Africa's favorite sport is soccer, and the best way to show your support for your team is to blow on your vuvuzela—a long plastic horn that plays a loud vibrating note. Vuvuzelas are cheap to buy and easy to play, and South Africa's soccer fans often bring them to matches. So a soccer stadium was the perfect place to set a new world record for most vuvuzelas being played at once! It happened on July 23, 2009, at the Nelson Mandela Stadium in Port Elizabeth. 12,511 spectators blew their vuvuzelas all together, and entered the record books.

THE SOUND OF THE VUVUZELA HAS BEEN DESCRIBED AS BEING LIKE A SWARM OF ANGRY WASPS.

BY the NUMBERS

PYRAMIDS AT GIZA

The Pyramids at Giza in Cairo, Egypt's capital, are among the most famous buildings in the world.

The ancient Egyptians built the three largest pyramids as tombs for three pharaohs, Khufu, Khafre, and Menkaure. They were made by cutting and stacking layer upon layer of big, heavy stone blocks, probably by dragging them up ramps of earth. It was an incredible feat, especially so long ago, when there were no power tools, cranes, or bulldozers!

HEIGHT OF THE GREAT PYRAMID TODAY:

449.5 FEET (137 M)

AGE OF THE PYRAMIDS:

OVER 4,500 YEARS

WIDTH OF THE GREAT PYRAMID:

756 FEET (230 M)

—AS LONG AS TWO SOCCER FIELDS

HOW LONG THE GREAT PYRAMID STOOD AS THE WORLD'S TALLEST BUILDING:

3,871 YEARS

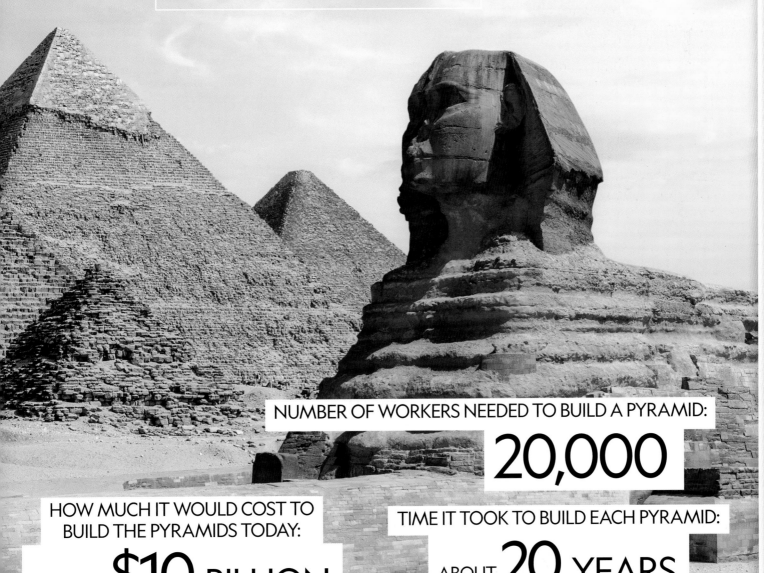

WEIGHT OF EACH STONE BLOCK:

AT LEAST **2.5** TONS (2.3 t)

—AS MUCH AS 35 PEOPLE, OR ONE SMALL ELEPHANT

NUMBER OF STONE BLOCKS IN THE GREAT PYRAMID:

2.3 MILLION

NUMBER OF WORKERS NEEDED TO BUILD A PYRAMID:

20,000

HOW MUCH IT WOULD COST TO BUILD THE PYRAMIDS TODAY:

AROUND **$10** BILLION

TIME IT TOOK TO BUILD EACH PYRAMID:

ABOUT **20** YEARS

CREATIVE CRITTERS

Elephant Street Art
South Africa

Falko One is a street artist who is making his mark on Cape Town, South Africa—literally! He is the man behind an outbreak of elephants popping up in unexpected places all over the city. His art adorns some weird canvases including boats, staircases, and even old dumpsters! And quite often, the art incorporates elements of the surroundings in unusual ways—one of his elephants might appear to be holding up an air-conditioning unit like a boombox or plucking a piece of fruit from a nearby tree. Falko One began painting when he was 16 years old. After painting an elephant from memory (to hide another picture of chickens), he quickly found his style and has been painting colorful elephants ever since!

There's room for one more!

Sociable Weaver
Southern Africa

Do you know the expression "There's no place like home"? Well, the sociable weaver, native to the dry savannas of southern Africa, has proven just that. These incredible crafters design the most popular residences around—each nest acts like a huge apartment building for an entire colony. Some of their artsy creations are home to up to 100 different families—that could mean as many as 400 birds in a single nest! Sometimes stretching more than 20 feet (6 m) wide and almost 10 feet (3 m) tall, single nests have been known to be inhabited for up to 100 years. This avian art combines fashion *and* function!

I call this "Portrait of the Artist as a Young Pig"!

Pigcasso
Franschhoek Valley, South Africa

Meet Pigcasso, who could trot into a gallery near you! Since being rescued in 2016 by her co-artist, Joanne, Pigcasso has been creating masterpieces that have been admired worldwide. Joanne first encouraged the piggy painter when she noticed the hog's interest in some paintbrushes that had been left lying around. While Pigcasso holds the brush in her mouth and paints across the canvas, Joanne applies colors to the brush. The art they create together has an admirable goal—Joanne hopes it will help people think more carefully about the negative effects of animal agriculture. All the money made from the artwork goes to Farm Sanctuary South Africa, a nonprofit organization.

Cool CONSTRUCTIONS !

Big Pineapple

SpongeBob SquarePants may live in a pineapple under the sea, but this real-life pineapple building is on land, in Bathurst, South Africa. It was built in the 1980s to celebrate the local pineapple-growing industry, which took off in the 1800s after farmers realized how well pineapples grew there. This pineapple isn't actually a house, however. Inside, its four floors contain a pineapple-themed museum and shop. Though there are other pineapple buildings in the world, this one is the tallest, so it holds the record for the biggest pineapple on Earth!

Villaggio Vista

These landmark buildings, which include the tallest residential tower in West Africa, have an amazing design inspired by their location. If you are into bold colors, then these luxury apartments will be right up your alley. The eye-catching structures are part of Villaggio Vista, an innovative project to create high-rise living in a place where earthquakes and a hot climate have made building upward difficult in the past. Its striking patterns are inspired by Kente (Ghanaian textile) weaving patterns. You could even say the buildings are dressed for success!

Lemon Squeezer Church

Is it a rocket? Is it an upside-down flower? No—it's a lemon squeezer! Or at least that's the nickname given to the Church of St. Anthony in Maputo, Mozambique. Built in 1962, it's made of smooth sheets of concrete that look as if they've been folded up like origami. The shape is exactly the same on the inside as on the outside. There's just one big circular room, with a zig-zagging, folded ceiling, and a view all the way up the tall, cone-shaped spire, lit up by beautiful stained-glass windows.

Hotel With Wings

Would you like to stay in a hotel room that sticks out in midair? This amazing hotel is the Hotel du Lac in Tunis, the capital of Tunisia. The floors get longer and longer as you go up, with the top floor measuring twice as long as the bottom floor. It was built in the early 1970s—and not long after that, the makers of the first *Star Wars* movie came to Tunisia to film in the desert. Some say they saw the hotel and it inspired the shape of the Sandcrawler, a huge desert vehicle that appears in the movies. Sadly, the hotel is no longer used, so you couldn't stay in it even if you wanted to!

The Bibliotheca Alexandrina

It might look like a massive cheese grater, but this vast building is actually a library. An amazing example of modern architecture, it pays tribute to the former renowned ancient Library of Alexandria, which contained hundreds of books, including the original work of ancient Greek poets such as Sophocles and Euripides. The main library was accidentally burned down by Julius Caesar in 48 B.C. when he was helping Cleopatra in her war against her own brother. This modern reimagining of the library sits close to the Mediterranean Sea in the Egyptian city of Alexandria. It was designed by Norwegian architecture firm Snøhetta, who gave the design hidden meaning and purpose: The circular shape reflects the flow of time and knowledge, the windows are designed to let the light in but prevent glare, and the outside walls are carved with characters from all known alphabets.

WEIRD WONDERS

This staggering sight is the colossal sand dunes of Namibia! The striking, uninhabited peaks almost look like a painting. Situated on the Atlantic coast, the Namib Desert is the oldest desert in the world. The sand gets its rich red color from a coating of iron oxide. Dune 45 (so named because it's located 45 km from the main entrance to the Namib-Naukluft National Park where the dunes are found) is aptly nicknamed "Big Daddy." Although not the highest dune around, it stands 262 feet (80 m) tall and offers spectacular views from the top.

These dunes are some of the tallest in in the world. The highest measures **1,256 FEET (383 M)—** around the same height as the Eiffel Tower!

JAW-DROPPING SAND DUNES

Namib-Naukluft National Park, Namibia

REMARKABLE ROCKS

White Desert

Farafra, Egypt

In the middle of Egypt's Western Desert, which is part of the Sahara, is a smaller, much stranger desert. It's as white as snow, and covered in tall chalk-white rocks in all kinds of weird shapes. The formations have been compared to mushrooms, meringues, and even modern art. They are made by the wind blasting desert sand over rocks and wearing them away over thousands of years. They're said to look especially magical at sunset and by moonlight—so tourists often come here for an overnight stay and sleep under the stars.

Mount Nyiragongo Volcano

Virunga National Park, Democratic Republic of the Congo

The Nyiragongo volcano, one of the most active in Africa, has erupted at least 34 times since 1882. Despite the constant threat, there are thriving communities residing in towns and cities below. The world's largest lava lake—formed by large volumes of molten lava collecting in a vent, depression, or crater—sits right at the top. You wouldn't want to get too close, though—the bubbling cauldron contains liquid lava that can travel up to 40 miles an hour (64 km/h), gaining speed when traveling down the volcano's steep slope.

Balancing Rocks
Harare, Zimbabwe

These rocks in Zimbabwe look so carefully balanced, it seems like a deliberate design, but they're actually natural. They, and many other massive boulders, can be found piled up in teetering towers in a park in Harare, Zimbabwe's capital. The incredibly hard rocks formed there long ago, when volcanic lava pushed up from underground, then cooled and solidified. They ended up on top of softer rock, which crumbled and wore away over time, leaving the boulders behind. They're so well known in Zimbabwe that they are featured on some of the country's paper money.

DATING SHOWS THAT THE STONE CIRCLES COULD BE UP TO 1,000 YEARS OLD.

Senegambian Stone Circles
Senegal and Gambia

If you love mysterious ancient stone circles, forget Stonehenge and head to West Africa! In a smallish region of Senegal and Gambia, you'll find not just one stone circle, but more than 1,000 of them—the biggest group of stone circles in the world. The stones in each circle are neatly carved and shaped into square or round blocks to match one another. No one knows who made them, and the locals have a variety of different stories. Some legends say ancient gods put them here when time began, or that the blocks are ancient humans who turned to stone. Others say they are the graves of kings or giants who lived long ago. Excavations have found skeletons buried in the circles, but the mystery of who built them remains.

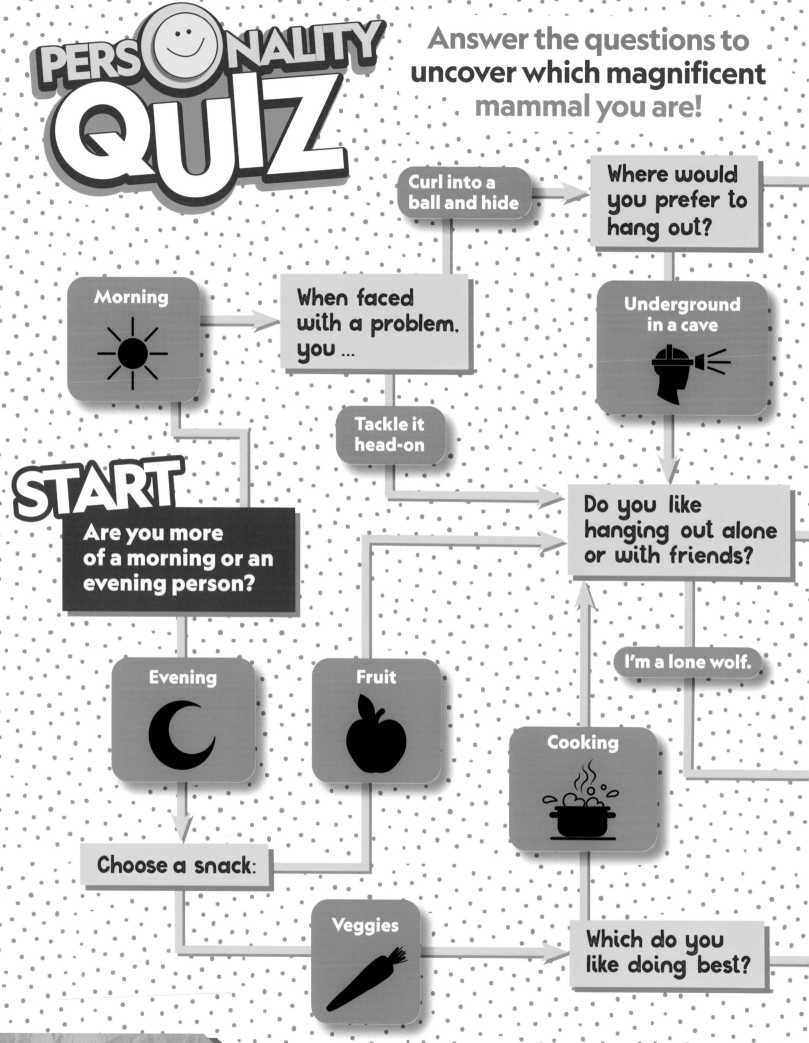

PERSONALITY QUIZ

Answer the questions to uncover which magnificent mammal you are!

Curl into a ball and hide

Where would you prefer to hang out?

Morning

When faced with a problem, you ...

Underground in a cave

Tackle it head-on

START

Are you more of a morning or an evening person?

Do you like hanging out alone or with friends?

Evening

Fruit

I'm a lone wolf.

Cooking

Choose a snack:

Veggies

Which do you like doing best?

Up high in a tree house

Aardvark

You're down to earth, hardworking, and always busy! Even so, like the aardvark, you're never too busy for a snack. You're true to yourself and adapt well to different circumstances.

I'm a little clumsy.

How would you describe your balance?

Aye-Aye

This nighttime dweller enjoys a treetop adventure, and its balance is top level, which makes navigating branches a piece of cake. Although snoozing is high up on the agenda, like this cool creature, you're a true adventurer who loves exploring the high ground. Life's good, *aye*?

Friends! I'm a social butterfly.

I have ninja stealth!

Pigcasso

Like this artistic creature, you wear your heart on your sleeve! You love creative challenges and speak up for what you believe in. You're happy to be with others, but you don't mind alone time either. You're a talented individual—there's no *snout* about it!

Yes, I tell it like it is.

Are you someone who speaks their mind?

No, I don't like to ruffle feathers.

Making art

Pangolin

You sometimes prefer to be alone, and you don't like conflict. You're most likely to hide when trouble comes your way, but you have a thick skin, too! Like the pangolin, you have your own style and are not afraid to be unique.

WEIRD WONDERS

Watch the annual trek of millions of creatures as they journey to find food.

WILDEBEEST MIGRATION

Tanzania and Kenya

Some have referred to it as the greatest show on Earth—and you can see why.
Every year, 1.5 million wildebeests journey about 1,860 miles (3,000 km) in a loop across Tanzania and Kenya. At the end of the rainy season, the wildebeests begin their journey, following the seasonal rains in search of greener pastures. Two hundred thousand zebras also join the wildebeest on the journey. The zebras feast on longer grass, whereas the wildebeests prefer shorter grass, so they're happy to travel and live together without being in direct competition for the same food.

BY the NUMBERS

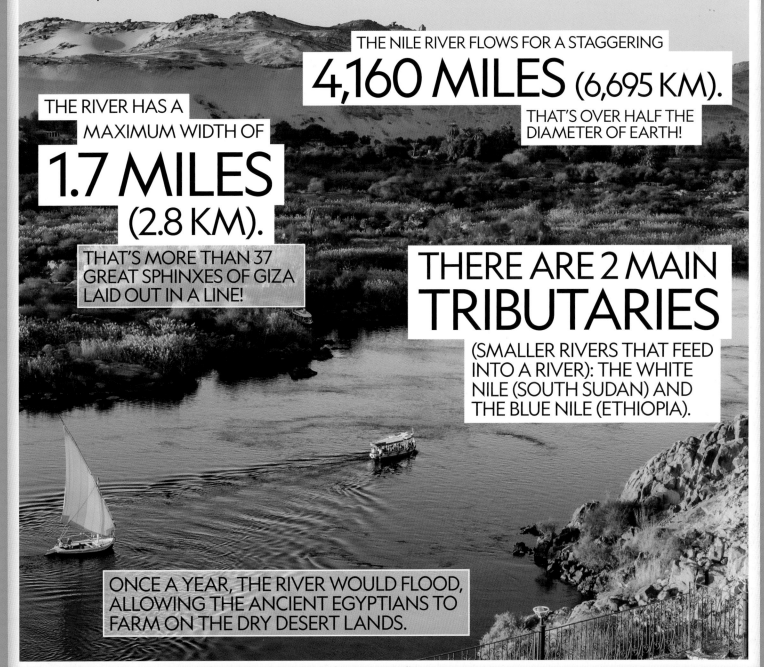

THE NILE

It's the longest river in the world ... or is it? Experts have deliberated the question again and again. The Nile is only slightly longer than the world's second-longest river, the Amazon. For now, the Nile holds on to the title. But many say it depends on where you classify the start and end points of each river.

THE NILE MEANDERS THROUGH
11 COUNTRIES
ACROSS THE AFRICAN CONTINENT.

95% OF EGYPTIANS LIVE WITHIN A FEW MILES OF THE RIVER.

THE NILE RIVER FLOWS FOR A STAGGERING
4,160 MILES (6,695 KM).
THAT'S OVER HALF THE DIAMETER OF EARTH!

THE RIVER HAS A MAXIMUM WIDTH OF
1.7 MILES (2.8 KM).
THAT'S MORE THAN 37 GREAT SPHINXES OF GIZA LAID OUT IN A LINE!

THERE ARE 2 MAIN TRIBUTARIES
(SMALLER RIVERS THAT FEED INTO A RIVER): THE WHITE NILE (SOUTH SUDAN) AND THE BLUE NILE (ETHIOPIA).

ONCE A YEAR, THE RIVER WOULD FLOOD, ALLOWING THE ANCIENT EGYPTIANS TO FARM ON THE DRY DESERT LANDS.

Weird but true!

The plant *Pachypodium namaquanum,* or elephant's trunk, is **covered with spines** and can reach up to **16 feet** (5 m) in height.

To avoid being eaten by desert animals, *LITHOPS* PLANTS are CLEVERLY DISGUISED as rocks!

When the creepy, gross-smelling *HYDNORA AFRICANA* FLOWER opens up, it looks like a fleshy red hand trying to grab you!

The *Welwitschia,* or "TWO-LEAF-CANNOT-DIE," as it's known in Afrikaans, can live for up to **2,000 YEARS!**

AFRICAN PLANTS

THE **QUIVER TREE** ISN'T **REALLY A TREE**—IT'S A SPECIES OF **ALOE** THAT GROWS UP TO **30 FEET** (9 M) TALL.

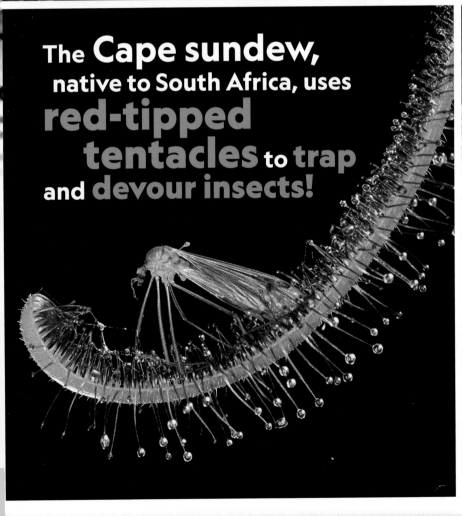

The **Cape sundew,** native to South Africa, uses **red-tipped tentacles** to trap and **devour insects!**

THE **COCO DE MER** PALM TREE OF THE SEYCHELLES IS FAMOUS FOR ITS GIGANTIC **BUTT-SHAPED NUT!**

WEIRD WONDERS

There's not much snow in the Sahara, but you can still go snowboarding—or sandboarding, to be exact. Using either a snowboard or a special sandboard, riders zoom, carve, and jump down the gigantic sand dunes in Morocco's *ergs*. An erg, also called a dune sea or sand sea, is an area of loose sand in the desert, blown by the wind into a landscape of dunes. Some of these sand mountains can be 1,000 feet (300 m) high! And they're not just used for boarding—you could try off-roading in a four-wheeler, quad bike racing, or, the toughest challenge of all, running desert marathons.

Time to catch some waves—er—sand!

SAND SURFING

Sahara desert, Morocco

The Sahara desert covers

3.5 MILLION SQUARE MILES
(9 million sq km).

WILD MADAGASCAR!

Mice to meet you.

Madame Berthe's Mouse Lemur
Menabe Region

This mini marvel holds the title of smallest primate in the world! They average a modest 3.5 inches (9 cm) long. Their large eyes, which enhance their night vision, and small stature make them not only incredibly cute but also perfectly suited to their nocturnal lifestyle. They have been said to have the smallest brains of all primates, weighing .07 ounce (2 g)—around the same as half a teaspoon of sugar!

Lowland Streaked Tenrec
Lowland Forests

This peculiar creature resembles some sort of punk-rock shrew as it scuttles around the rainforest floor. It's a lowland streaked tenrec—a little insectivore covered in quills. Its spiky yellow crown is perfect for deterring predators. But some of its quills are used to communicate, too: The tenrec vibrates certain quills until they make noise!

Aye-Aye
Tropical Forests

Meet the aye-aye, probably the only animal in the world that's famous for its fingers! This scruffy-looking nocturnal lemur creeps around between tree branches, tap-tap-tapping on the bark with its super-skinny middle finger. It can tell where tasty grubs are hiding by listening to the sound this makes. When it gets lucky, it gnaws a hole, then uses its extra-long fourth finger, which has a hooked claw on the tip, to pull out the prey.

Darwin's Bark Spider
Rainforest Rivers

Imagine canoeing happily along a river in Madagascar, when suddenly your face gets caught in the world's biggest spiderweb! It's the work of Darwin's bark spider, which spins webs across rivers by letting a long thread of silk float through the air to the opposite bank on the breeze. In the middle, it constructs a web up to 10 feet (3 m) across to catch water-loving insects such as dragonflies. Besides weaving the biggest webs, it has the strongest spider silk on Earth. But the spider itself is small—only about half an inch (1.5 cm) long.

I may be itsy-bitsy, but my web isn't!

Brookesia micra
Nosy Hara Island

This is the teeniest, tiniest chameleon in the world. When fully grown, *Brookesia micra* is just over an inch (2.5 cm) long. During the day, it hides in leaf litter on the ground, climbing trees at night to sleep in safety, and feeds on tiny fruit flies. It was discovered on Nosy Hara, a small island off the coast of Madagascar, in 2007. It's no wonder that scientists hadn't spotted it until then!

Weirdly Cute!
Giraffe-Necked Weevil

Giraffes don't live on the island of Madagascar. Instead, their mini-me lives there—the tiny but incredibly long-necked giraffe weevil! This plant-eating beetle is found in leafy rainforest trees. Females use their long necks to help them roll up leaves to make safe holders for their eggs. Males have even longer necks—longer than their bodies—which they use to fight and push each other away in battles over females.

WEIRD WATER

Water Harvesting
Morocco

If you think cloud fishing sounds like a thing of dreams, then think again! This awesome system has been designed to catch water droplets from fog in a collection of large nets. These droplets are then mixed with groundwater and piped into surrounding villages. An incredible 1,386 gallons (6,300 L) are captured daily—that's enough for up to 100 households. The system has transformed lives throughout southwestern Morocco, limiting the need to travel long distances for water.

This process is also called fog catching, fog harvesting, and—oddest of all—fog milking!

Devil's Pool, Victoria Falls
Zambia and Zimbabwe

Swimming right up to the edge of the world's biggest waterfall might seem like a bad idea. But at Victoria Falls, between Zambia and Zimbabwe, you really can do this, thanks to a natural pool known as the Devil's Pool, near the edge of the falls. It has a rocky ledge that stops you from slipping off, so you can swim up to the edge and peer over to see the water plunging more than 350 feet (108 m) into the gorge below. However, you can't just jump into the pool on your own. People who want to experience the thrill have to take a guided tour, with expert staff to make sure they're safe.

Danakil Depression
Ethiopia

A depression is an area that's lower than its surroundings, and Ethiopia's Danakil Depression is very low—more than 400 feet (120 m) below sea level. It's formed by three tectonic plates, the chunks of rock that make up Earth's crust, pulling away from one another—and it's packed with volcanic activity. Among the spouting geysers, bubbling hot springs, and acidic lakes, the land is covered with crusty white, yellow, and green minerals. Danakil also has some of the hottest average temperatures on the planet, so coming here feels like a trip to an incredibly hot, strange, and colorful alien world.

Boiling Lake Bogoria
Kenya

Kenya's Lake Bogoria has dozens of springs around the edges, some of them so hot you can actually see areas of water bubbling and boiling. Although the lake is quite hard to get to, tourists come here to eat lunch, and use the hot springs to boil eggs for their picnics (taking care not to fall in, of course!). Nearby there's a river where the hot spring water mixes with cooler water. This creates the perfect temperature of a warm bath, and it's safe to take a nice relaxing dip.

THERE CAN BE AS MANY AS **TWO MILLION FLAMINGOS** FEEDING IN **LAKE BOGORIA** AT ONCE.

ANCIENT MYSTERIES

Giraffe Carvings
Niger

In the Sahara desert in Niger, carved into a big, flat, sloping rock, are two beautiful giraffes, a male and a smaller female. There are other rock carvings here too, but the giraffes are the biggest, with the male around 18 feet (5.5 m) tall—life-size! They date from around 8,000 years ago, when the Sahara was a lush grassland with rivers, trees, and many more animals than it has now, including giraffes. No one knows who made these artworks or why. What's more, the giraffes appear to have leashes, or reins. Did the ancient people of the Sahara have tame or pet giraffes? It's a mystery!

Is there water in my ear?

Heracleion
Alexandria, Egypt

In 1933, a pilot flying over the bay of Alexandria, on the coast of Egypt, looked down and saw ruins under the water. Later, divers explored the seafloor and found statues, columns, coins, sunken ships, and the remains of a temple. These ruins were remnants of the city of Heracleion, one of ancient Egypt's most important ports, which stood on islands in the bay 2,500 years ago. At some point, the islands were washed away, and the buildings collapsed and sank into the sea. No one knows exactly when or how. It might have been a tsunami, earthquakes, or rising sea levels, or maybe all of the above! And there's probably much more of Heracleion waiting to be found under the muddy seafloor.

Mystery of Mount Lico
Mozambique

In 2018, a team of scientists and climbers set out on a daring mission: to climb Mount Lico, a tall mountain surrounded by vertical cliffs on every side. Why? To explore the rainforest on top. Thanks to the ancient volcano's sheer sides, the top of the mountain was unexplored. Its crater contained an ancient forest that had remained undisturbed for centuries. The explorers discovered a pristine habitat, with several previously unknown species. But they also found something weirder: some ancient human-made pottery, half-buried in the ground. Someone had been here before, in ancient times—but who they were, and how they reached the top, is unknown.

A **DRONE** WAS USED TO TAKE IMAGES OF THE FOREST INSIDE THE CRATER BEFORE THE TEAM CLIMBED INTO IT.

Pyramids of Meroë
Sudan

Now those are some spectacular structures! These unique-looking pyramids represent a lost civilization of Sudan, from the Kushite Kingdom. Built between 2,700 and 2,300 years ago, these pyramids show the marks of time. They stand as a memory of a once bustling city, but they've suffered under the hands of relic hunters and excavators. In 1880, Italian explorer Giuseppe Ferlini even blew the tops off several pyramids in search of treasure. With almost 200 of them in total, these tombs of kings and queens remain a historical marvel.

177

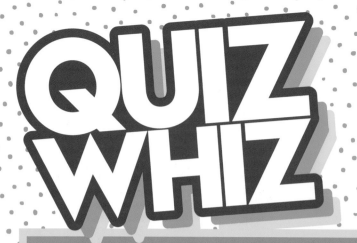

QUIZ WHIZ

How many questions can you answer? Grab a pencil and paper to find out.

1 **How many countries does the Nile pass through?**

a. Two
b. Five
c. 11
d. 20

2 **What is special about some springhares?**

a. They can communicate with birds.
b. They can use tools.
c. They glow in the dark.
d. They can travel really fast.

3 **What can you find in the middle of the street in Kinshasa?**

a. Metal trees
b. Traffic robots
c. People giving out free candy
d. Wild animals

4 What can you ride on at Moses Mabhida Stadium?

a. A big swing
b. A big horse
c. A big car
d. A big roller coaster

5 What is the name of the smallest primate in the world?

a. Monsieur Jacques's shrew monkey
b. Madame Berthe's mouse lemur
c. Mademoiselle Amelie's tiny loris
d. Professeur Singe's mini gorilla

6 How long does the *Welwitschia* plant live?

a. Up to 2,000 hours
b. Up to 2,000 days
c. Up to 2,000 months
d. Up to 2,000 years

7 What is "Big Daddy" in Namibia?

a. The nickname of a sand dune
b. The nickname of an old male elephant
c. The nickname of a shipwreck
d. The nickname of a very tall tree

8 What weather feature is being harvested in Morocco?

a. Lightning
b. Wind
c. Fog
d. Rain

Answers: 1. c, 2. c, 3. b, 4. a, 5. b, 6. d, 7. a, 8. c

179

6
ASTOUNDING ASIA

Radical restaurants, sensational structures, curious creatures, **and more.**

It's weirdly wonderful!

If this GIANT TEAPOT could be filled, it would hold about 7.4 MILLION GALLONS (28 million L) OF TEA!

It took the artist TWO DAYS TO set up the scene and PAINT HIMSELF TO PERFECTLY MATCH his surroundings.

WEIRD in the WORLD

Check out some of the INCREDIBLE, UNIQUE, and totally JAW-DROPPING ANIMALS, OBJECTS, and PLACES across ASIA.

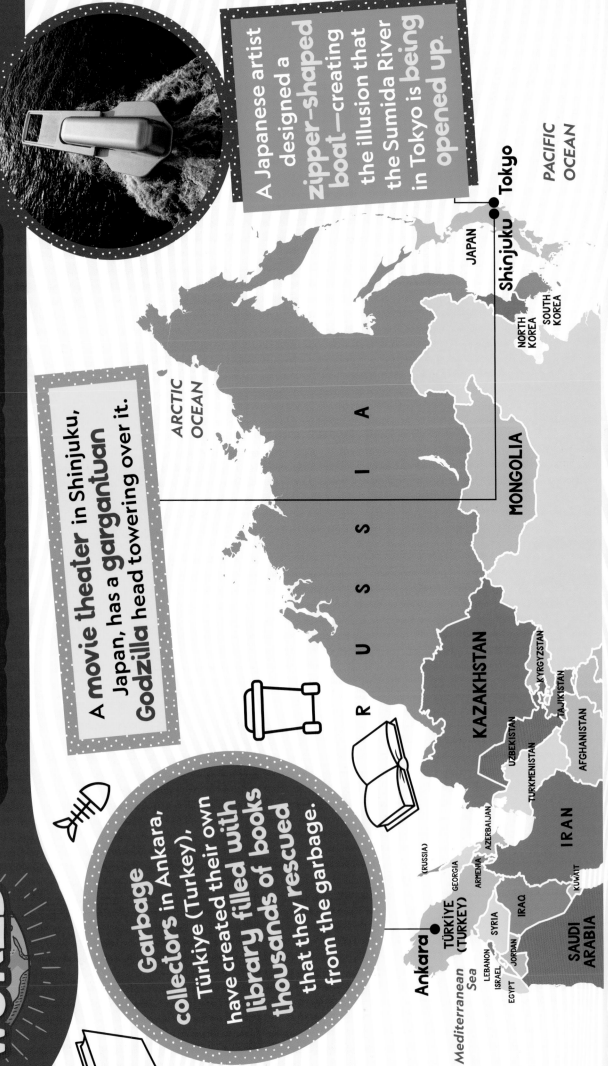

A Japanese artist designed a zipper-shaped boat—creating the illusion that the Sumida River in Tokyo is being opened up.

A movie theater in Shinjuku, Japan, has a gargantuan Godzilla head towering over it.

Garbage collectors in Ankara, Türkiye (Turkey), have created their own library filled with thousands of books that they rescued from the garbage.

ARCTIC OCEAN

R U S S I A

MONGOLIA

KAZAKHSTAN

UZBEKISTAN

TURKMENISTAN

KYRGYZSTAN

TAJIKISTAN

AFGHANISTAN

IRAN

NORTH KOREA

SOUTH KOREA

JAPAN

Tokyo

Shinjuku

PACIFIC OCEAN

(RUSSIA)

GEORGIA

ARMENIA

AZERBAIJAN

TÜRKIYE (TURKEY)

Ankara

Mediterranean Sea

LEBANON

SYRIA

ISRAEL

JORDAN

EGYPT

IRAQ

KUWAIT

SAUDI ARABIA

Arctic Ocean
EUROPE
AFRICA
ASIA
Indian Ocean
AUSTRALIA
Pacific Ocean

CHINA

TAIWAN

PHILIPPINES

VIETNAM
LAOS
THAILAND
CAMBODIA
MYANMAR (BURMA)

BHUTAN
NEPAL
BANGLADESH

INDIA

PAKISTAN

QATAR
UNITED ARAB EMIRATES
BAHRAIN
OMAN
YEMEN

Arabian Sea

Bay of Bengal

SRI LANKA

MALDIVES

INDIAN OCEAN

South China Sea

BRUNEI

MALAYSIA

SINGAPORE

INDONESIA

Java Sea

TIMOR-LESTE (EAST TIMOR)

That's weird!

The world's largest book is in Myanmar. It consists of 730 marble tablets, each of which is more than five feet (1.5 m) tall and five inches (12.7 cm) thick.

Paper, gifts, and stationery made from elephant poop are made in Thailand. Don't worry—they're odorless!

ANIMAL MAGIC

Muju Firefly Festival
South Korea

Light shows at festivals may be pretty common, but this one is far from average. At the Muju Firefly Festival, the skies are illuminated by tiny beetles. That's right—fireflies, and there's an entire eco-friendly festival dedicated to them. Each year, thousands of visitors flock to Muju, South Korea, for music, storytelling, reenactments of traditional weddings, and more. But the real fun starts after dark, when the fireflies light up the night sky. Muju is a perfect natural habitat for the fireflies; because fireflies inhabit only superclean places, these critters represent Muju's unspoiled environment.

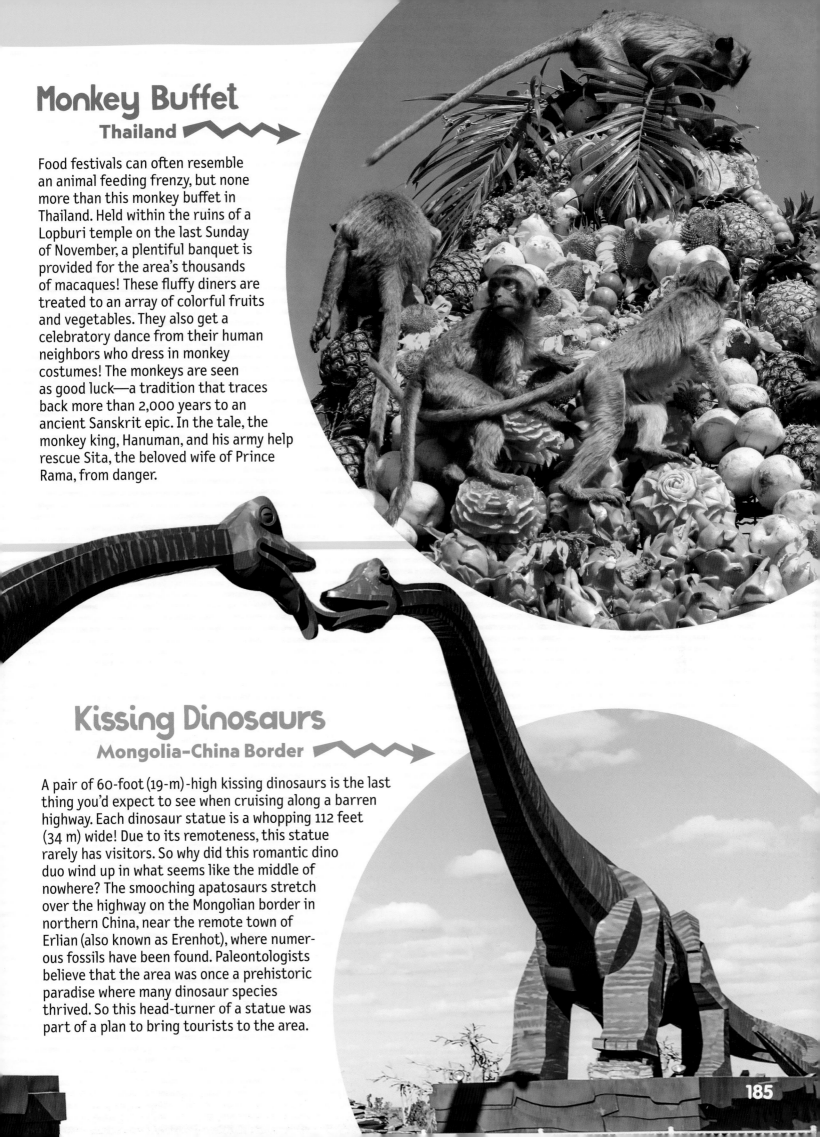

Monkey Buffet
Thailand

Food festivals can often resemble an animal feeding frenzy, but none more than this monkey buffet in Thailand. Held within the ruins of a Lopburi temple on the last Sunday of November, a plentiful banquet is provided for the area's thousands of macaques! These fluffy diners are treated to an array of colorful fruits and vegetables. They also get a celebratory dance from their human neighbors who dress in monkey costumes! The monkeys are seen as good luck—a tradition that traces back more than 2,000 years to an ancient Sanskrit epic. In the tale, the monkey king, Hanuman, and his army help rescue Sita, the beloved wife of Prince Rama, from danger.

Kissing Dinosaurs
Mongolia-China Border

A pair of 60-foot (19-m)-high kissing dinosaurs is the last thing you'd expect to see when cruising along a barren highway. Each dinosaur statue is a whopping 112 feet (34 m) wide! Due to its remoteness, this statue rarely has visitors. So why did this romantic dino duo wind up in what seems like the middle of nowhere? The smooching apatosaurs stretch over the highway on the Mongolian border in northern China, near the remote town of Erlian (also known as Erenhot), where numerous fossils have been found. Paleontologists believe that the area was once a prehistoric paradise where many dinosaur species thrived. So this head-turner of a statue was part of a plan to bring tourists to the area.

185

COLOR POP!

Picasso Moth
Southeast Asia

This spectacular insect looks as if its vibrant designs have been carefully hand-painted on its wings by famous artist Pablo Picasso. But this miraculous wonder of nature actually evolved to look this way. Found mainly in northern India and Southeast Asia, the moth's two-inch (5-cm) wingspan is covered in bold, colorful geometric prints. Although moths don't have noses, they have an incredible sense of smell. They use their antennae sensors to pick up chemical cues from their surroundings! What pictures can you see on its wings?

Has anyone seen my moth-er?

Danxia Landforms
Gansu Province, China

Have you never seen multicolored mountains? Well, take a trip to China's Zhangye Danxia Landform Geological Park and you will have a chance to do just that. The natural wonder has boardwalks and viewing platforms for visitors to take in the awesome site. These famous Rainbow Mountains are all shades of red, blue, yellow, and orange. It's hard to believe they haven't been painted! So how did these mountains get their stripes? The shape and vivid colors of the Danxia landforms are a result of weathering, as well as tectonic plates shifting over millions of years. Over millennia, the sandstone and minerals have eroded into fascinating textures, shapes, and patterns, creating a landscape that's out of this world.

Village of Color
Kampung, Indonesia

Painted every shade from pastel yellows to vibrant pinks, this village is wall-to-wall color—nothing escaped the paintbrush! Welcome to Kampung Warna Warni Jodipan, or the Village of Color. Today, it might be one of the brightest villages on the planet, but not so long ago, this was a typical-looking Indonesian village. So why did it get a magnificent makeover? Kampung was painted these vivid colors by artists, students, and residents as part of a project to improve the area and bring tourists in. And it worked! Turning this traditional village into a work of art has attracted visitors eager to snap photos and share selfies.

Pink Palace

Jaipur, India

If you want a palace that looks like it's straight out of a storybook, then look no further than the magnificent Pink Palace in Jaipur. The palace's 953 honeycombed windows allow for a gentle breeze to move through it—a welcome relief in the hot climate. The intricate latticework on the windows was also designed so that royal women could watch over the life going on outside of the palace without being seen. This ornate masterpiece is five stories high and built from sandstone, which gives the palace its pink hue. In fact, the city of Jaipur itself is known as the Pink City because so many of its buildings are rose-colored.

THE PALACE'S HINDI NAME IS **HAWA MAHAL,** MEANING "PALACE OF THE WINDS."

FANTASTIC FACTS ABOUT

Weird but true!

THE GREAT WALL is called **"THE EARTH DRAGON"** because it seems to snake across the mountains like **A SLEEPING DRAGON.**

STICKY RICE was one of the **MANY MATERIALS** used to **CONSTRUCT THE ORIGINAL WALL!**

Contrary to popular belief, **THE GREAT WALL OF CHINA CANNOT BE SEEN FROM SPACE** with the naked eye—you would need **A HIGH-POWERED TELESCOPE.**

The **Great Wall** winds for over **13,000 MILES** (21,000 km). To cover that **distance** on a **running track**, you'd have to run **52,000 LAPS!**

THE GREAT WALL OF CHINA

A **legend** suggests that a **HELPFUL DRAGON** marked out the wall's path for the **seventh-century workers** who originally built it.

IN 2019, A **RESTORATION PROJECT** USED **3D MAPPING, DRONES,** AND A **COMPUTER ALGORITHM** TO HELP ENGINEERS FIGURE OUT WHERE THE WALL **NEEDED MAINTENANCE.**

BULLET MARKS can still be seen in the wall at Gubeikou, from a conflict between **CHINA** and **JAPAN IN THE 1930s.**

DURING THE **MING DYNASTY,** SOLDIERS MAY HAVE **BURNED WOLF DUNG** IN THE WALL'S WATCHTOWERS TO CREATE **SMOKE SIGNALS.**

COOL CRITTERS

Giant Technicolor Squirrels
India

These orange-black-and-purple creatures are magnificent Malabar giant squirrels. The rainbow rodents can grow up to three feet (1 m) long from head to tail and weigh four pounds (2 kg). They are skilled leapers (much like their smaller squirrel relatives!) and can jump an impressive 20 feet (6 m) between trees in their forest home. While many squirrel species keep their supplies of nuts and seeds underground, Malabar giant squirrels store their food up high in trees. You might think that their striking coloring makes these squirrels stand out, but it actually helps them camouflage in the sunny and shady patches created by the forest canopy.

Mossy frogs sometimes play dead when they are frightened.

Mossy Frog
Vietnam

It's not hard to see how this bumpy-skinned green critter got its name. The mossy frog's textured markings make it look just like a patch of moss! Besides being able to hide in the undergrowth easily, these little frogs have another cool trick: They can make it sound as though they're 10 to 13 feet (3–4 m) away from where they really are, sending predators off in the wrong direction.

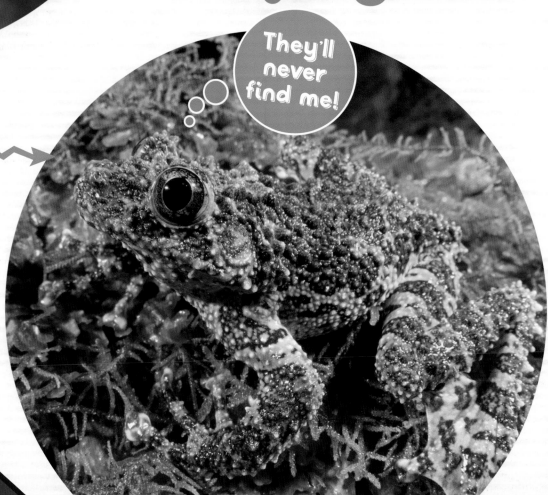

They'll never find me!

Japanese Spider Crab
Japan

Just how big can a crab be? Well, this one is big enough to fill an average-size living room! The Japanese spider crab has 10 incredibly long, skinny legs and has a leg span of up to 12.5 feet (3.8 m). Its body is quite small, though—only about the size of a trash can! But don't panic: The spider crab doesn't spin a web, and it's not interested in catching or eating you. Found in the Pacific Ocean around Japan, it's a slow-moving gentle giant, eating only small fish and scavenging dead animals. And if you ever want to spot one of these spider crabs, grab yourself a submarine—they live up to 1,640 feet (500 m) underwater on the seafloor.

JAPANESE SPIDER CRAB EGGS ARE ONLY .03 INCH (.76 MM) LONG—SIMILAR TO A GRAIN OF RICE!

Weirdly Cute!

Irrawaddy Dolphin

This unusually expressive round-faced character is the Irrawaddy dolphin. These curious creatures have many distinctive features, but it's their happy faces that most people notice first. Their lips and small beaks often make it look like they're smiling! They can frequently be found waving and slapping the water, but possibly the weirdest thing about these endangered dolphins is how they catch their dinner: They spit at it! These jets of water help them herd their fishy prey, making their meal easier to catch.

BY the NUMBERS

GARDENS BY THE BAY

This breathtaking collection of architecture and gardens is found by the Marina Bay Waterfront in Singapore. Among the attractions are a Flower Dome (a greenhouse busting at the seams with flowers), a Cloud Forest (a mist-filled conservatory teeming with tropical plants), and a Floral Fantasy (a fairy-tale-inspired hanging garden.) However, it's more than just a tourist attraction. This park also provides biodiversity and protects endangered species.

THERE ARE OVER
250 ACRES (101 HA)
SPLIT OVER **THREE** GARDEN AREAS.

THE CLOUD FOREST CONSERVATORY TOWERS AT A HEIGHT OF
115 FEET (35 M).

OVER **15,000** PRESERVED BLOOMS HANG FROM THE FLORAL FANTASY CONSERVATORY CEILING.

THE **FLOWER DOME** HOLDS PLANTS AND FLOWERS FROM **5 CONTINENTS,** INCLUDING **1,000-YEAR-OLD** OLIVE TREES.

THE TALLEST SUPERTREE IS EQUIVALENT IN HEIGHT TO **A 16-STORY BUILDING.**

11 OF THE **SUPERTREES** (GIANT VERTICAL GARDENS) HAVE TECHNOLOGY TO PRODUCE **ENVIRONMENTALLY FRIENDLY POWER,** SUCH AS **SOLAR POWER.**

ROCKIN' RESTROOMS

Modern Toilet Restaurant
Taipei, Taiwan

Forget your regular dining furniture and crockery—here diners eat out of toilet-shaped bowls while sitting on toilet-shaped seats! Yes, you heard right. The creators started out by selling ice cream in toilet-shaped containers and grew a loyal fan base from there. In 2014, they opened up the Modern Toilet Restaurant. The owner, Wang Zi-Wei, was inspired by a Japanese cartoon character who liked playing with poop!

Poopoo Land
Seoul, South Korea

Poopoo Land is a museum celebrating what you flush down the toilet! You can explore everything from flatulence to the science of poop—all while getting the chance to pose for selfies on toilet seats and more! At the end, visitors wander through a digestion maze with obstacle courses, and boogie to tunes in the Poo Party Zone before exiting speedily down a steep slide. After all that fun, visitors can refuel at a café packed with, you guessed it, toilet-themed food and drink.

Toilet Bowl Waterfall
Foshan, China

Some might say this sculpture is a total washout, but there's a lot to love about it! China's Shiwan Park is home to many ceramic sculptures, including this epic toilet bowl waterfall. It took two months for Chinese artist Shu Yong and his team to install this wall of 10,000 repurposed ceramic toilets, sinks, and urinals. No, we're not yanking your chain! The fabulous fountain stretches 330 feet (100 m) long and 16 feet (5 m) high, and it can be flushed to create the effect of a calming waterfall.

Does anyone have toilet paper?

TOILET PAPER IS A POPULAR HOUSEWARMING GIFT IN SOUTH KOREA.

Most Remote Toilet in the World
Altai Mountains, Siberia

Only explorers daring enough to venture 8,530 feet (2,600 m) up in the Altai Mountains can find the world's most remote toilet. The precarious-looking restroom is part of Siberia's highest weather station, Kara-Tyurek. This lonely latrine is not for the faint of heart—as you can see, it stands teetering over a cliff edge and is about as remote as you can get. The nearest village is 60 miles (100 km) away, which means toilet paper deliveries come by helicopter!

WEIRD WONDERS

Panjin Beach is home to **OVER 260** bird species, including the endangered crown crane and black-beaked gull.

CHINA'S RED BEACH

Panjin, China

As beaches go, this one in Panjin is pretty extraordinary. Forget sand or pebbles—China's red beach is carpeted with a plant called seepweed that turns vibrant crimson each autumn. It's part of one of the world's largest wetlands, found along the Liaohe River Delta. The area is also home to lots of endangered wildlife and has been protected since 1988. Most of it is closed to tourists, but a 6,500-foot (1,980-m)-long wooden boardwalk jutting out into the sea allows visitors to bird-watch and enjoy the spectacular red hues.

JUST JAPAN

Star Sand Beach
Islands of Japan

Twinkle, twinkle, little star! Have you ever stopped to examine what's beneath your feet while strolling along the beach? Well, if you ever find yourself at Hoshizuna-no-Hama, meaning Star Sand Beach, then make sure you do just that. Unlike other beaches, which are made up of rocks and minerals, this unique coastline has a certain star quality. Scattered within the sand are tiny star-shaped exoskeletons (left by single-celled organisms known as foraminifera). Many refer to it as "living sand," which although not technically accurate, reflects that it was once part of a living organism in the ocean.

Shin-Yokohama Ramen Museum
Yokohama, Japan

It might seem a little odd to have a whole museum dedicated to a single type of food, but who doesn't love ramen? Tourists have been traveling far and wide to visit this noodle lover's dream since it opened in 1994. It offers up the chance to learn about all things ramen, including the opportunity to sample different ramen dishes from all over Japan. The museum is lined with shops, exhibits, and even a miniature historical theme park showcasing a bustling 1958 neighborhood with real ramen restaurants.

More than 95 billion packs of ramen are consumed around the world every year.

What's **Weird** About This **?**

That's weird!

Have you ever heard of a forest that can make its own music?

This is the Sagano Bamboo Forest on the edge of Kyoto, Japan, the home of the Tenryu-ji Temple, a UNESCO World Heritage site. When the long bamboo stalks sway in the wind they create a swishing *zawa-zawa* noise—a sound considered so important by the Japanese government that it has become a national protected soundscape. Visitors come to this 6.2-square-mile (16-sq-km) site to experience the peaceful tranquility of this forest. As well as the relaxing sounds, the way that the sunlight filters through the leaves gives the forest a serene green glow.

PERSONALITY QUIZ

What is your ideal day trip in Asia?

Take this quiz, write down your answers, and reveal where you'd most like to be.

1 You can only pick one item to take on vacation—what would it be?

a. Walking shoes
b. Swimwear
c. Camera

2 Which do you most enjoy watching?

a. Nature documentaries
b. Action movies
c. Costume dramas

4 Which school subject do you like most?

a. Science
b. P.E.
c. History

Mostly A's
Gardens by the Bay, Singapore
You're curious about the world around you and love exploring. This budding botanist's dream would make a perfect destination for you. You'll enjoy strolling through the enchanted conservatories and taking in the huge variety of wildlife living there.

3 Which description suits you best?

a. Nature lover
b. Star athlete
c. Inquisitive investigator

5 Which of these animals would you want to be?
a. A macaque monkey
b. An Irrawaddy dolphin
c. A Japanese spider crab

6 Which type of art do you like best?
a. Wildlife photography
b. Paintings of the sea
c. Historic masterpieces

7 What hobby would you like to learn?
a. Gardening
b. Diving
c. Archaeology

8 Which activity would you most enjoy?
a. Trekking through a rainforest
b. Snorkeling in the ocean
c. Exploring ancient ruins

Mostly B's
Deep Dive Dubai
You seem to gravitate toward the ocean and all things active, so grab your flippers and head for the depths of this super-deep pool (see p. 207). You'll love exploring the imaginative underwater worlds of this awesome attraction.

Mostly C's
Angkor Wat
With your passion for the past, this abandoned temple in Cambodia overgrown with jungle roots (see p. 209) would allow you to put your investigative skills to good use. You'd enjoy exploring this 1186 building and piecing together its fascinating history.

Breathtaking BUILDS!

Robot Building
Bangkok, Thailand

It may look like it's escaped from a sci-fi movie, but this sleepy-looking robot is actually a bank. The 20-story-high building was completed in 1987 for the Bank of Asia. The design was meant to highlight the way technology was taking over the banking world. The striking building was created by architect Sumet Jumsai, who was inspired by his son's toy robot.

I'm a lean, mean workplace machine!

Bottle House of Ganja
Ganja, Azerbaijan

As the name suggests, this amazing house is decorated with glass bottles—48,000 in total! Bottles of various shapes and sizes, along with colorful stones, make up a giant mosaic on the outside of this private house. But the Bottle House is far more than just decorative. It was built by the Jafarov family as a shrine to their brother, Yusif, who was lost in World War II. The house features a portrait of Yusif, along with words and patterns that tell the story of this family. The best time to see this masterpiece is when the sun is shining through the colorful glass!

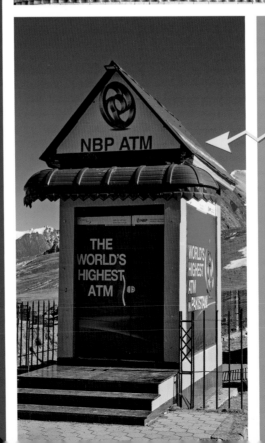

Highest ATM in the World
Gilgit Baltistan, Pakistan

Way up in Khunjerab Pass sits the highest-altitude ATM in the world. Found at the dizzying height of 15,396 feet (4,693 m) above sea level—you'd need to trek a long way to get cash out here! So why did the National Bank of Pakistan choose this unlikely location for an ATM? The bank wanted to make an ATM powered by solar panels and wind turbines. The record-breaking ATM opened to the public in 2016.

Meitan Tea Museum
Meitan, China

This towering teapot is really causing a stir. The bizarre building is a hot destination: It set a world record for tallest teapot, at a height of 243 feet (74 m) and with a whopping 54,000 square feet (5,000 sq m) of floor area. The titanic teapot is accompanied by a matching mega teacup, too. The oversize pair celebrate the Meitan region's storied tea culture. With its thriving tea industry, Meitan is a perfect place to have a museum showcasing tea history.

Hanging Temple of Hengshan
Shanxi Province, China

Talk about precarious—this fifth-century temple is built into the side of an almost vertical cliff. It was built around 1,500 years ago by a Chinese Buddhist monk named Liao Ran. The Hanging Temple, or Xuankong Si, sits 190 feet (58 m) above the riverbed and is made up of a series of bridges and corridors with a total of 40 rooms. Originally it was held in place with just wooden beams in the rock, but thankfully it has been made stronger over the years.

The Khan Shatyr Entertainment Center
Nur-Sultan, Kazakhstan

This incredible structure may remind you of a gigantic tent, but if you take a closer look, it's so much more. It is located in Nur-Sultan, Kazakhstan, where the unforgiving climate ranges from minus 31°F (-35°C) in the winter to 95°F (35°C) in the summer! The Khan Shatyr Entertainment Center provides an enclosed world with a steady microclimate no matter what the weather is like outside. It is controlled by a special chemical coating added to the outside of the building that lets sunlight through but protects it from weather extremes. The building provides an all-year-round sheltered environment where people can enjoy jogging tracks, shopping, movie theaters, and restaurants. It even has a water park with slides and wave pools!

BY the NUMBERS

TURBO TRAIN

Shanghai Maglev in China is the world's fastest passenger train. How does it move so fast? Well, it floats ... kind of! It's called a magnetic levitation train, which means the train is propelled using electromagnets. They create magnetic fields to push or pull the train along guideways rather than tracks. Shanghai Maglev runs from Shanghai's Pudong International Airport to the Longyang metro station on the outskirts of Shanghai.

OPENED:
2004

NUMBER OF LINES: **1**

NUMBER OF STATIONS: **2**

DISTANCE:
19 MILES (30 KM)

SPEED:
267 MPH (431 KM/H)

JOURNEY TIME:
UNDER 8 MINUTES

AT THIS SPEED, IT WOULD TAKE 96 HOURS TO TRAVEL AROUND THE WORLD—THAT'S FOUR DAYS!

What's **Weird** About This ?

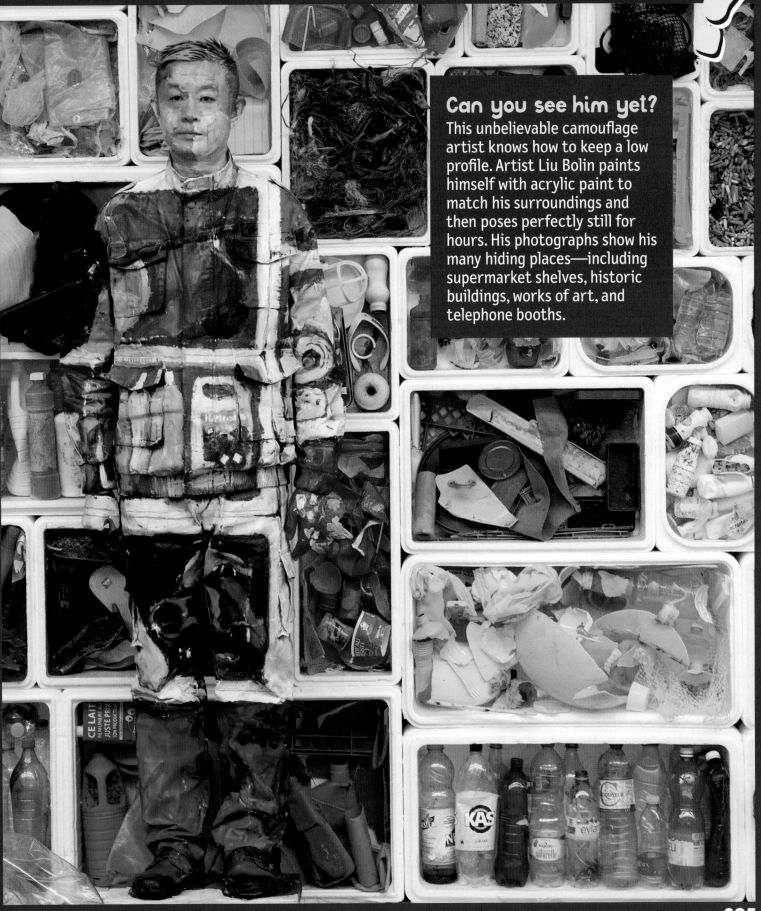

Can you see him yet?
This unbelievable camouflage artist knows how to keep a low profile. Artist Liu Bolin paints himself with acrylic paint to match his surroundings and then poses perfectly still for hours. His photographs show his many hiding places—including supermarket shelves, historic buildings, works of art, and telephone booths.

MAKING A SPLASH

Lake Baikal
Siberia, Russia

Lake Baikal is a record breaker in more ways than one. First, it's been around for a jaw-dropping 25 to 30 million years, making it the oldest lake in the world. And it's also the world's largest freshwater lake. That's even more special than it sounds—only .007 percent of the world's water comes from fresh-water lakes, and Lake Baikal is responsible for 22 percent of that freshwater—more than any other lake on Earth!

300 rivers flow into Lake Baikal, but only one flows away from it—the Angara River.

Rain Vortex
Singapore

Located at the heart of Changi Airport, this record-breaking indoor waterfall is a breathtaking wonder. The water cascades down a whopping 131 feet (40 m). At night, things get even more impressive as a light and sound show are projected onto the waters, bringing them alive. Since Singapore experiences a great number of thunderstorms, all the water is sourced from captured rainwater. That's 10,000 gallons (37,850 L) of reused water getting pumped through every minute!

THERE ARE OVER 200 PLANT SPECIES AROUND THE BASE OF THE WATERFALL.

Deep Dive Dubai
Dubai, U.A.E.

Hold your breath, because you won't believe the depth of this incredible record-breaking dive pool. Deep Dive Dubai holds the current record for the deepest swimming pool for diving—an incredible 196 feet 10 inches (60.02 m). That's as much as 11 giraffes stacked up on top of one another! It is filled with 3.7 million gallons (14 million L) of freshwater— the equivalent volume of six Olympic-size pools! But there's more to the pool than its depth: During your dive, you can visit human-made features such as a sunken abandoned city, an arcade with pinball machines, and even an underwater film studio. For those who prefer dry land, Deep Dive Dubai offers a viewing restaurant fitted with large glass windows where diners can peek inside the magical underwater world.

NATURE VS. ARCHITECTURE

The Root Bridges of Cherrapunji
Cherrapunji, India

During monsoon season, the valleys and gorges of Meghalaya are some of the wettest places on the planet. Its fast-flowing rivers become impossible to cross, cutting off whole villages. Luckily, the Khasi tribes who live here have found a solution. The Indian rubber trees that grow in the forest have incredibly strong roots, which can be nurtured into living bridges, known locally as *jing kieng jri*. While manufactured materials can weaken with age, the roots become stronger. The Khasi plant trees on each side of the river and build a frame to connect them using bamboo. Over time, the roots are woven through the bamboo to make a crossing strong enough to hold more than 35 people at a time.

It took six years to construct the amazing artificial island.

Palm Jumeirah
Dubai, U.A.E.

Palm Jumeirah, an artificial island in Dubai, was built to solve overcrowding. The palm tree–shaped island is more than three miles (5 km) in diameter and adds almost 50 miles (80 km) to Dubai's coastline, making it one of the biggest artificial islands in the world. As you can imagine, there's a lot to think about when building an island—like how to make sure it doesn't get washed away, or sink. In order to construct Palm Jumeirah, more than three billion cubic feet (85 million cubic m) of sand were dredged up from the Persian Gulf and sprayed into place using special equipment. To stop the island from drifting, millions of tons of rock were used to create its sturdy foundations.

WEIRD WONDERS

Visit the temple where the trees have taken over!

TEMPLE OF TREES

Siem Reap, Cambodia

When you look at Ta Prohm, it's hard to tell where the building ends and tree roots begin. This ancient Buddhist temple in Angkor was built in 1186, but it was abandoned and left to become entwined with the roots and branches of jungle trees. Over the centuries, the sacred site has continued to evolve and grow alongside nature—making the site all the more magical. The temple is a collection of courtyards, walkways, and towers, packed with carved stone blocks.

EXTREME EATERIES

Bird's Nest Restaurant

Koh Kood, Thailand

Ever wondered what it would be like to be a bird? Well, imagine no more. This unique restaurant at Soneva Kiri Resort allows you to dine in a nestlike bamboo pod high above the tropical rainforest of Koh Kood, an island in the Gulf of Thailand. Once you are sitting snug in your pod, you are carefully raised by the staff, high above the spectacular shoreline. The dangling dining rooms are suspended around 16 feet (5 m) above the ground. As you hang around, you can soak up the views of the ocean and take in the rainforest, where you may be lucky enough to spot some local wildlife.

Zauo Fishing Restaurant

Tokyo, Japan

Everyone loves a discount dinner, but there aren't many places where you can save money by catching your own chow. At the Zauo Fishing Restaurant, you can literally fish for your food. You rent your fishing rod, pick your fish, catch it, and then let the chef know how you'd like it prepared. And it really is cheaper when you catch it yourself than if you order straight off the menu!

AT THE ZAUO FISHING RESTAURANT, YOU MUST EAT WHAT YOU HOOK— YOU CAN'T PUT IT BACK IN THE WATER.

Foodom

Guangzhou, China

When you think of a busy restaurant, you probably imagine crashing pans, flustered chefs, and the odd accidental spill. That's not the case in this radical robot restaurant opened by Qianxi Robotics Group! This eatery is staffed entirely by robots. It has over 20 different types of robot workers, ranging from AI chefs to droid waiters! According to Foodom, the cyber staff can serve up to 600 diners at once and cook a wide range of cuisines, from stir-fry to burgers. Some customers even receive their food less than two minutes after ordering. That's some seriously speedy snacking!

Labasin Waterfall Restaurant

Quezon, Philippines

This restaurant is certainly making a splash! What could be more refreshing than sitting by cascading waters, kicking off your shoes, and cooling your feet in the water that flows below your table? This unusual eatery offers diners the opportunity to feast at bamboo tables submerged at the base of a spectacular rushing waterfall. Despite the fact that you might get drenched as you dine, this experience is not one to be missed.
A colorful buffet, served from cooking stations set in the water, offers fresh fish, rice, chicken, and fruit all served on banana leaves. Beyond the waterfall, providing a beautiful backdrop, visitors may also be lucky enough to spot birds peeping out of the surrounding jungle. After dining, many take the opportunity to take a dip in the falling water.

BIZARRE BODY PARTS

Giant Glass Slipper Church
Budai, Taiwan

This ultra-modern glass structure, known as the High Heel Church, doesn't exactly blend in with its surroundings! The Cinderella-inspired construction is 55 feet (16 m) high and over 36 feet (10 m) wide, and it stands proudly in a fishing village called Budai in Taiwan. Although it's called a "church," this neon blue structure is used only for wedding ceremonies and photo shoots. It cost $686,000 to build and was completed in 2016, when it earned a Guinness World Record for being the largest building shaped like a shoe.

Talk about finding your footing!

The slipper is constructed out of 320 tinted-glass panels fitted into a metal frame.

The Foot of Zeus
Afghanistan

Step into the past with this severed, sandaled statue. Unearthed in 1968, this incredible find revealed that there had once been a Greek city in Afghanistan. Historians believe it dates from one of Alexander the Great's conquests in the fourth century B.C. Found below a ruined temple in Ai Khanum, this left foot belonged to a 10-foot (3-m)-high seated statue of Zeus. How did they know it was Zeus, you ask? Well, two winged thunderbolts on each strap of the sandal gave a clue—Zeus was known as the god of sky, lightning, and thunder!

Eye of the Sky
Guizhou Province, China

Check out the largest radio telescope in the world ... the FAST! At 1,640 feet (500 m) in diameter, the FAST is the world's largest single-dish radio telescope. Its full name is the Five-hundred-meter Aperture Spherical radio Telescope, and its nickname is Tianyan, which means Eye of the Sky. Since 2016, it has been monitoring the skies, on the look-out for undiscovered stars, new galaxies, and alien life. It took more than 20 years of planning and five years to build—not surprising considering it contains 4,450 giant triangular aluminum panels.

EYE OF THE SKY IS THE MOST SENSITIVE LISTENING DEVICE IN THE WORLD!

Golden Bridge
Hoa Phu, Vietnam

When it comes to crossing this bridge in Vietnam, you're in safe hands ... literally! In the hills of Vietnam, you can cross the spectacular Cau Vang (Golden Bridge) and enjoy spectacular views of the Annamese Mountains. The breathtaking construction is 500 feet (152 m) long and stands 4,600 feet (1,402 m) above sea level. But unlike your average bridge, this one is held up by two humongous stone hands. It is said that these mighty mitts represent the hands of a mountain god. Despite their size, the moss-covered hands seem to belong to the landscape, and the bridge's curving path appears to flow with the shape of the mountains.

QUIZ WHIZ

Bursting with bizarre info?

Answer the questions to see how much you can remember!

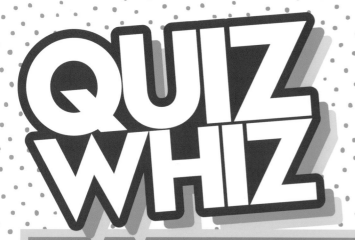

1 Which famous artist is this moth named after?

a. Salvador Dalí
b. Vincent van Gogh
c. Georgia O'Keefe
d. Pablo Picasso

3 What do Vietnamese mossy frogs do when they're scared?

a. Grow sharp claws
b. Make a rattling sound
c. Play dead
d. Spit

2 What foodstuff was used to build part of the Great Wall of China?

a. Sticky rice
b. Dim sum
c. Noodles
d. Soy sauce

4 What kind of waiters would you find at Foodom in China?

a. Monkeys
b. Robots
c. Children
d. Opera singers

5 How many legs does a Japanese spider crab have?

a. Six
b. Eight
c. 10
d. 12

6 What shape is the tea museum in Meitan, China?

a. A tea bag
b. A teaspoon
c. A tea leaf
d. A teapot

7 Where can you find the most remote toilet in the world?

a. On a mountain
b. On a desert island
c. In an underwater hotel
d. At the top of a really tall tower

8 What unique-shaped sand can be found at a special beach in Japan?

a. Triangular
b. Star-shaped
c. Donut-shaped
d. Crescent moon–shaped

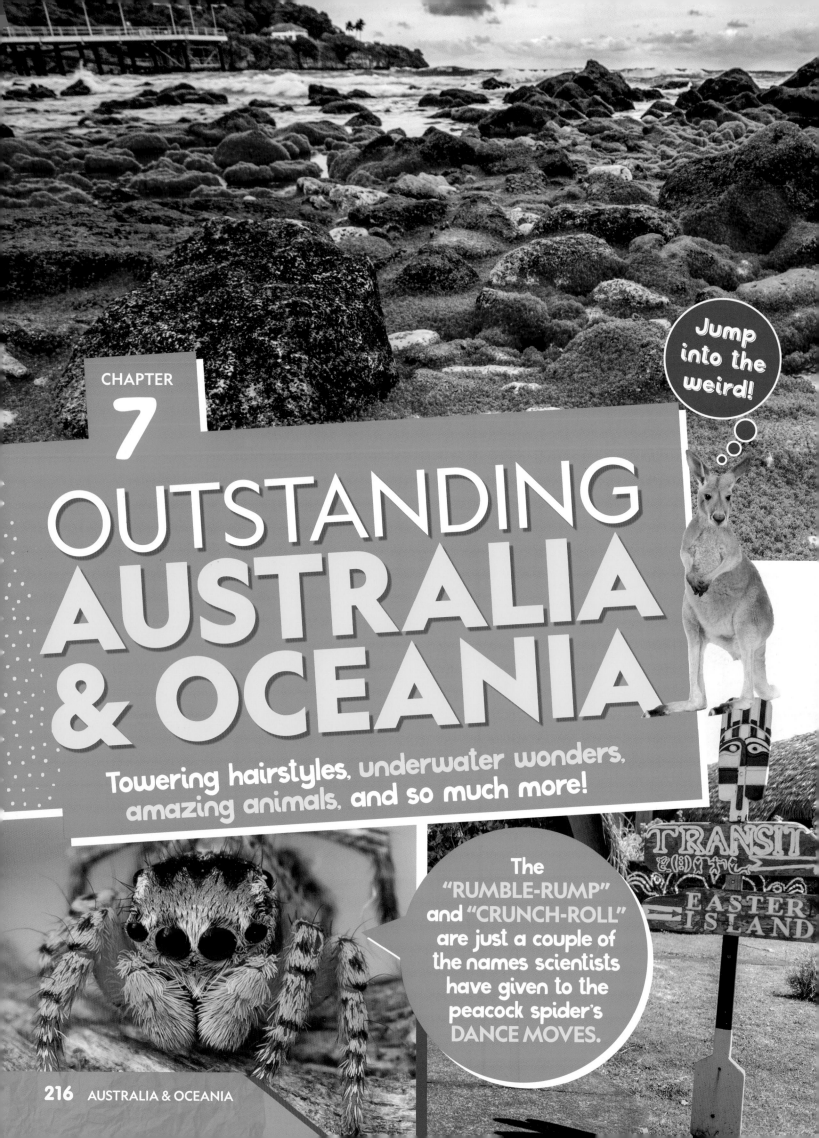

OUTSTANDING
AUSTRALIA
& OCEANIA

Towering hairstyles, underwater wonders, amazing animals, and so much more!

Jump into the weird!

The "RUMBLE-RUMP" and "CRUNCH-ROLL" are just a couple of the names scientists have given to the peacock spider's DANCE MOVES.

TRANSIT

EASTER ISLAND

Tree kangaroos are SOMETIMES known as "GHOSTS OF THE FOREST."

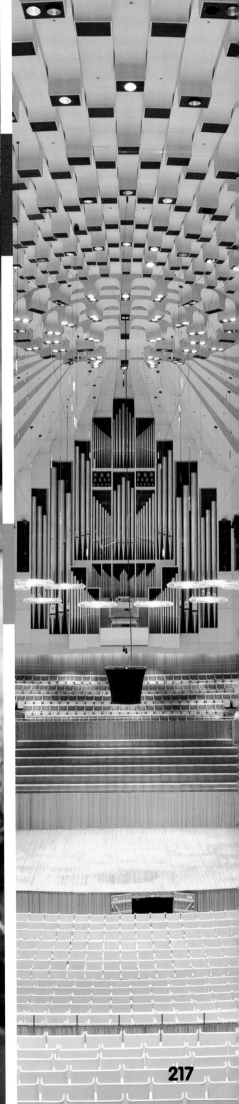

AUSTRALIA is the SMALLEST of the seven continents,

and only Antarctica is home to fewer people. But that doesn't mean it isn't

packed with INCREDIBLE ANIMALS, LUDICROUS LANDSCAPES, and BIZARRE BUILDINGS!

Emerald Island was "discovered" in 1821 and appeared on some maps until the 1980s—even though it never existed!

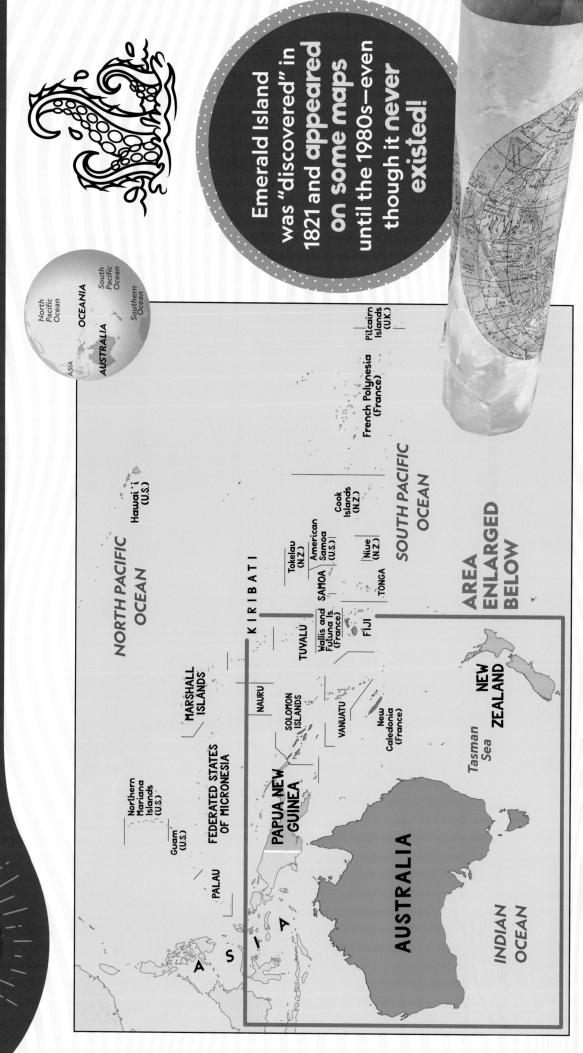

OCEANIA

North Pacific Ocean

South Pacific Ocean

AUSTRALIA

ASIA

Southern Ocean

NORTH PACIFIC OCEAN

Hawai'i (U.S.)

Northern Mariana Islands (U.S.)

Guam (U.S.)

FEDERATED STATES OF MICRONESIA

PALAU

MARSHALL ISLANDS

NAURU

KIRIBATI

TUVALU

Tokelau (N.Z.)

American Samoa (U.S.)

SAMOA

Wallis and Futuna Is. (France)

FIJI

Niue (N.Z.)

TONGA

Cook Islands (N.Z.)

French Polynesia (France)

Pitcairn Islands (U.K.)

SOUTH PACIFIC OCEAN

SOLOMON ISLANDS

VANUATU

New Caledonia (France)

PAPUA NEW GUINEA

ASIA

AUSTRALIA

Tasman Sea

NEW ZEALAND

INDIAN OCEAN

AREA ENLARGED BELOW

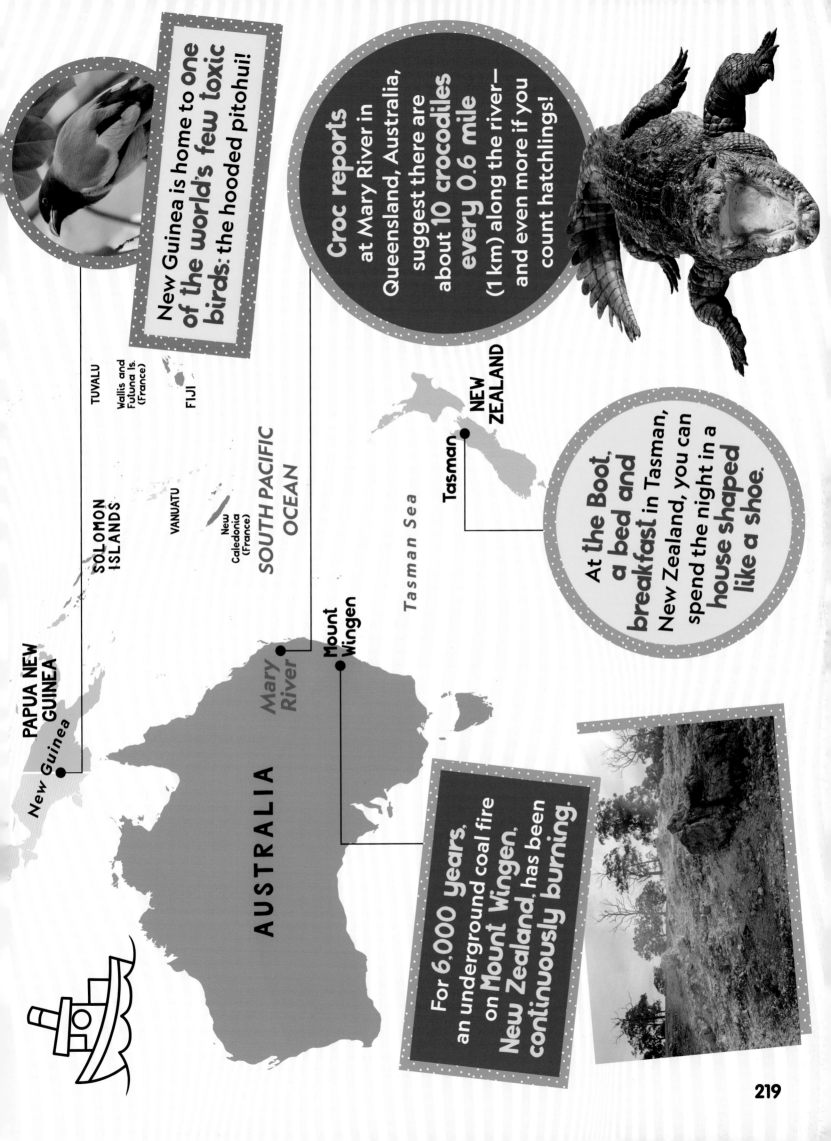

New Guinea is home to one of the world's few toxic birds: the hooded pitohui!

Croc reports at Mary River in Queensland, Australia, suggest there are about 10 crocodiles every 0.6 mile (1 km) along the river—and even more if you count hatchlings!

At the Boot, a bed and breakfast in Tasman, New Zealand, you can spend the night in a house shaped like a shoe.

For 6,000 years, an underground coal fire on Mount Wingen, New Zealand, has been continuously burning.

TUVALU

Wallis and Futuna Is. (France)

FIJI

SOLOMON ISLANDS

VANUATU

New Caledonia (France)

SOUTH PACIFIC OCEAN

PAPUA NEW GUINEA

New Guinea

NEW ZEALAND

Tasman

Tasman Sea

Mary River

Mount Wingen

AUSTRALIA

ISLANDS OF AUSTRALIA AND OCEANIA

Ball's Pyramid
Pacific Ocean

Rising out of the Pacific Ocean, Ball's Pyramid is the remains of a shield volcano. It was originally part of Zealandia—a "lost continent" that is now almost entirely underwater. At 1,844 feet (562 m) tall, the pyramid is higher than the Empire State Building, and the world's tallest volcanic stack. The isolated rock is a favorite among climbers, who need a permit to visit. But they aren't as alone as they might think out there. In 2001, scientists found a colony of 24 Lord Howe Island stick insects living 330 feet (100 m) above sea level. This creature, thought to be extinct since 1920, is as long as an adult human hand. Also known as the tree lobster or land lobster, it's the world's rarest and most endangered insect.

The Island Out of Time
Howland Island

International Date Line West— also called "Anywhere on Earth"— is the official given time zone of the banana-shaped Howland Island. As a result of it being uninhabited, this island does not actually have an official time zone. Instead, it is one of only two areas (the other being nearby Baker Island) in the world on this special calendar system. Their unique calendar marks that a period of time has ended when that date has passed in every other place in the world. Talk about being late to the party!

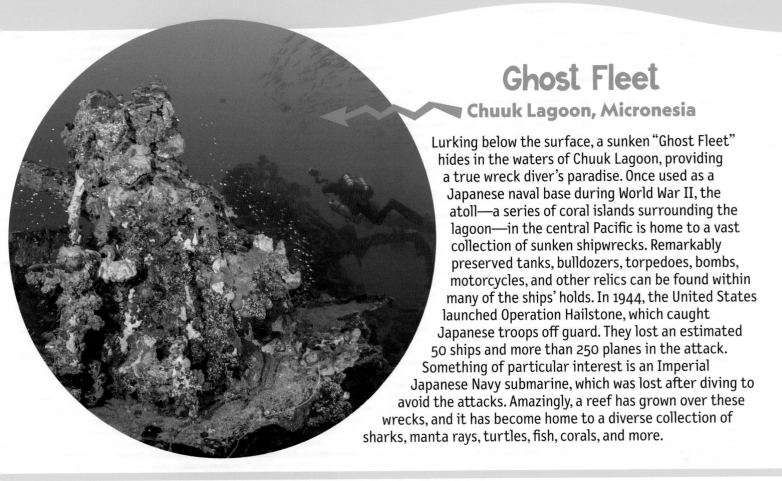

Ghost Fleet
Chuuk Lagoon, Micronesia

Lurking below the surface, a sunken "Ghost Fleet" hides in the waters of Chuuk Lagoon, providing a true wreck diver's paradise. Once used as a Japanese naval base during World War II, the atoll—a series of coral islands surrounding the lagoon—in the central Pacific is home to a vast collection of sunken shipwrecks. Remarkably preserved tanks, bulldozers, torpedoes, bombs, motorcycles, and other relics can be found within many of the ships' holds. In 1944, the United States launched Operation Hailstone, which caught Japanese troops off guard. They lost an estimated 50 ships and more than 250 planes in the attack. Something of particular interest is an Imperial Japanese Navy submarine, which was lost after diving to avoid the attacks. Amazingly, a reef has grown over these wrecks, and it has become home to a diverse collection of sharks, manta rays, turtles, fish, corals, and more.

Baby **echidnas** are called **puggles.**

Monotremes
Australia and Papua New Guinea

Most mammals give birth to live young, but monotremes obviously didn't get the memo! These animals, found only in Australia and Oceania, lay eggs instead. There are only five species of monotreme alive today. Four of those are varieties of echidnas (like the one pictured), also known as spiny anteaters. A female echidna carries its egg around in a pouch on its belly until it hatches. Predators quickly learn not to mess with an echidna—if it is under attack, it uses its claws to speedily dig a hole to hide in. Only its sharp spikes stick out, which don't provide much of a mouthful! The fifth kind of monotreme is the bizarre-looking duck-billed platypus, which is only found in eastern Australia.

SURPRISING FACTS ABOUT

Weird but true!

More than **10.9 MILLION** PEOPLE visit the SYDNEY OPERA HOUSE **EVERY YEAR.**

Over 200 architects competed to design the **Sydney Opera House,** and **Jørn Utzon's** design was chosen as the **winner.**

The **original budget** to build the Opera House was **$7 million** Australian dollars. It ended up costing **$102 million**—that's more than $74 million in U.S. dollars today.

In **2015,** genius physicist **STEPHEN HAWKING** appeared live onstage as a **HOLOGRAM.**

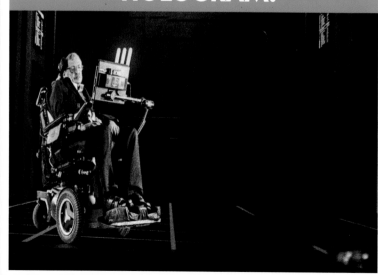

In 1960, American actor and singer **PAUL ROBESON** became the first person to perform at the Sydney Opera House when he climbed the scaffolding and sang to the construction workers!

THE SYDNEY OPERA HOUSE

The building is **cooled using seawater** taken directly from the harbor.

After a **chicken** fell on a **cellist** during an opera in the 1980s, a **net was installed** above the orchestra pit in one theater!

The **ROOF** is covered in more than **ONE MILLION** tiles.

When the **Sydney Symphony Orchestra** plays there, the **temperature** in the **Concert Hall** must be kept at **72.5°F (22.5°C)** to keep the instruments in tune.

It took **14 YEARS** to **CONSTRUCT** the building— **10 MORE YEARS** than expected.

The **GRAND ORGAN** in the Concert Hall has **10,244 PIPES,** making it the **LARGEST MECHANICAL ORGAN** in the **WORLD.**

CRAB INVASION

Christmas Island

There are around

50 MILLION

CLAMBERING CRABS

on the island!

WEIRD WONDERS

No, Christmas Island hasn't had a festive makeover—look closer to discover what causes this vibrant red carpet.

This little Australian territory is home to an array of interesting creatures. But none steal the spotlight quite like the Christmas Island red crab (*Gecarcoidea natalis*)—a bright red land crab. These crustaceans are not found anywhere else on Earth. Once a year, they leave their cooler homes in the forest and begin a mammoth trek to the coast. Because their larvae can survive only in water during their first weeks of life, these crimson crawlers must travel to the ocean to breed. This dangerous trek can take up to 18 days. During that time, they swarm the island. The human residents (close to 2,000) do their best to assist—building tunnels and crab crossings to help them navigate dangerous roads.

I'm seeing red!

WATERY WEIRDNESS

Henley on Todd Regatta

Todd River, Northern Territory, Australia

All aboard—it's time for a regatta! Not a fan of the water? Well, fear not, this bizarre boating event is the world's only dry riverbed boating regatta! That's right, you can mimic the moves of Fred Flintstone in this epic competition. Regatta teams put on their best costumes and race along a dusty riverbank in a bottomless boat. This fast-paced fun day offers a range of unusual events, ending with the "Battle of the Boats," in which three motorized vessels loaded with water bombs and water cannons have a giant water fight!

One year, the regatta was canceled—because of flooding!

Waitomo Glowworm Caves

Waitomo, North Island, New Zealand

Picture yourself drifting on a raft on an underground river. As the light from outside fades, all you have are candles to illuminate the way. As your journey continues, somehow you see more clearly. You look up and gasp in wonder at the glowing lights covering the cave ceiling. That's what happened to Maori chief Tane Tinorau and Englishman Fred Mace in 1887, when they used a small raft to go exploring. The light was provided by thousands of glowworms called *Arachnocampa luminosa*, which are found only in New Zealand. Today, visitors can still catch a glimpse of this breathtaking sight.

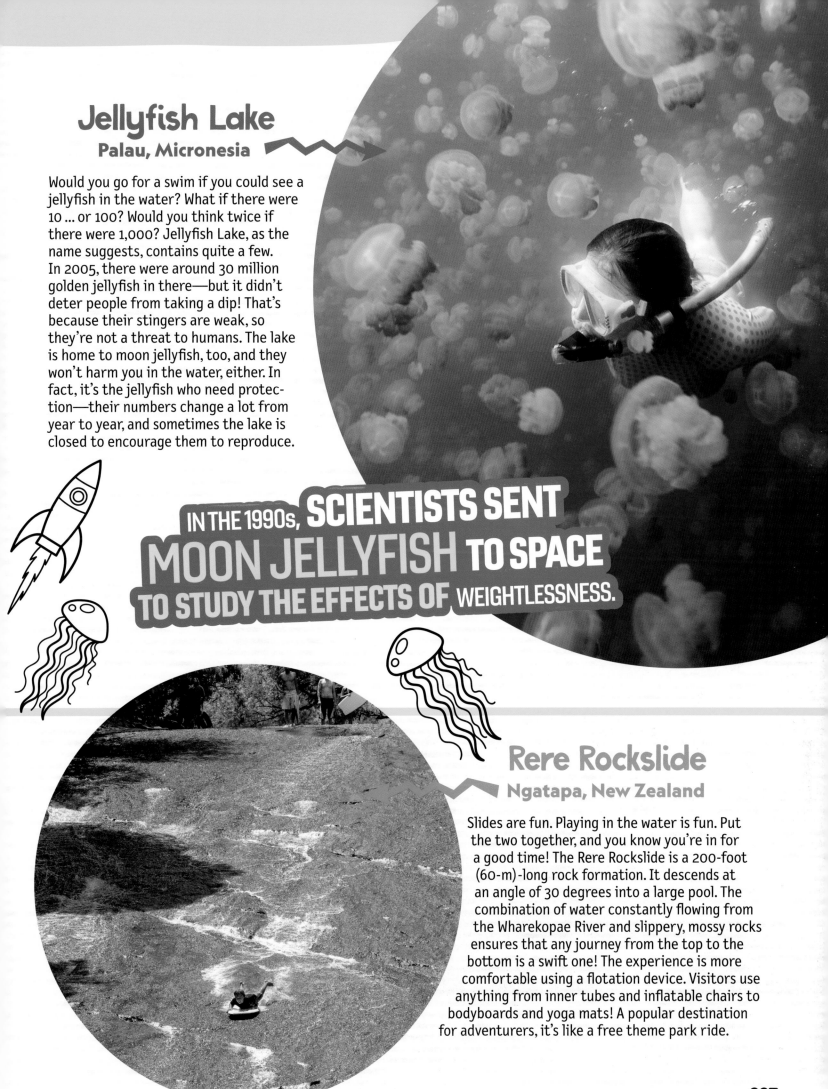

Jellyfish Lake
Palau, Micronesia

Would you go for a swim if you could see a jellyfish in the water? What if there were 10 ... or 100? Would you think twice if there were 1,000? Jellyfish Lake, as the name suggests, contains quite a few. In 2005, there were around 30 million golden jellyfish in there—but it didn't deter people from taking a dip! That's because their stingers are weak, so they're not a threat to humans. The lake is home to moon jellyfish, too, and they won't harm you in the water, either. In fact, it's the jellyfish who need protection—their numbers change a lot from year to year, and sometimes the lake is closed to encourage them to reproduce.

IN THE 1990s, SCIENTISTS SENT MOON JELLYFISH TO SPACE TO STUDY THE EFFECTS OF WEIGHTLESSNESS.

Rere Rockslide
Ngatapa, New Zealand

Slides are fun. Playing in the water is fun. Put the two together, and you know you're in for a good time! The Rere Rockslide is a 200-foot (60-m)-long rock formation. It descends at an angle of 30 degrees into a large pool. The combination of water constantly flowing from the Wharekopae River and slippery, mossy rocks ensures that any journey from the top to the bottom is a swift one! The experience is more comfortable using a flotation device. Visitors use anything from inner tubes and inflatable chairs to bodyboards and yoga mats! A popular destination for adventurers, it's like a free theme park ride.

HEADS, SHOULDERS, KNEES, AND TOES

"Quasi" Sculpture
Wellington, New Zealand

New Zealand artist Ronnie van Hout is well known for his sculptures that combine household objects with human body parts. He describes his 16.4-foot (5-m)-tall work "Quasi," which was made from scanning bits of his own body, as a partial self-portrait. A stern face stares out from the back of a hand, which stands upright on two fingers. The sculpture's name was inspired by Quasimodo in *The Hunchback of Notre-Dame.* The tragic bell ringer in that famous book was shunned because of his appearance, and opinion is split on his bizarre-looking namesake. Some locals have called him weird, but others think he's funny and a hero!

Cassowary
New Guinea and Australia

If you've ever wished you could fly, spare a thought for the poor cassowary. It does have wings, but they are tiny and their feathers aren't adapted for flight. That means the cassowary must rely on its feet for getting around. But those feet aren't only used for locomotion—they're deadly weapons, too! If they think their territory is being invaded, they'll fight to defend it. A cassowary can be 6.6 feet (2 m) tall, and has strong, muscular legs—it can run faster than a human, so it's difficult to escape from one. It will also kick out powerfully if threatened. Luckily, these big birds are shy and aren't keen on fighting. If you're lucky enough to see one, just keep your distance—it pays to be cassowary-wary!

The **claw** on a **cassowary's** inner toe can be **five inches** (13 cm) long and cuts like a **dagger!**

BY the NUMBERS

KANGAROO

Meet the world's largest marsupial. If you're thinking of challenging one to a race, you had better do some hardcore training—their incredibly strong hind legs allow kangaroos to move fast. And you wouldn't want to challenge one to a boxing match, either. Male kangaroos pack a powerful punch and often "box" each other, propping themselves up on their tails and duking it out with punches and kicks.

AVERAGE WEIGHT:

200 POUNDS (91 KG)

HOW HIGH THEY CAN JUMP:

6 FEET (1.8 M)

*THE AVERAGE HEIGHT OF A REFRIGERATOR

A BABY JOEY STAYS IN ITS MOTHER'S POUCH FOR

2 MONTHS.

LIFESPAN:

UP TO **25** YEARS

THEY CAN LEAP

25 FEET (8 M)

FORWARD IN A SINGLE JUMP.

SPEED:

35 MILES AN HOUR (56 KM/H)

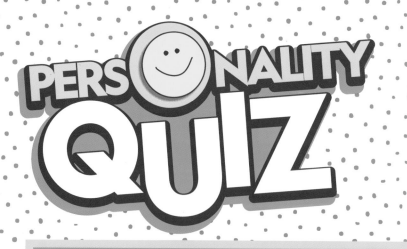

PERSONALITY QUIZ

Which Australia and Oceania activity would you enjoy?

Answer the questions **to discover your perfect day!**

1 **Where are you usually found?**

a. Playing sports with friends

b. Surrounded by animals

c. At home, playing games online

2 **What are you most afraid of?**

a. Heights

b. The dark

c. Water

3 **How would others describe you?**

a. A friend who's always up for fun

b. A daring explorer

c. A prankster

4 **Which sport would you most enjoy?**

a. A team sport like basketball

a. Something extreme like kitesurfing

c. Snowboarding

5 **You're heading out the door— what item do you grab?**

a. A camera, so you can get some pics of you and your friends

b. A skateboard—no walking for you; you like to travel at top speed!

c. A portable game console, because you never know when you'll need entertainment

6 What would you wear to a costume party?

a. My favorite team's uniform
b. A funny animal costume
c. Something extravagant—I want to be noticed.

7 What's your ideal day out?

a. A busy day full of activities
b. Adrenaline-filled!
c. Trying out new skateboarding tricks with friends

8 If you could step into a job for a day, what would it be?

a. An athlete
b. A park ranger
c. A stuntperson

Mostly A's
Racing Regatta

With your love of fun and your competitive spirit, you'll love racing in the Henley on Todd Regatta. Get dressed up in your silliest sailing attire, and hop on board with your friends as you race to victory in a wearable bottomless boat.

Mostly B's
Croc Spotting

You love being around animals, so you'll be in your element exploring the banks of the Mary River. Take a cruise on the wetlands, and test your nerves as you try to track down a snapper lurking only feet away.

Mostly C's
Coconut Canons

You're big on adrenaline and practical jokes, so you would love the party tricks of the locals at Alofaaga Blowholes, Samoa. They'll try to take you by surprise when they launch coconuts high into the air using the blowholes' powerful jets of water. (Turn the page to find out more!)

TAKING FLIGHT

Mataveri International Airport
Rapa Nui

This isolated airport on Rapa Nui (also known as Easter Island) is the most remote airport in the world! Famous for its mysterious stone *moai*, or statues, this island certainly gets a lot of visitors. However, it is a long, lonely 2,336 miles (3,759 km) away from the next nearest airport in Santiago, Chile. That's farther than the distance between Washington, D.C., and Los Angeles! Despite being remote, it draws around 100,000 travelers per year!

Gisborne Airport
New Zealand

If you're a nervous flier, you may want to look away now! Gisborne Airport has to share its runway with the Palmerston North-Gisborne train line. It is one of the few airports in the world to have active train tracks running straight through the middle of its main runway. Although regular passenger and freight trains no longer run on the track, classic locomotive steam trains cross the runway as they travel their short distance of around 10 miles (16 km) from Gisborne to Muriwai.

Flying Coconuts
Samoa

Look into the skies of the Samoan island of Savai'i, and you may see a soaring coconut launching high into the sky. The amazing Alofaaga Blowholes are formed by lava creating underwater caves below the surface. The caves slowly grow toward the surface until they become direct tunnels to the ocean below. The tunnels (named the Taga Tunnels) transport the breaking water at rocketing speeds, sending it erupting into the air. This water can shoot up to 66 feet (20 m) into the sky. For a small fee, locals will toss in a coconut just before the eruption, catapulting the coconut around 100 feet (30 m) into the sky— that's the height of seven cars stacked up on top of one another end to end!

Can I have this dance?

Bird of Paradise
Papua New Guinea

Forget angry birds. Here, it's all about the boogie birds. The Vogelkop superb bird of paradise has some serious moves. To impress onlooking females, the male puffs out his chest with his cape flipped up and dances around the female in semicircles. The bird is dressed to impress, too: Its striking blue eyes and vibrant blue breastplate stand out against the blackness of its feathers. Because of its color pattern, though, this bird has been given the nickname "sliding frowny face"!

DISTINCTIVE DWELLINGS

SiloStay
Little River, New Zealand

Want to stay somewhere that goes against the grain? Well, take a look at this unusual accommodation. In the small town of Little River, New Zealand, you can spend the night in one of their converted grain silos (large towers that stored grain). That's right, each of the silos fits a bed, kitchen, living room, and bathroom—all tucked into a metal tower. What's even cooler is that the bathroom toilet and sink are combined! It's not as gross as it sounds: When you flush, freshwater runs into a small sink for washing your hands, and this water then drains directly into the toilet flush tank to be reused. And the environmental thinking doesn't stop there—all the food waste, toilet paper, and poop from the site is used to feed tiger worms (little wrigglers that are experts in turning organic waste into compost).

Korowai Tree Houses
Papua, Indonesia

The Korowai tribe in Papua live in tree houses, most of which are between 20 and 39 feet (6–12 m) off the ground. Some of the buildings are as high as 131 feet (40 m) up in the air! Constructing one involves finding a sturdy tree and removing the top. The building materials all come from the jungle. The frame is made from branches bound together with rattan palms, and the roof is made from large leaves. A ladder carved from a tree trunk hangs from the bottom of the house for access. The treetop homes sit high above seasonal floodwaters to protect the inhabitants from biting insects at ground level. Over the past few years, many Korowai have moved to live in villages, so this generation may be the last to call the aerial accommodations home.

Coober Pedy
South Australia

More than a century ago, in 1915, a 14-year-old boy discovered an opal in the outback of South Australia. Miners flocked to the area and found large quantities of the precious gemstone. The town of Coober Pedy, named in 1920, sprang up to house the settlers, and today it supplies most of the world's gem-quality opals. The town is known for something else, too—its incredible temperature. In summer, it can reach 113°F (45°C) in the day, with the temperature plummeting at night! To cope with the heat, half the town's inhabitants live underground, which is much cooler. As well as homes, there are churches, a museum, hotel rooms, and even a campsite. Creating new dugouts can have unexpected rewards—one man building a place to live found enough opals to pay for his new home!

Baldwin Street
Dunedin, New Zealand

Baldwin Street is officially the steepest road in the world. Even the houses look like they are sliding down it! That's because they have to be built up at one side to compensate for the street's slope. On this street, every 9.4 feet (2.86 m) you walk horizontally, you're going up 3.3 feet (1 m)! Who on Earth would plan such an offbeat street? Someone who had never been there, of course! The Dunedin streets were planned in London in the 19th century, with no thought for the hilly terrain. In fact, some of the roads on the blueprints were so steep, they couldn't be laid.

EVERY YEAR, THOUSANDS OF ROUND CHOCOLATE CANDIES ARE ROLLED DOWN THE STREET IN A CHARITY RACE!

ANIMAL ANTICS

Peacock Spider
Australia

This little spider, *Maratus banyowla,* is just one of many kinds of colorful, spirited arachnids known as peacock spiders. In fact, the total number of known peacock spiders is up to 108 and counting. These tiny, large-eyed crawlers are only .16 to .24 inch (4–6 mm) in size. Beyond their colorful appearances, peacock spiders are also known for their fancy footwork. Male peacock spiders perform dances to attract a mate, but despite the males' best efforts, sometimes their finest moves just don't cut it. If the females are unimpressed, they have been known to simply gobble up the males right then and there—talk about harsh critics!

Kākāpō
New Zealand

Also known as the "mighty moss chicken" (because of its fluffy plume of green feathers), the kākāpō is the world's only flightless parrot! Its inability to fly could make it vulnerable to attack, but when threatened, it simply freezes, tries to blend into the background, and pretends to be a plant! Recognized as both the world's heaviest and longest-living parrot, the kākāpō can reach an estimated 90 years in age. However, due to habitat loss and the arrival of new predators, such as cats and stoats, these birds plunged to seriously low populations. In the 1990s, the total number of kākāpōs was as low as just 50! The good news is that the population of these little fighters has more than quadrupled since then, and many have been relocated to predator-free islands to help conserve them further.

Comb-Crested Jacana
Australia

Now that's a scarily large number of limbs! Or is it? The jacana is well known as a leggy bird with distinct long, spindly toes that allow it to traverse across floating lily pads. These incredibly long toes allow it to spread its weight and stop it from breaking the water's surface tension. So they can literally walk on water! Don't worry, though—the bird's alien-like extra legs actually belong to its chicks. When the father believes that his babies are in danger, he will scoop them up under his wings with only their little legs dangling down! They seem to have plenty of space there, seeing as some have been spotted carrying two chicks under each wing!

THIS BIRD IS ALSO KNOWN AS THE LOTUS BIRD OR LILY TROTTER!

Weirdly Cute!

Huan Tree Kangaroo

This incredible creature might not be what you first think of when someone says the word "kangaroo." It doesn't hop around the outback and is much smaller than its red kangaroo cousins, but it sure knows how to live the high life! Found only in the forests of Australia, Papua New Guinea, and West Papua, these kangaroos actually live in trees! Although it is unknown when these mammals evolved into tree dwellers, their bodies are well adapted to it. They have long, gripping claws and a long tail to help them balance. Their thick mahogany fur is perfect for insulating them against damp weather, and it helps them camouflage against predators.

WEIRD WONDERS

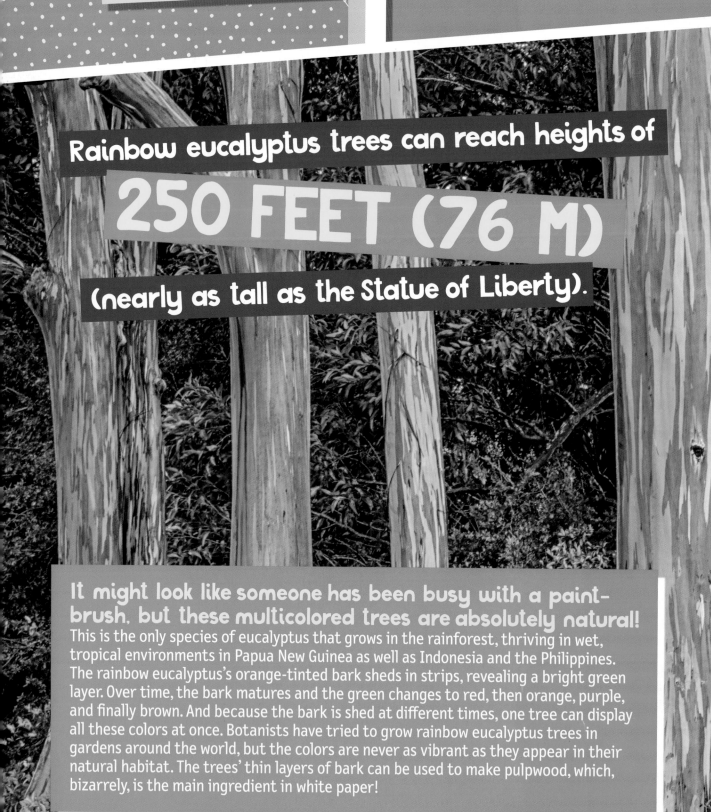

Rainbow eucalyptus trees can reach heights of

250 FEET (76 M)

(nearly as tall as the Statue of Liberty).

It might look like someone has been busy with a paint-brush, but these multicolored trees are absolutely natural! This is the only species of eucalyptus that grows in the rainforest, thriving in wet, tropical environments in Papua New Guinea as well as Indonesia and the Philippines. The rainbow eucalyptus's orange-tinted bark sheds in strips, revealing a bright green layer. Over time, the bark matures and the green changes to red, then orange, purple, and finally brown. And because the bark is shed at different times, one tree can display all these colors at once. Botanists have tried to grow rainbow eucalyptus trees in gardens around the world, but the colors are never as vibrant as they appear in their natural habitat. The trees' thin layers of bark can be used to make pulpwood, which, bizarrely, is the main ingredient in white paper!

RAINBOW EUCALYPTUS

239

AUSSIE ODDITIES

Gnomesville
Ferguson Valley, Australia

An area of land near a roundabout in southwestern Australia is gnome—sorry, home—to a huge collection of tiny statu-ettes. Gnomesville began in 1995 when the roundabout was being built. First one gnome appeared. (Although it's unclear whether it was watching over the work or protesting against it.) Soon more little folk arrived, dis-tracting drivers from the road. So the statuettes were moved nearby. The collection began to attract visi-tors who brought their own gnomes to help the tiny town grow, and it wasn't long before gnomes started to arrive from all around the world. The number grows every year. Well, gnome wasn't built in a day, was it?

Hairy Food
Melbourne, Australia

Unless you're looking for a hair ball, you wouldn't want to bite into these delicious-looking dos. Hot dogs, pretzels, and pizzas are just a few of the incredible styles that Mykey O'Halloran has created to raise money for the Make-A-Wish Foundation. Although some creations can take around eight hours to construct, the results are magical! O'Halloran recruits volunteers online and then uses a combination of vibrant colors and clever sculpting to make these hairy versions of popular dishes. The stylist has traveled the world using vegan and cruelty-free products on a tour called the Rainbow Road Trip.

O'Halloran has used powdered sugar and hair dye to make toppings for his creations.

Pink Slugs
Mount Kaputar, Australia

This magnificent mollusk is found only at the top of Mount Kaputar in New South Wales. The mountaintop is a unique ecozone formed by a volcanic eruption that happened 17 million years ago, and there are at least 20 species of slugs and snails that aren't found anywhere else in the world. These amazing pink slugs are eight inches (20 cm) long. They live in beds of snow gum eucalyptus leaves, where their color helps to camouflage them from predators. However, the pink slugs emerge in the hundreds after it rains to feed on tree moss—and they definitely stand out from their surroundings then! A lot of poisonous animals are brightly colored to warn predators. Although the pink slug isn't toxic, its amazing color might discourage hungry hunters.

Quokkas
Rottnest Island, Australia

Found on islands off the coast of Western Australia, the quokka has been nicknamed the "happiest animal in the world" because of its big grin. When Dutch explorer Willem de Vlamingh first saw them in 1696, he thought they were giant rats! He named their island Rotte Nest, meaning "rats' nest" in Dutch. Today, Rottnest Island is the best place to see this cute marsupial. Of about 14,000 wild quokkas, between 10,000 and 12,000 of them live here. Though small—about the size of a cat—they are not afraid of humans and will often allow people to get close. They became famous worldwide when they started appearing in selfies with visitors to the island, including celebrities, though this practice is now discouraged.

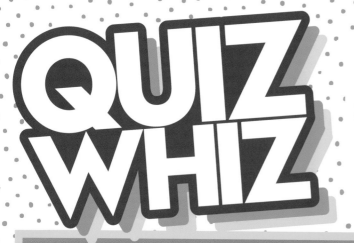

It's hard to keep track of all this weirdness!

See how much you can remember with this quiz. Grab a piece of paper and write down your answers.

1 What does a comb-crested jacana carry under its wings?

a. Spare change
b. Snacks
c. Nesting materials
d. Its babies

2 What does one talented Australian hairdresser sculpt clients' hair to look like?

a. Plants
b. Food
c. Footballs
d. Game consoles

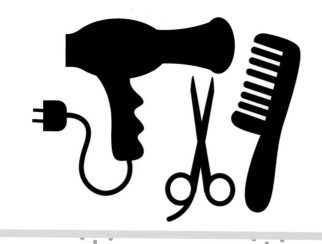

3 Which creatures "invade" Christmas Island en masse each year?

a. Crabs
b. Squid
c. Spiders
d. Mosquitoes

4 **What can you find crossing the runway at Gisborne Airport?**

a. Sheep
b. A huge piece of art
c. Flashing lights
d. A railroad track

5 **Which Australian animal can reach speeds of over 35 miles an hour (56 km/h)?**

a. Koala
b. Cassowary
c. Kangaroo
d. Peacock spider

6 **What can you find under the waters of Chuuk Lagoon in Micronesia?**

a. A ghost fleet
b. A mysterious cave
c. The wreck of a pirate ship
d. The biggest shell in the world

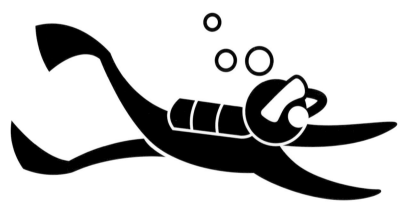

8 **Which is a nickname for the kākāpō?**

a. Small green turkey
b. Mighty moss chicken
c. Camouflage king
d. Duck duck goose

7 **What strange shape is a bed-and-breakfast in Tasman, New Zealand?**

a. A shoe
b. A hat
c. A cat
d. A boat

Answers: 1.d, 2.b, 3.a, 4.d, 5.c, 6.a, 7.a, 8.b

Does it feel weirdly cold?

CHAPTER 8
AMAZING ANTARCTICA

Steaming ice towers, striped icebergs, frozen fruitcakes, and more!

At the South Pole, the temperature can plummet to **MINUS 112°F (-80°C)!**

245

WEIRD in the WORLD

Check out some of the WACKIEST, COOLEST, and DOWNRIGHT WEIRDEST PLACES and ANIMALS across ANTARCTICA!

At the South Pole, it's dark all the time for six months in the winter, then there's daylight for six months in the summer!

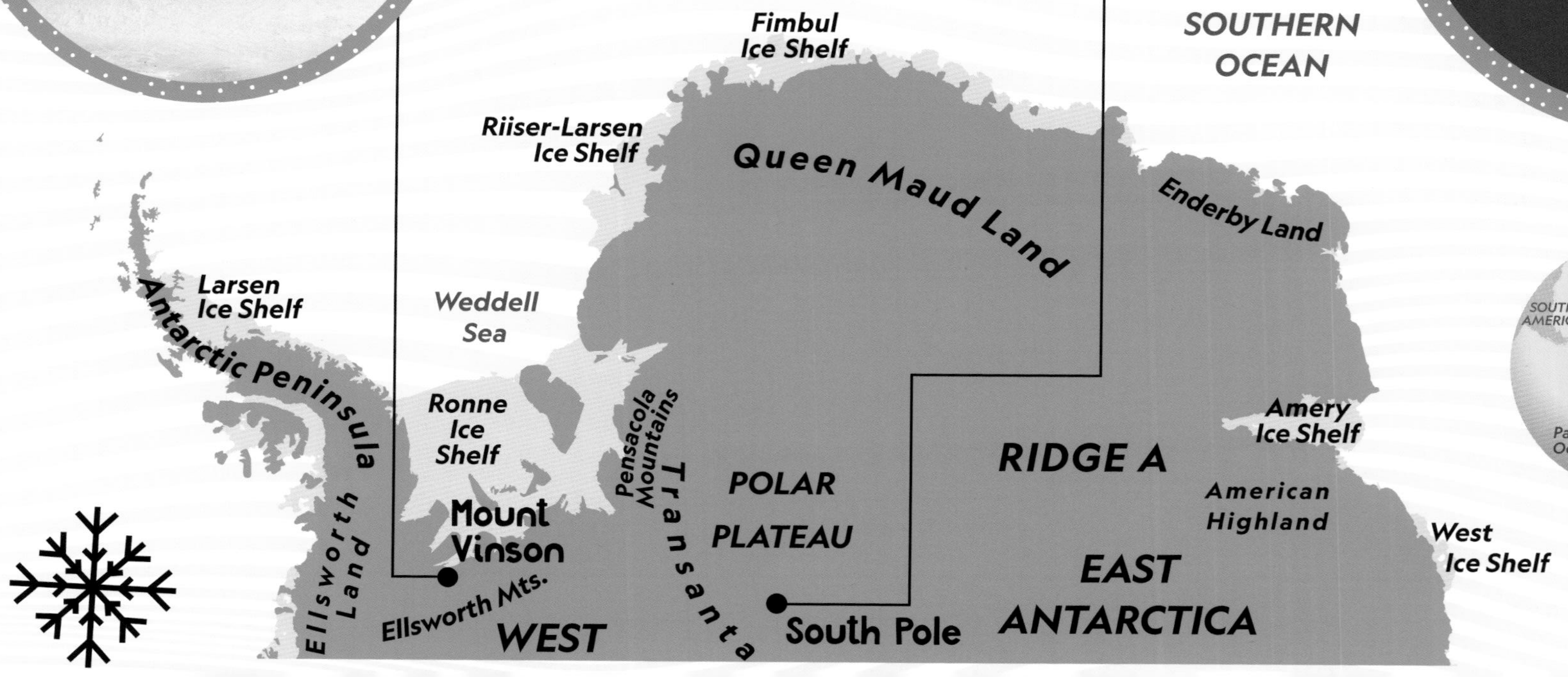

Antarctica isn't just big, it's high! Mount Vinson, its tallest peak, soars to 16,050 feet (4,892 m).

AFRICA
Atlantic Ocean
SOUTH AMERICA
Pacific Ocean
ANTARCTICA
Indian Ocean
AUSTRALIA
Southern Ocean

SOUTHERN OCEAN

Enderby Land

Amery Ice Shelf

American Highland

West Ice Shelf

RIDGE A

EAST ANTARCTICA

Queen Maud Land

Fimbul Ice Shelf

POLAR PLATEAU

South Pole

Transanta

Pensacola Mountains

Riiser-Larsen Ice Shelf

Weddell Sea

Ronne Ice Shelf

Mount Vinson

Ellsworth Mts.

WEST

Ellsworth Land

Larsen Ice Shelf

Antarctic Peninsula

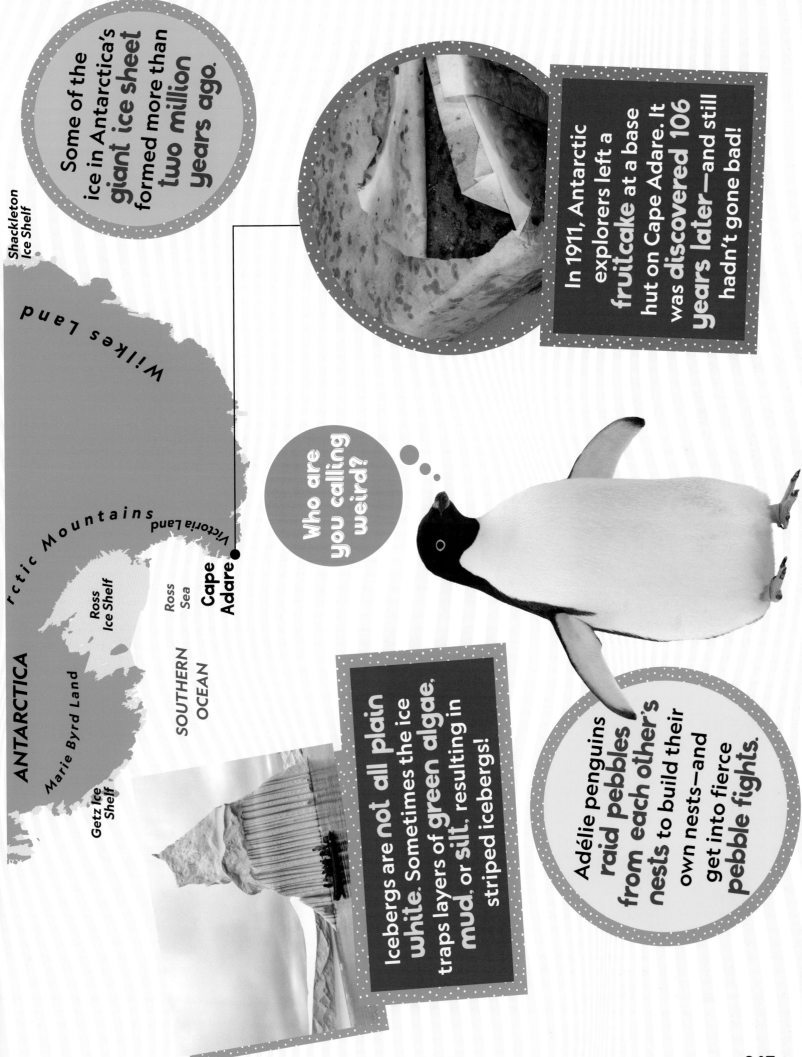

Some of the ice in Antarctica's giant ice sheet formed more than two million years ago.

In 1911, Antarctic explorers left a fruitcake at a base hut on Cape Adare. It was discovered 106 years later—and still hadn't gone bad!

Who are you calling weird?

Icebergs are not all plain white. Sometimes the ice traps layers of green algae, mud, or silt, resulting in striped icebergs!

Adélie penguins raid pebbles from each other's nests to build their own nests—and get into fierce pebble fights.

Shackleton Ice Shelf

Wilkes Land

Transantarctic Mountains

Victoria Land

Cape Adare

ANTARCTICA

Marie Byrd Land

Getz Ice Shelf

Ross Ice Shelf

Ross Sea

SOUTHERN OCEAN

WEIRD WONDERS

Around Antarctica, there are several huge ice shelves, where thick ice covers the sea. There are also countless free-floating icebergs and ice floes, or flat sections of ice. Although the water is freezing cold, it's not empty: Under the ice, there's a whole ecosystem of amazing Antarctic wildlife living in a beautiful blue-green world. Tiny shrimps and krill feed on algae that grows on the underside of the ice, and they in turn become food for sardines, squid, and whales. Penguins zoom and dart around at high speeds to catch fish, chased by hunters such as the fierce leopard seal. There are sometimes humans here, too: scuba divers with cameras exploring, wildlife-spotting, and snapping breathtaking shots like this one!

The water temperature around Antarctica can drop **AS LOW AS 28°F (–2°C)!**

UNDER THE ICE

A Mysterious Underwater Realm

COOL FACTS ABOUT THE HALLEY VI

The station is built on a **426-FOOT (130-M)-THICK FLOATING ICE SHELF** in the Weddell Sea.

There are **no fruit trees** in Antarctica—**fruit mainly comes in cans.** If a delivery plane brings fresh fruit, **it's gone in minutes!**

For **105 days a year,** it's **DARK** for **24 hours a day.**

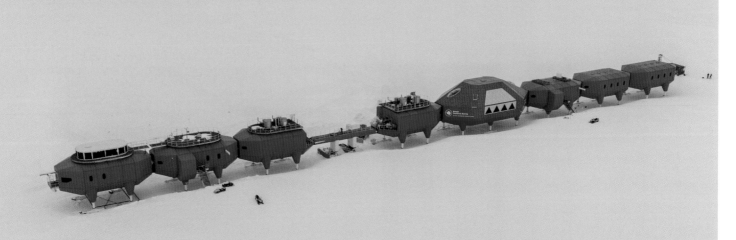

EIGHT MODULES make up the RESEARCH FACILITY.

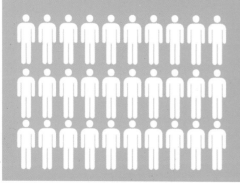

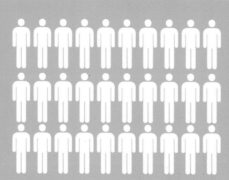

Up to **70 STAFF** work at **Halley** over the **SUMMER.**

RESEARCH STATION

Since Halley is so **remote,** the European Space Agency uses it to study how **people cope with darkness** and **isolation.** This helps them plan for future long-distance space journeys.

Halley researchers **FREQUENTLY** spot **EMPEROR PENGUINS, MINKE WHALES,** and **WEDDELL SEALS** near the station.

Antarctic **SCIENTISTS WITH BEARDS** often find that their **BREATH FREEZES ONTO THEIR FACIAL HAIR,** giving them a face full of **"HAIR-CICLES"!**

NOT EVERYONE living at Halley is a scientist. There are also lots of other staff: mechanics, electricians, plumbers, radio operators, and medical staff.

RESEARCHERS EAT LOTS OF **CHOCOLATE BARS** FOR ENERGY—THEY HAVE TO BE STUFFED IN A POCKET TO KEEP THEM FROM **TURNING ROCK HARD IN THE COLD.**

TEMPERATURES AROUND THE BASE DROP **AS LOW AS MINUS 67°F (-55°C)** IN WINTER.

UNUSUAL UNDERWATER CREATURES

Antarctic Sun Sea Stars

Growing up to 24 inches (60 cm) across, this monster sea star is always on the prowl. It climbs up on top of sponges, rocks, or even human-made underwater equipment and waves its long arms—up to 50 of them—around in the water. Its arms and body are covered in little jawlike grabbers called pedicellariae, which can snap together like a trap to grab prey such as shrimps or small fish. Then it uses its arms to pass the food into its mouth. The tiny traps give this sea star its other name—the "wolftrap" sea star.

Rotifers

Without a microscope, it would be almost impossible to see one of these—scientists think that around 100 rotifers could fit into one drop of water! Rotifers are zooplankton—tiny marine animals—usually between .004 and .02 inch (0.1–0.5 mm) in size. "Rotifer" means "wheel bearer," after the circle of hairlike structures around their mouth. These "hairs"—known as cilia—ripple one after the other, like a rotating wheel helping rotifers to move around and to eat. Bdelloid rotifers can survive being dried out completely and then rehydrated—a handy adaptation for life in Antarctica!

Antarctic Icefish

Meet the icefish, which doesn't just live in the icy Southern Ocean, it also looks like ice! Partly snow-white and partly see-through, it's the only type of fish that has no red blood cells. Instead, its blood is thin and clear like water. Scientists aren't sure why, since without red blood cells, its blood can't carry much oxygen. To make up for this, the fish has an extra-large heart and blood vessels, and more blood than a normal fish. And to save energy, it doesn't chase its prey. It lies in wait instead, grabbing shrimps or small fish as they pass by.

FEATHER STARS
TAKE BETWEEN THREE AND SIX MONTHS TO REGROW MISSING
BODY PARTS.

Feather Stars

These pretty plantlike creatures from the deep have been around for 488 million years! Some feather stars swim, and others crawl along the seafloor using their arms, which they can regrow when damaged or injured. Once fully regrown, there is no sign of an injury ever occurring. In fact, they can regrow most body parts as long as the disk in the center of their body, called the centradorsal, is not too damaged. Many different organisms, such as tiny shrimps, make their homes on these magical-looking living structures. The feather stars provide these animals with food (which gets stuck in the feathery arms) and shelter.

PERFECT PENGUINS

Adélie Penguin

The Adélie penguin has some impressive leaping skills! Zooming up out of the water to land on sea ice, an Adélie can shoot 10 feet (3 m) into the air—several times its own height! Adélies also live in *enormous* colonies, or groups. In 2018, a new Adélie colony was discovered using satellite images —it was made up of a mind-boggling 1.5 million birds.

Macaroni Penguin

How did macaroni penguins get their name? It's not because they like mac and cheese. (All penguins are carnivores and eat only other sea creatures.) Instead, the name comes from the macaronis of 18th-century England, a group of men who wore frilly high-fashion styles— including caps with plumes similar to the macaroni penguin's crest of bright yellow-orange feathers. Despite their stylish looks, though, macaronis don't always have great manners. The males often fight for space in their crowded colonies by slapping each other with their flippers. Grumpy macaronis have been known to give passing scientists a good slap, too!

BY theNUMBERS

LIFE ON THE ICE

Antarctica is one of the coldest places on the planet, but that doesn't deter the emperor penguin. These ultimate survivors spend their entire lives on the ice and in the frigid water. Take a look inside the supercool life of an emperor penguin.

WEIGHT:

UP TO **88** POUNDS

(40 KG)

DIVE DEPTH:

1,850 FEET (564 M)

DISTANCE A FEMALE WILL TRAVEL TO FIND FOOD:

ABOUT **50** MILES

(80 KM)

TIME EMPEROR PENGUINS CAN STAY UNDERWATER:

20 MINUTES

SWIMMING SPEED:

46 MPH (74 KM/H)

ICE AND FIRE

Lava Lake

Mount Erebus

On Ross Island, you will find the southernmost active volcano on Earth. This is the place where fire and ice meet! Lava has flowed from Mount Erebus, but unlike many volcanoes, its slopes are covered in snow and ice. This frozen volcano was discovered in 1841 on an expedition led by Sir James Clark Ross. It started to form 1.3 million years ago and now stands at 12,450 feet (3,800 m) high. The extreme climate ranges from minus 4°F (-20°C) in summer to as low as minus 58°F (-50°C) in winter. While most volcanoes are dormant (non-active) most of the time, this one is always bubbling and sometimes even hurls exploding lava bombs! The lava lake may bring up magma from miles beneath Earth's surface.

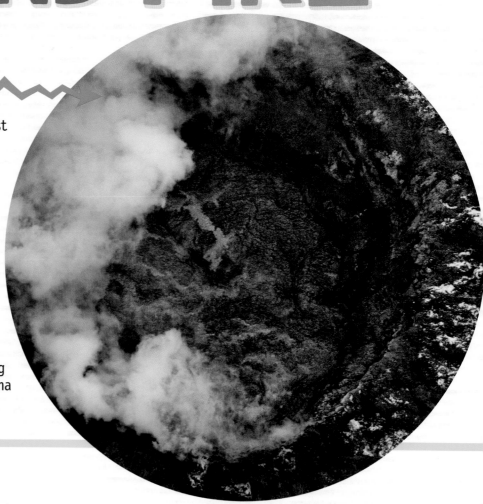

Antarctic Fire Department

Ross Island

Even a continent covered in ice needs a fire service! Antarctic Fire Department (AFD) is the fire and rescue service for McMurdo Station (United States Antarctic Program), Amundsen-Scott Station (New Zealand's research station), and United States Air Force airfields. These busy places have lots of machinery, plus large stores of toxic chemicals, and that means lots of potential risk. When a fire does start, the extreme dry, cold, and windy climate means that flames spread quickly, and water—a basic necessity to fight most fires—soon freezes solid. To combat this, the fire engines have pumps to keep the water continually moving.

Incredible Ice Towers

Volcanoes in warmer places have fumaroles: vents or cracks in the ground around the volcano where hot volcanic gases and steam shoot out. On Mount Erebus, thanks to the subzero temperatures, fumaroles become huge fumarolic ice towers! These crooked pillars of ice can be between 10 and 12 feet (3–4 m) across and up to 33 feet (10 m) tall. How do they happen? As the boiling hot gas and steam flow out of the ground, they instantly melt the ice and snow above. But then they hit the cold air and freeze onto the ice around the edge of the melted hole. Over time, more and more ice builds up, creating a towering chimney. Once in a while, the top of a tower collapses or topples over—don't get too close!

MOUNT EREBUS ERUPTS MULTIPLE TIMES A DAY, FIRING OUT AROUND 50 LAVA BOMBS.

257

Ocean ODDITIES!

Hoff Crab

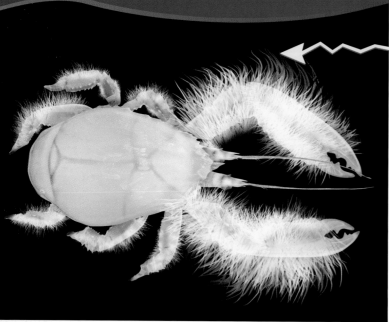

Imagine a small, blind, white deep-sea crab with a very hairy chest, and you have a Hoff crab! This curious creature was discovered in 2010, living in the icy deep seas around Antarctica. It's found near hydrothermal vents, where hot mineral-filled water seeps out of the seafloor. Special vent bacteria live here, and the Hoff crab feeds on them. To make this easier, its underside is covered with hairlike parts that give the bacteria a place to live—and the crab just scrapes a few off whenever it feels like a snack! So why "Hoff"? Scientists gave the crab this name because its hairy-looking chest reminded them of actor David Hasselhoff, known as "the Hoff"—and he was happy to be linked to the cool new discovery!

Orca

Orcas, the largest of the dolphins, have big brains to match, and they're super smart. A bit like humans, they can come up with new ideas to solve problems, then share them and learn from one another. This has happened in Antarctica, where some orcas have invented a way of catching seals that sit on floating ice floes to stay safe. The orcas team up in a group of three or four, then charge toward the ice floe, making a big wave that tips it over or washes the seal completely off!

My lips are sealed!

Leopard Seal

Many people think of seals as cute, chubby, and cuddly creatures who like munching fish and flopping around on the beach. That's until they see a leopard seal! This seal gets its name because of its spotted coat, but that's not the only way it resembles a big cat. Leopard seals are huge—up to 12 feet (3.6 m) long—and fierce, with their giant jaws full of *T. rex*–style long, sharp teeth. They're streamlined and agile underwater, where they chase and grab penguins, octopuses, squid, and other smaller seals to eat. They can be dangerous to humans, too, and have even been known to chase explorers across the Antarctic sea ice.

Snowy Sheathbill

Meet the birds known as the "garbage collectors" of the Antarctic. Snowy sheathbills, which look like extra-large white pigeons with pink warty faces, get this nickname because they'll eat absolutely anything! Unlike most Antarctic birds, they don't have webbed feet and aren't great swimmers. So instead of diving into the sea to catch fish, they vacuum up any kind of food they can find on land. That ranges from insects and worms to other birds' eggs, animals that have died, and stinky, fish-flavored seal poop! They'll even gang up on penguins to steal whatever food they've caught. And they've also learned to bother humans, hanging around outside research bases, ready to grab snacks from passing scientists!

Krill

It looks like a small, pink, slightly see-through shrimp about the size of your little finger, but this is actually a krill, superstar of the Antarctic seas. To say krill are common in Antarctic waters would be an understatement. There are *gazillions* of them! They form vast shoals called superswarms that are so big, they can be seen from space. In a swarm, a bathtub-size amount of water can contain 20,000 krill! And if you put all the world's krill together, they'd weigh more than all the humans. Krill are also incredibly important, since they are a vital food for countless other Antarctic animals—from fish, penguins, and seabirds to squid, seals, and massive whales.

Basket Star

This creepy creature of the Antarctic deep looks like some kind of sci-fi alien monster, but don't panic—it's just a basket star! That's a sea star, or starfish, that resembles a basket because of the way its five main arms divide and branch off into many smaller arm tips (sometimes as many as 5,000 of them!). Its scientific name, *Gorgonocephalus*, means "Gorgon head," after the Gorgon of Greek mythology, who had writhing deadly snakes for hair. But these basket branches don't bite: Instead, the basket star waves them around like a net to catch passing prey, such as small shrimps.

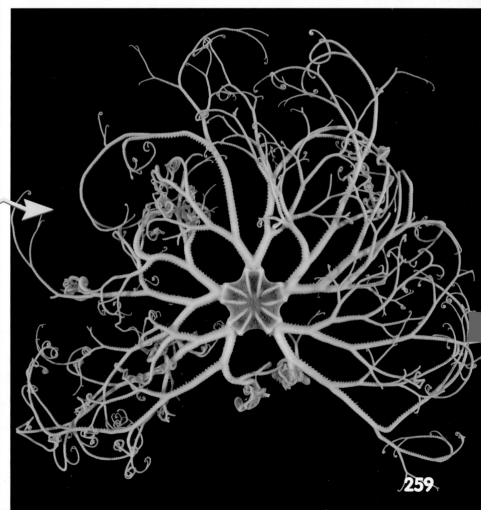

259

ICY TRAVEL

 Mini-Trac

Things have moved on a lot since early polar explorers took ponies and dogsleds on their Antarctic adventures more than 100 years ago. Today, scientists mainly get around using planes, trucks, snowmobiles, and Sno-Cats, which have caterpillar tracks for crossing the ice. But back in the 1960s, a very different vehicle could be seen trundling around the polar wilderness: a tiny, iconic Mini car. Instead of driving along on its equally tiny tires, the Mini was given its own caterpillar tracks, along with a heater to keep the crew inside warm, and the "Mini-Trac" was born. Sadly, it wasn't used for long, and the Wilkes Antarctic Station where it was based has now closed down. But we still have the photos!

Bicycling to the South Pole

As you may know if you've ever tried riding a bike in freezing temperatures, ice and bicycling aren't a great combination. Add in the blasting Antarctic wind and endless snowdrifts, and bicycling from the edge of Antarctica to the South Pole might seem like a definite no-go. But it has been done! In fact, in 2013, three different bicyclists attempted the feat at the same time. The first to make it was British adventurer Maria Leijerstam, who set a record by covering 396 miles (638 km) in 10 days, 14 hours, and 56 minutes. Instead of a normal two-wheeler, she rode a special low-lying three-wheeled bicycle, the ICE Polar Cycle, which she helped design.

What's **Weird** About This **?**

The ice that covers Antarctica's Ross Ice Shelf sings! Unfortunately, humans can't actually hear the eerie, low humming sound it makes. Researchers discovered this fascinating fact by using seismometers, which are microphones for the ground, to study the snow and ice. They recorded the sound for two years and found that the hum is caused by wind blowing over the surface of the ice. Interestingly, they also discovered that the sound changes slightly depending on the weather conditions. For example, if wind moves the snow around and changes the shape of the snow dunes, or if areas of the ice melt, the sound's pitch changes. This means that scientists can track the ice's singing to monitor how stable the ice is, and whether it's in danger of cracking or collapsing.

QUIZ WHIZ

Think you're a whiz at weird but true?

Test your knowledge with these quirky questions!

2 **An orca is a type of ...**
a. Shark
b. Dolphin
c. Seal
d. Fish

1 **Which of these does Mount Erebus NOT have?**

a. Lava bombs
b. A lava lake
c. A cable car
d. Ice towers

3 **Why are some icebergs striped?**

a. Layers of dead leaves get trapped in them.
b. Layers of mud and algae get trapped in them.
c. They scrape against each other, carving striped lines.
d. Scientists paint stripes on them.

5 How many wheels did Maria Leijerstam's "Polar Cycle" have?

a. Two
b. Three
c. One
d. Five

4 What does an Antarctic icefish's blood look like?

a. Water
b. Milk
c. Glitter
d. Pea soup

6 What are "hair-cicles"?

a. Weird hairy Antarctic sea stars
b. Bicycles designed for use in the Antarctic
c. Very thin icicles that look like hair
d. Icicles that grow on someone's hair or beard

7 Why are leopard seals called leopard seals?

a. Because they eat zebras.
b. Because they climb trees.
c. Because they have spots.
d. Because they have long furry tails.

8 How long can an emperor penguin stay underwater?

a. two minutes
b. three hours
c. 20 minutes
d. one day

The GREAT BLUE HOLE of Belize measures 980 FEET (300 m) across!

That's wheely weird!

9
SENSATIONAL
SEA &
SPACE

Deep dives, revolutionary robots, sunken sculptures, and more!

SUPERNOVAE are the result of STARS EXPLODING— they can outshine ENTIRE GALAXIES!

WEIRD in the WORLD

Travel beyond the human domain into the **DARKEST DEPTHS** of the OCEAN and the **DISTANT REACHES** of OUTER SPACE...

More people have been to the moon than have been to the bottom of the Mariana Trench.

There is a supermassive black hole at the heart of virtually every galaxy.

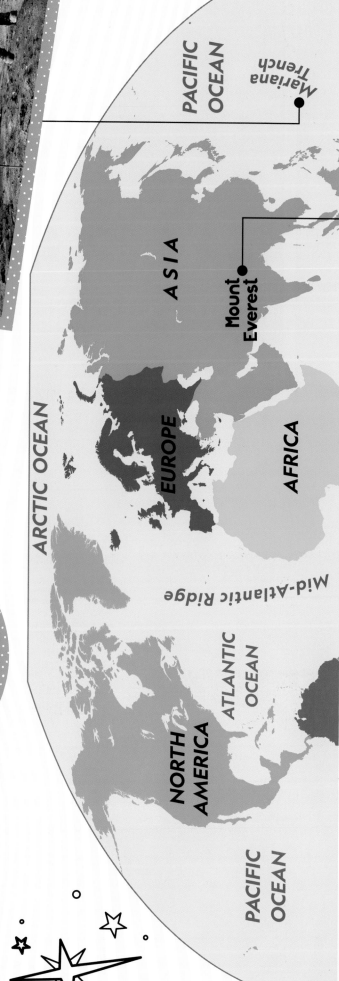

PACIFIC OCEAN

Mariana Trench

ASIA

Mount Everest

EUROPE

AFRICA

ARCTIC OCEAN

Mid-Atlantic Ridge

ATLANTIC OCEAN

NORTH AMERICA

PACIFIC OCEAN

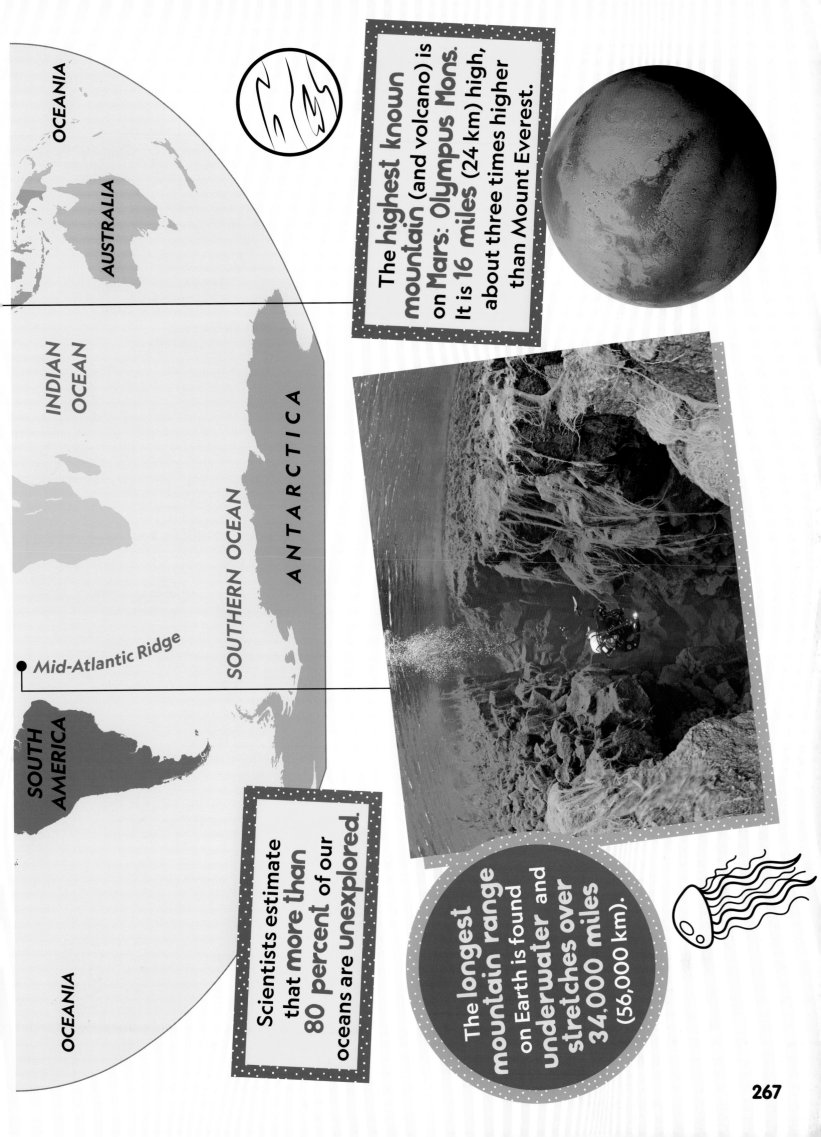

OCEANIA

AUSTRALIA

INDIAN OCEAN

SOUTHERN OCEAN

ANTARCTICA

Mid-Atlantic Ridge

SOUTH AMERICA

OCEANIA

The highest known mountain (and volcano) is on Mars: Olympus Mons. It is 16 miles (24 km) high, about three times higher than Mount Everest.

Scientists estimate that more than 80 percent of our oceans are unexplored.

The longest mountain range found on Earth is underwater and stretches over 34,000 miles (56,000 km).

UNDERWATER WEIRDNESS

Pufferfish Circles

Pacific Ocean, Japan

When divers first found strange circular patterns on the seafloor near Japan, they were stumped. The circles have rings of ridges around them, so neat and detailed that they look like something a human artist might make. Eventually, however, the real artist was spotted at work—and it was a fish! It turns out that the male of a species of pufferfish makes the patterns. He creates the ridged circles by swimming in and out around the circle, shaping the sand as he goes. The resulting pattern is actually a nest, which a male makes to impress a female pufferfish. If she likes it, she'll lay her eggs in the middle, and the male then guards them until they hatch.

The intricate **circular patterns** made by a pufferfish are up to **6.5 feet (2 m) across.**

Underwater Fireworks

Eastern Pacific Ocean

Halitrephes jellyfish wouldn't look out of place in the sky on the Fourth of July—hence explorers describing them as "deep-sea fireworks." But despite the jellyfish's big bell, which can reach up to four inches (10 cm), and big burst of colorful tendrils, it would be hard to find in its natural habitat. It lives 1,000 feet (620 m) down in the ocean where there's almost no light, so it can be photographed only when a camera light illuminates it.

Pink See-Through Fantasia

Pacific Ocean, Indonesia

This alien-like creature of the deep is a swimming sea cucumber unlike any you've ever seen before. Pink see-through fantasias don't leave much to the imagination—their transparent skin means that their intestines are all on display. One of the coolest things about them is that they light up. They can even shed flakes of their glowing skin to confuse pesky predators—essential for critters this fragile. Their bellies have fingerlike webbing that allows them to swim and move along the seafloor as far down as 8,200 feet (2,500 m) deep.

WEST MATA WAS ONE OF THE VERY FIRST UNDERWATER ERUPTIONS TO BE CAUGHT ON CAMERA.

Undersea Volcano

Tonga Trench, Pacific Ocean

This is a picture of volcano West Mata erupting at the bottom of the Pacific Ocean, between Fiji, Tonga, and Samoa. Just like a volcano on land, it churns out red-hot molten rock, or lava. But instead of flowing down the volcano's sides, the lava hits the cold water immediately. This causes it to suddenly cool and solidify, turning the lava into lumps of volcanic rock that cover the seafloor. Though we rarely see them, there are more volcanic eruptions under the sea than on land—which makes sense, as Earth has a lot more sea than land.

DOWN TO THE DEPTHS

Deepest Submersible Dive

Mariana Trench, Pacific Ocean

The deepest any human has ever been is 35,872 feet (10,934 m)—almost to the bottom of Challenger Deep in the Mariana Trench. The record was set in 2019 by American explorer Victor Vescovo. He made the trip alone in a deep-sea submersible—a type of small submarine strong enough to resist the deep ocean water pressure. Right at the bottom, he spotted shrimplike sea creatures and, sadly, a plastic bag.

Talk about an all-time low!

Deepest Scuba Dive

Dahab, Red Sea

The world's deepest open-circuit scuba dive reached a staggering 1,090 feet 4.5 inches (332.35 m) down. Open circuit is the most common type of scuba diving and involves using a traditional breathing apparatus called a regulator, which doesn't recycle any of the gas you exhale. Ahmed Gabr set this epic record in the Red Sea in September 2014. The feat required a team of 30 people to support Ahmed, including divers, medical staff, and technicians. A dive like this takes tons of organizing—it took 10 years of preparation but only 15 minutes to descend to the bottom. Coming back up however, took a whole 13 hours and 35 minutes.

BY the NUMBERS

THE DEEP SEA

How deep does the ocean go? In most places, the seafloor slopes gently away from the coast, forming the continental shelf, which then falls steeply away into the deeper ocean. The very deepest point in the whole ocean is called Challenger Deep, in the Mariana Trench, near the island of Guam in the Pacific Ocean. This area is so deep that it takes several hours to get there in a submarine, it's pitch-black, and if you weren't protected inside a submarine, the water pressure there would squash you in a split second.

DEEPEST DEPTH SUNLIGHT CAN REACH:

3,280 FEET (1,000 M)

HEIGHT OF THE BURJ KHALIFA, THE WORLD'S TALLEST BUILDING:

2,717 FEET (828 M)

AVERAGE DEPTH OF THE SEA-FLOOR AROUND THE WORLD:

12,100 FEET (3,688 M)

DEEPEST EVER SCUBA DIVE:

1,090 FEET (332 M)

AMOUNT OF WATER IN ALL THE WORLD'S OCEANS:

321 MILLION CUBIC MILES (1.3 BILLION CUBIC KM)—WHICH IS MORE THAN 10 TRILLION BATHTUBS!

HEIGHT OF MOUNT EVEREST, THE WORLD'S HIGHEST MOUNTAIN:

29,032 FEET (8,849 M)

MONSTERS OF THE DEEP

Vampire Squid
Deep Waters Around the World

Does it have scary fangs and a taste for blood? No. The vampire squid got its name because it has a red cape and lives in the dark! Photographed by the team at the Monterey Bay Aquarium Research Institute (MBARI), this harmless creature lives in the deep sea where oxygen is low and predators are few. It's related to squids and octopuses, and feeds using two skinny tentacles to catch bits of food that drift down from the ocean surface. Its eight arms are connected by sheets of skin, resembling a cloak. When in danger, the squid can turn its "cape" inside out and hide inside, displaying the large spines on the insides of its arms to ward off attack.

Barreleye Fish
Warm and Tropical Ocean Waters

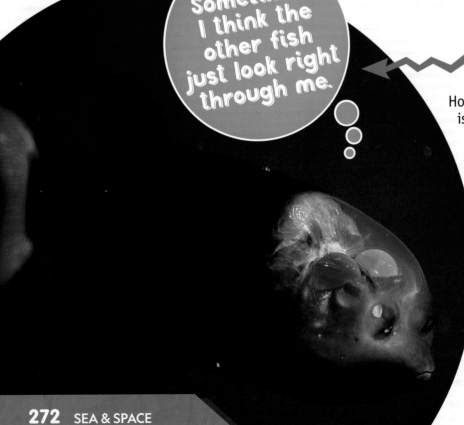

Sometimes I think the other fish just look right through me.

Hovering silently in the murky ocean depths is a fish with a dome-shaped see-through head and two tube-shaped green eyes that rotate to point forward or straight up. It's not made-up—this really is a fish, named the barreleye, and it's one of the weirdest animals in the world. Where it lives, there's only a little light filtering down from above. So it's thought the barreleye looks upward to spot the silhouettes of prey, such as smaller fish, as they pass overhead. Then, according to researchers at MBARI, the fish rotates its eyes forward to see its meal while it chows down. But why the transparent dome? The barreleye sometimes swims through jellyfish tentacles to steal the food they've caught—and the dome protects its eyes from stings!

Sea Butterfly

Atlantic Ocean, off Cabo Verde

These graceful marine snails are called sea butterflies and yes, they do have wings! Their delicate wings propel the creatures along in a zigzag path—mainly up to the water's surface for food at night. During the day, sea butterflies float back down to safety, farther away from predators. The way that they swim up and sink down depends on the size and shape of their shell, so each moves in its own individual way.

Weirdly Cute!

Sea Pig

Just as land pigs snuffle around in the mud, sea pigs snuffle their way along the deep seafloor in search of food. And like a real pig, a sea pig is plump, pinkish, and pretty cute! But that is where the likeness ends. A sea pig is actually a type of sea cucumber. And confusingly, a sea cucumber is not a cucumber, but a small animal related to sea stars. They use their tentacles to "walk" and feel their way around, and they feed on the rotting bodies of other creatures that have died and sunk to the seafloor. According to MBARI, sea pigs are some of the most common critters on the seafloor, making them quite the cleanup crew! And if that's not weird enough for you, get this: They breathe through their butts!

273

WEIRD WONDERS

The Great Blue Hole of Belize is a scuba diver's dream. Its pristine waters are bursting with tropical marine life and out-of-this-world coral formations. At its deepest, the underwater sinkhole goes as far down as 400 feet (122 m), so it's not an expedition for the faint of heart. The Great Blue Hole is part of the Barrier Reef Reserve System, which is a World Heritage Site. It formed during the last ice age when water filtered through the rock over many, many years, creating stalactites and stalagmites. Over time, these formations caved in on one another. At the end of the ice age, sea levels rose as the ice melted, resulting in the hole becoming engulfed by the Caribbean Sea.

GREAT BLUE HOLE

Belize, Caribbean Sea

The Great Blue Hole is the

BIGGEST
NATURAL FORMATION

of its kind in the world.

275

WHO PUT THAT THERE?

Musical Mermaid
Rudder Cut Cay, Bahamas

A grand piano is the last thing you'd expect to find at the bottom of the sea. But that's exactly what some lucky divers and snorkelers may encounter on a clear day in the Bahamas. The steel sculpture also includes a life-size mermaid and is nestled near some private islands about 15 feet (4.5 m) down. The wistful mermaid appears to sit on the seafloor, longing for a diver to play her a tune on the piano. The sculpture was sunk to the seafloor to surprise guests enjoying boat trips or snorkeling while staying on the luxury islands.

Sunken Art Gallery
British Virgin Islands

Divers can marvel at the sight of this epic kraken sculpture at the bottom of the ocean. The mighty 80-foot (24-m) kraken was built clinging to an old boat, which was then deliberately sunk. Why? To create a one-of-a-kind reef. The idea behind the underwater art gallery was to create an ideal environment to support endangered marine life. So not only is it lots of fun, but it's also eco-friendly! And it's not just any old ship, either—it's a World War II U.S. Navy fuel barge named the *Kodiak Queen*.

Underwater Pyramid
Yonaguni Jima, Japan

Mystery and controversy surround these stone ruins discovered beneath the waves. Some scholars believe that they are the ancient remains of a Japanese Atlantis that sunk following an earthquake 2,000 years ago. Others say that there's no evidence that the site is human-made. According to their research, the rocks are a natural geological phenomenon. The site was first discovered in 1986 by a local diver. Tourists and researchers continue to dive here today.

Largest Underwater Sculpture
Nassau, Bahamas

This is the colossal "Ocean Atlas"— a sculpture of a girl carrying the weight of the ocean. It is the biggest sculpture ever constructed underwater, and it's so huge that it had to be put together in sections. It stretches from the seafloor to the water's surface at 18 feet (5 m) tall. This means that it could be highly hazardous for passing ships, so there is a flag and light at the very top. Besides looking impressive, "Ocean Atlas" is also there to create a reef for creatures to inhabit, while aiming to attract tourists away from polluted reefs to allow time for their recovery.

THIS SCULPTURE IS BASED ON THE ANCIENT GREEK MYTH OF ATLAS (THE GOD THAT HELD UP THE HEAVENS).

Bizarre BEHAVIOR

Stinger Thief

When it comes to resourcefulness, these sea slugs are up there with the best of them. Without shells for protection, aeolid nudibranchs must rely on other ways to stay safe from predators, such as being camouflaged or being brightly colored to signal danger. Besides these run-of-the-mill defense mechanisms, they have their own kind of superpower—they can eat jellyfish and other poisonous sea creatures without being stung. Better still, they can then use the jellyfish tentacles as weapons to fight off their own enemies. Waste not, want not, as they say ... The stinging cells of their prey are digested and stored in the white tips along their back, ready to be fired out and reused when the time comes.

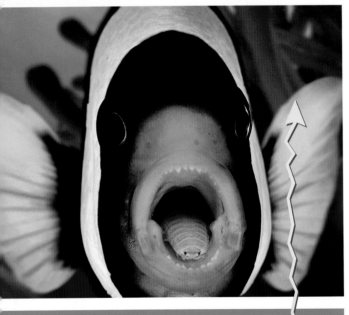

Uninvited Guest

The tongue-eating louse is a parasite—a creature that survives on or inside another living thing. It swims in through the fish's gills, attaches itself to the base of its tongue, and bites through the blood vessels. The real tongue dies and falls off, and is replaced by the louse! The fish now has a living louse for a tongue, feeding on its blood. Luckily, this doesn't kill the fish or stop it from eating.

Blowing Bubbles

By puffing a big bubble of air out of its blowhole underwater, a dolphin can make a spinning bubble ring that hovers in the water. Then the dolphin chases the ring, bats it around with its flippers, pokes it with its snout, or, if it's big enough, swims right through it. Playing is a sign of intelligence, and dolphins are known for being very smart creatures. They sometimes make and play with bubble rings, and one dolphin can even learn to make rings by watching another.

Master of Disguise

The mimic octopus of Indonesia can do impressions of other animals—and not just one or two, but around 12 of them! Like other octopuses, it can change the color and texture of its skin. But it can also change its shape, disguising itself as venomous or dangerous sea creatures to keep predators away. It imitates the deadly lionfish by arranging its tentacles like spiky fins, and becomes a sea snake by hiding most of its body and sticking out two tentacles in a long line. To mimic a flounder, which lies on the seafloor, it arranges is body and tentacles into a flattened fish shape.

Slow Mover

It may sound surprising for an underwater animal, but leafy sea dragons are in fact very bad swimmers—not ideal when there are hungry predators galore lurking in the depths. Luckily, leafy sea dragons got it right when it comes to camouflage! They blend in perfectly with their algae-covered environment, thanks to their plantlike tendrils. Surprisingly, they don't use these structures to swim (they're purely for camouflage), but instead rely on two super-thin, transparent fins to move along.

Bubble Bullets

You don't want to get on the wrong side of a pistol shrimp—they're one of the most powerful creatures in existence and can kill their enemies with bubbles. Not just any old bubbles, though—these are 8000°F (4400°C) jet-propelled bubbles! Besides looking threatening, their enormous claws can move as fast as 60 miles an hour (97 km/h). This action creates a serious amount of noise—210 decibels, to be precise, noisier than a gunshot. The sheer speed of this snap makes a bubble shoot out with such force that it often immobilizes and kills the target.

279

BY the NUMBERS

INTERNATIONAL SPACE STATION

For most people, the idea of space travel feels like a million miles away (literally!). It's hard to picture what living aboard the International Space Station (ISS) would really be like, but these facts and stats should fill in some blanks.

MORE THAN

50 COMPUTERS

CONTROL THE SYSTEMS ON THE SPACE STATION.

NUMBER OF SPACESHIPS THAT CAN BE CONNECTED TO THE SPACE STATION:

8 AT A TIME

SIZE OF THE STATION:

356 FEET (109 M) LONG

IT'S ALMOST AS LONG AS A FOOTBALL FIELD.

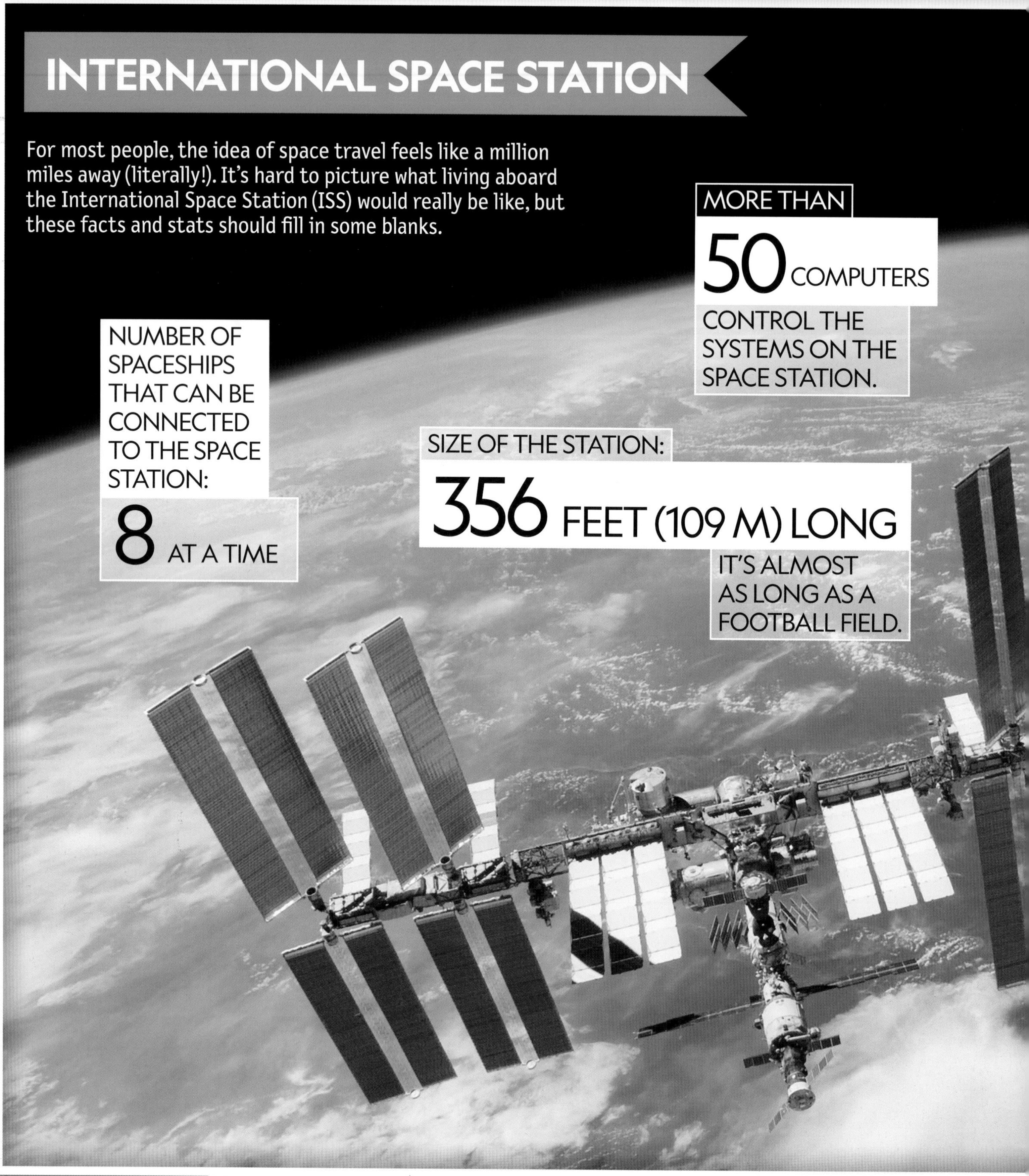

NUMBER OF TIMES THE ISS ORBITS EARTH:

16 TIMES IN 24 HOURS

TIME ASTRONAUTS EXERCISE:

2 HOURS PER DAY MINIMUM

THIS KEEPS ASTRONAUTS FROM LOSING TOO MUCH MUSCLE OR BONE MASS IN MICROGRAVITY.

NUMBER OF SPACE AGENCIES OPERATING THE ISS:

5 SPACE AGENCIES FROM
15 COUNTRIES

7 ASTRONAUTS

LIVE AND WORK ABOARD THE SPACE STATION AT ONCE.

I'm feeling out of this world!

NUMBER OF ROOMS:

6 SLEEPING QUARTERS
2 BATHROOMS
1 GYM

JOKES IN SPACE

Space Gorilla

U.S. astronaut Scott Kelly took the idea of monkeying around to a whole new level. When his twin brother bought him a gorilla suit for his birthday, Kelly decided to make good use of the unusual gift by taking it aboard the International Space Station. Cue hilarious videos of a big gorilla breaking free from a bag before flying around the station.

Suit-Free Space Walk

One April Fools' Day, three crew members aboard the International Space Station played a prank on mission control that would go down in history. The joke was a photograph of all three of them outside the space station, waving through the window. That doesn't sound all that unusual for astronauts until you notice that they're wearing T-shirts and sunglasses ... no space suits in sight! They joked that they were safe, though, because they all had their sunscreen on and couldn't float away since they were tethered to the spacecraft. Now that's an April Fools' prank that's out of this world!

What's **Weird** About This

This famous photo, taken in 1984, shows U.S. astronaut Bruce McCandless floating in space, completely alone. Unlike most space walks, on this one McCandless was not tethered to anything. He was just floating free in the vastness of the universe. Luckily, though, he wasn't actually lost. The photo was taken from the nearby spacecraft, and McCandless was making his space walk using a special jet pack. It allowed him to control his direction, so he could return safely after flying 320 feet (98 m) away from the shuttle.

SPACE ROBOTS

Robonaut 2 ⟿

Exploring space is extra difficult because, like the sea, humans can't survive in it without help. We need space suits and breathing equipment, and have to bring food and water supplies along, too. So it makes sense that NASA has a robot crew member who needs none of these things! Meet Robonaut 2, the latest version of this humanoid robot assistant. On board the International Space Station, it can clean, flip switches, and solve problems using artificial intelligence. In the future, robots like this will also be able to do risky space walks. And to help it get along with its human team, Robonaut has been programmed to high-five when it completes a task!

Shall I load the dishwasher next?

⟿ Canadarm2

This is a very different type of robot, which doesn't resemble a human at all. It's a huge, 60-foot (18-m)-long robot arm, attached to the outside of the International Space Station. It's not for waving at other spacecraft: This arm is busy doing all kinds of important tasks, such as moving supplies around the outside of the ISS, attaching new parts and modules, and locking on to visiting spacecraft when they deliver astronauts or food supplies. It can even detach and "walk" itself around the whole space station, holding on to different base points like a huge one-legged spider.

The arm is made of parts that can be replaced by astronauts in space.

RoboSimian

This versatile robot can walk, climb stairs, drive, and use a drill to boot! The RoboSimian has been designed to operate in challenging environments as part of a push to use robots to respond to human-made or natural disasters. One of RoboSimian's strengths is the ability to cope with tough terrain while handling dexterous tasks. It has seven sets of stereo cameras and a LiDAR (Light Detection and Ranging) device that means it can map its environment in 3D, so that those operating the robot can get a clear idea of the environment it's in.

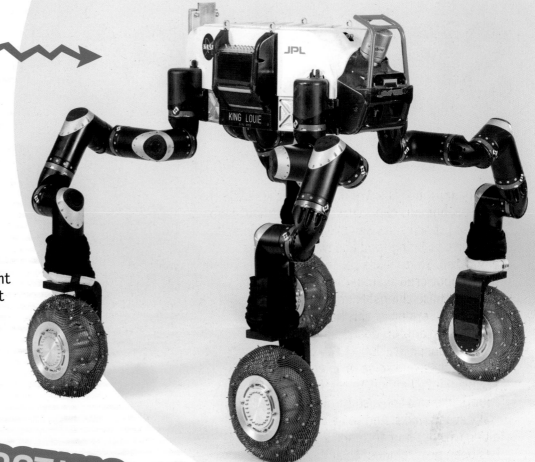

THE BOT HAS FOUR LIMBS, EACH WITH 28 ARTICULATED JOINTS THAT HELP IT HOLD AND USE TOOLS.

Weirdly Cute!

Kirobo

How cute is this mini space robot? Named Kirobo, Japanese for "Hope Robot," he's only 13 inches (34 cm) tall, and one of the friendliest robots you could meet. Kirobo was actually designed to be a friend—a chatty companion who can recognize your face and keep you company. He went to the International Space Station in 2013 as a companion for Japanese astronaut Koichi Wakata. It was part of an experiment to see how good robots are at helping with loneliness and befriending people—and the answer is, pretty good! In fact, more and more robots are being used this way on Earth as well as in space.

Far, Far AWAY!

Pillars of Creation

A nebula is a huge cloud of gas and dust in space. In some nebulae, new stars form, causing them to glow brightly. Nebulae are often named after their weird and wonderful shapes, which can resemble familiar objects. The beautiful Pillars of Creation are a small part of the Eagle Nebula. Tower-shaped masses of gas are filled with newborn stars. This famous nebula image was captured by the Hubble Space Telescope in 1995.

Black Eye Galaxy

When new galaxies are discovered, astronomers give them a number-based name such as NGC 4826, but also a nickname, usually chosen for what they look like. And here's one example! This galaxy, 17 million light-years away, has a band of dust that absorbs light, making it a galaxy with a dark side. It's known as the Black Eye Galaxy, or sometimes the Evil Eye Galaxy.

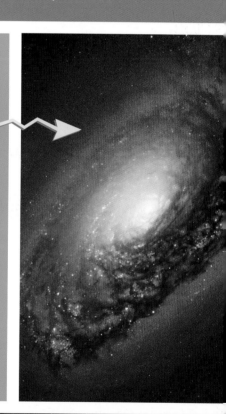

Birthday Tapestry

Created in honor of the Hubble Space Telescope's 30th birthday, this portrait of a nearby galaxy celebrates the incredible imagery that has given humankind a look into the sky. This image was nicknamed the "Cosmic Reef." Hubble has revolutionized astronomy and made it accessible to everyone, forever changing our understanding of the universe around us.

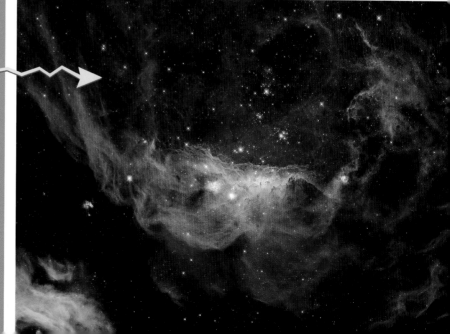

Cosmic Remains

This is the aftermath of a supernova, or explosion of a star—the biggest blast there is in space. These colorful cosmic ribbons of gas, known as DEM L249, are the remains of a Type 1a supernova, which occurs when a white dwarf star dies. Astronomers believe this dwarf star was larger than typical supernovae because its leftover gas was hotter and shone brighter. This probably means that it died earlier in its life cycle, too. White dwarf stars are generally stable and unlikely to explode, but when they are in a binary system where two stars are orbiting each other, they can start sucking matter away from their companions. Sooner or later, the white dwarf steals so much gas that it explodes!

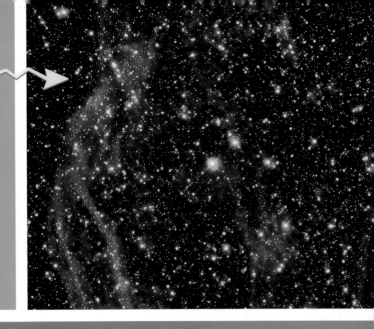

Rare Rings

The Hubble Space Telescope captured these super-rare Einstein rings—the most complete ever discovered in our universe. The unusual shape is due to gravitational lensing, a process that was accurately predicted by scientist Albert Einstein more than 100 years ago. It happens when light shining from far away is pulled and distorted by the gravity of another object before it reaches us.

New Perspective

The first full-color images and spectroscopic data from the James Webb Space Telescope were released during a televised broadcast on July 12, 2022. NASA's telescope is the biggest and most powerful space telescope in existence. So it's not surprising that it's already taken the sharpest images of the universe so far.

Galaxy Crash

This stunning galaxy, Centaurus A, seems to have several parts, resembling a giant jellyfish crashing through a galaxy-size pancake. That's because it's actually made up of two galaxies that have crashed together. This can happen when one galaxy's powerful gravity pulls on another galaxy nearby.

287

UNLIKELY ITEMS IN SPACE

Luke Skywalker's Lightsaber

In 2007, the space shuttle *Discovery* launched with the original prop lightsaber from the original 1977 *Star Wars* movie. The Jedi weapon was taken to the orbiting post and back as a way to mark the 30th anniversary of the franchise. Astronaut Jim Reilly greeted R2-D2 and collected the lightsaber before it was taken to the Kennedy Space Center. As you'd expect from hard-core *Star Wars* fans, plenty of people came dressed as their favorite characters to give it the send-off it deserved. The iconic lightsaber then spent two weeks in orbit.

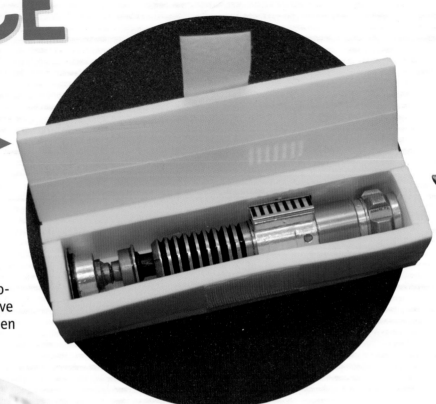

To infinity ... and the ISS!

Buzz Lightyear

Toy Story's favorite space-man, Buzz Lightyear, went to the International Space Station. The iconic Pixar character was part of NASA and Disney's mission to encourage more children to go into careers in science. The Buzz Lightyear toy took off in 2008 and spent a total of 15 months in space before returning back to Earth.

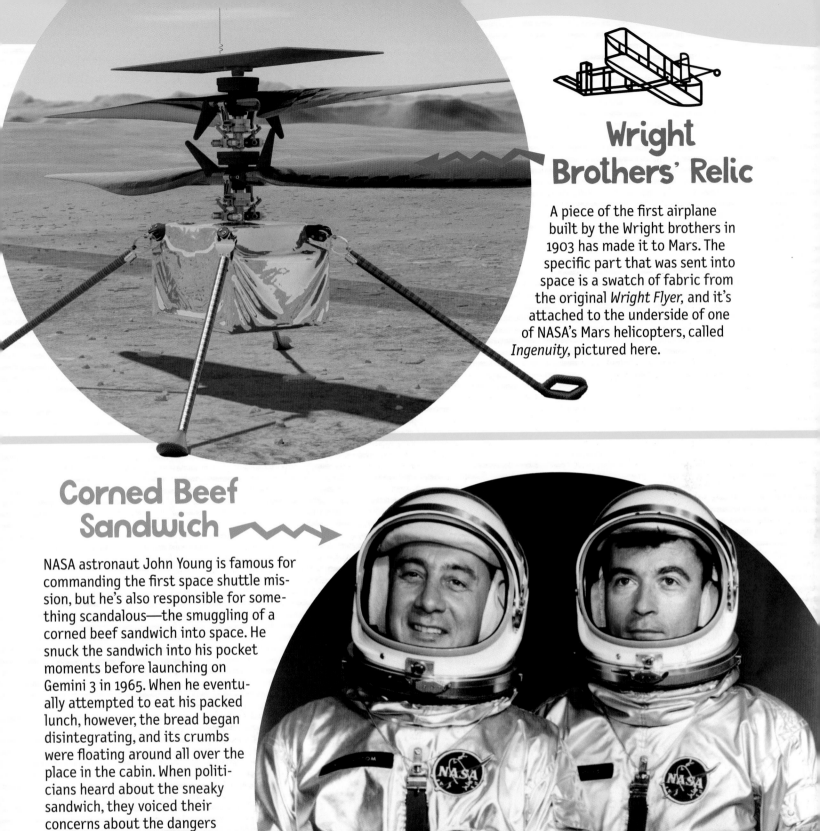

Wright Brothers' Relic

A piece of the first airplane built by the Wright brothers in 1903 has made it to Mars. The specific part that was sent into space is a swatch of fabric from the original *Wright Flyer*, and it's attached to the underside of one of NASA's Mars helicopters, called *Ingenuity*, pictured here.

Corned Beef Sandwich

NASA astronaut John Young is famous for commanding the first space shuttle mission, but he's also responsible for something scandalous—the smuggling of a corned beef sandwich into space. He snuck the sandwich into his pocket moments before launching on Gemini 3 in 1965. When he eventually attempted to eat his packed lunch, however, the bread began disintegrating, and its crumbs were floating around all over the place in the cabin. When politicians heard about the sneaky sandwich, they voiced their concerns about the dangers of crumbs interfering with the equipment.

SUPER-STELLAR FACTS ABOUT

As the **ISS ZOOMS** around **EARTH** every **92 minutes,** the **SUN** comes **up and goes down** about **16 times a day.**

ASTRONAUTS have to **DRINK OUT OF POUCHES WITH STRAWS** so their juice or coffee doesn't fly around everywhere!

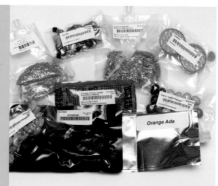

Astronauts' **PEE** goes into a **cleaning system** and is **turned back** into **DRINKING WATER!**

On the **International Space Station, SALT AND PEPPER** come in **LIQUID FORM** so they **don't float** off and **clog up the air vents.**

Crew members were treated to a **PIZZA NIGHT IN SPACE** when NASA sent them **a special meal kit.**

LIFE IN SPACE

When they **return to Earth,** astronauts can **BARELY WALK** because their **bones** and **muscles** have gotten so **WEAK** without gravity.

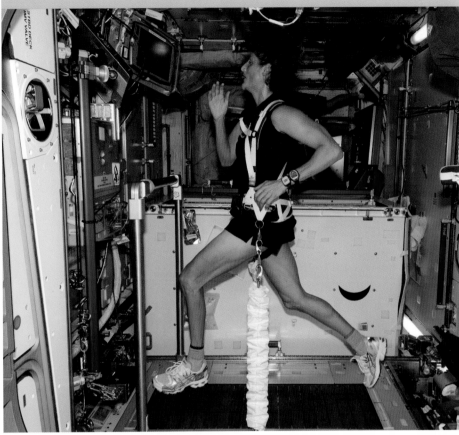

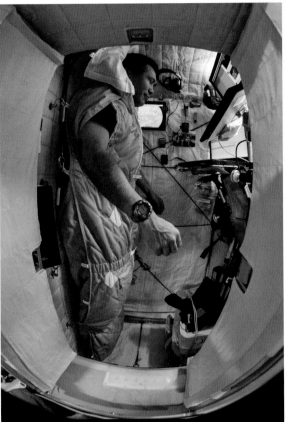

There's **no "down"** in space, so astronauts **can't lie down to SLEEP**— instead, they **strap themselves** and their **sleeping bag to a wall.**

OBJECTS AND TOOLS have to be **SECURED** with Velcro and duct tape so they **DON'T FLOAT AWAY.**

The **LACK OF GRAVITY** means that astronauts **GROW UP TO TWO INCHES TALLER** during a stay on the space station.

(5 cm)

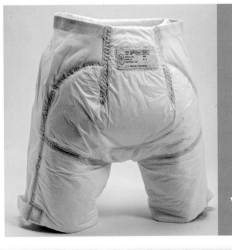

Working **SEVEN HOURS STRAIGHT** in mega-constricting suits means that astronauts must sometimes **WEAR DIAPERS.**

QUIZ WHIZ

You've read tons of **weird facts** about sea and space. The question is, can you remember them all?

1 An underwater mermaid sculpture in the Bahamas sits next to a ...
a. Violin
b. Piano
c. Guitar
d. Drum kit

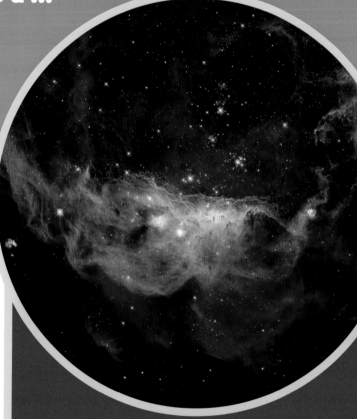

2 Which of these meal kits did NASA send to astronauts as a treat?
a. Pizza
b. Fajitas
c. Curry
d. Stew

3 What is the nickname of the Hubble Space Telescope's birthday tapestry?
a. "Space Waves"
b. "Outer-Space Ocean"
c. "Cosmic Reef"
d. "Celestial Seas"

4. What type of animal is an "underwater firework"?

a. Octopus
b. Crab
c. Sea star
d. Jellyfish

5. Astronauts must exercise for a minimum of ...

a. Two hours a week
b. Four hours a week
c. Two hours a day
d. Four hours a day

6. How do pistol shrimp keep predators at bay?

a. Spraying water
b. Making loud noises
c. Firing bubble bullets
d. Shooting sand balls

7. Aeolid nudibranchs use the stingers from jellyfish as ...

a. Camouflage
b. Weapons
c. Decoration
d. Medicine

8. Leafy sea dragons are known to be not very good at ...

a. Swimming
b. Camouflage
c. Sleeping
d. Eating

Answers: 1. b, 2. a, 3. c, 4. d, 5. c, 6. c, 7. b, 8. a

INDEX

INDEX

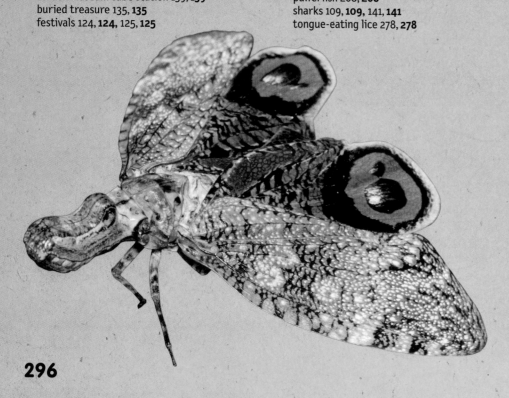

INDEX

INDEX

PHOTO CREDITS

FRONT COVER: (UP LE), Joel Sartore/National Geographic Image Collection; (UP RT), NASA/Roscosmos; (CTR LE), Butterfly Hunter/SS; (CTR RT), Joel Sartore/National Geographic Image Collection; (LO LE), Joel Sartore/National Geographic Image Collection; (LO RT), object_photo/SS; (blue craft paper texture), K.N.V./SS; (vector world tourist attractions), Katsiaryna Pleshakova/SS; (orange paper texture), Luria/SS; **SPINE:** Joel Sartore/National Geographic Image Collection; **BACK COVER:** (UP), Piotr Naskrecki/MP; (CTR), Catmando/AD; (LO), Jürgen Otto; **FRONT MATTER:** 1, Joel Sartore/National Geographic Image Collection; 4, Yousuf Khan/Anadolu Agency/GI; 5 (UP), Nikolay N. Antonov/AD; 5 (LO), Christian Schwarz; 6 (UP), Joel Sartore/Photo Ark/MP; 6 (LO), Roberto/AD; 7 (UP), © 2004 MBARI; 7 (LO LE), dennisvdw/iStock/GI; 7 (LO RT), George Steinmetz/National Geographic Image Collection; 8 (UP), Cathy Keifer/AD; 8 (LO LE), Kiyoshi Ota/Bloomberg/GI; 8 (LO RT), Catmando/AD; 8-9, Cavan Images/AL; 9 (UP), Alex Robinson/AWL Images Ltd; 9 (LO), Farinoza/AD; 10 (LE), ValentinValkov/AD; 10 (RT), ericlefrancais1/AD; 11 (UP), mrks_v/AD; 11 (LO), yutthana-landscape/SS; **CHAPTER 1:** 12 (UP), Renan Ozturk/National Geographic Image Collection; 12 (CTR), cynoclub/AD; 12 (LO LE), Dorte Mandrup A/S/MIR; 12 (LO RT), wacomka/AD; 13 (UP LE), Yousuf Khan/Anadolu Agency/GI; 13 (UP RT), Marcio Cabral/Caters News Agency; 13 (LO LE), bHaptics; 13 (LO RT), Zhou Hua/Xinhua/GI; 14 (calendar), linear_design/SS; 14 (UP LE), Dixi_/AD; 14 (UP CTR), streptococcus/AD; 14 (UP RT), michaelstephan-fotografie/SS; 14 (LO LE), Ruth Black/AD; 14 (LO CTR), Alexstar/AD; 14 (LO RT), exclusive-design/AD; 15 (UP LE), sdecoret/AD; 15 (UP RT), POYZ8080/SS; 15 (CTR LE), Bikej Barakus/AD; 15 (CTR RT), soupstock/AD; 15 (wolf), Miceking/AD; 15 (LO), Lindsay Garza/SS; 16, Vanguard Industries Inc.; 17 (UP), Caters News Agency; 17 (LO), bHaptics; 18 (UP), cynoclub/AD; 18 (CTR), Riko Best/AD; 18 (LO), wacomka/AD; 19, Wayhome Studio/AD; 20 (UP), Richard Ellis/AL; 20 (LO), AP Photo/Bob Brawdy; 21 (UP), Ton Koene/AL; 21 (LO), Pressmaster/SS; 22 (paw print), AAVAA/SS; 22, Lance/AD; 23 (UP), John G Mabanglo/EPA/SS; 23 (LO), Lance/AD; 24 (paw print), AAVAA/SS; 24 (UP), Doug Allan/NPL; 24 (LO), Sylvain Cordier/NPL; 25 (UP), D. R. Schrichte/Blue Planet Archive; 25 (CTR), Eko/AD; 25 (LO), Tony Wu/NPL; 26 (paw print), AAVAA/SS; 26 (UP), Phil Savoie/NPL; 26 (LO), Piotr Naskrecki/MP; 27, Konrad Wothe/NPL; 28 (camera), CAPToro/SS; 28, Steven Kovacs/Biosphoto/MP; 29 (UP), Lukas Gallo/Caters News Agency; 29 (CTR), Marcio Cabral/Caters News Agency; 29 (LO), Alan Murphy/Caters News Agency; 30 (camera), CAPToro/SS; 30-31, Renan Ozturk/National Geographic Image Collection; 32-33, m.elyoussoufi/AD; 34 (newspaper), T-Kot/SS; 34 (UP LE), Eric Isselée/AD; 34 (UP RT), Alfonso Fanjul Peraza; 34 (CTR), Courtesy National Museums of Scotland; 34 (LO LE), Eric Isselée/AD; 34 (LO CTR), Eric Isselée/AD; 34 (LO RT), Dorte Mandrup A/S/MIR; 35 (UP LE), Yousuf Khan/Anadolu Agency/GI; 35 (UP RT), Asif Hassan/GI; 35 (CTR), Zhou Hua/Xinhua via GI; 35 (LO LE), Hennen D.A., Means J.C., Marek P.E.; 35 (LO RT), Brian Friedman/SS; **CHAPTER 2:** 36 (UP), Rudolf Novak/GI; 36 (CTR), cynoclub/AD; 36 (LO LE), Oregon Coastal Flowers; 36 (LO RT), Victoria/AD; 37 (UP LE), Thomas Marent/MP; 37 (UP CTR), Matthew Micah Wright/GI; 37 (LO LE), Walter Bibikow/GI; 37 (LO CTR), dottedyeti/AD; 37 (RT), dpruter/iStock/GI; 38, rvlsoft/AD; 39 (UP), Uwe/AD; 39 (LO LE), Daniel/AD; 39 (LO RT), Richard Bloom/GAP Photos; 40 (UP), Oregon Coastal Flowers; 40 (LO LE), Aleksei/AD; 40 (LO RT), Heather Samelson/Courtesy of Will Weinhold; 41 (UP), Gunter Marx/HI/AL; 41 (LO), Life on white/AL; 42, Michael and Patricia Fogden/MP; 43, Court Whelan/iStock/GI; 44 (UP), Norman Pogson/AL; 44 (LO), Carlos Sanchez Pereyra/AWL Images; 45 (UP), Walter Bibikow/GI; 45 (CTR), Joseph Sohm/AD; 45 (LO), Walter Bibikow/AWL Images; 46 (UP), Matthew Micah Wright/GI; 46 (LO), Dudarev Mikhail/AD; 47 (UP), Krzysztof Wiktor/AD; 47 (LO), Victoria/AD; 48 (UP), Michael R Brown/SS; 48 (LO), CBS Photo Archive/GI; 49, Carsten Peter/National Geographic Image Collection; 50-51, Fractal7/SS; 51, Daria Rybakova/SS; 52 (UP), Mark Sykes/WAWL Images Ltd; 52 (CTR), Brian Cahn/ZUMA Press Wire/AL; 52 (LO), Brian Cahn/ZUMA Press Wire/AL; 53 (UP), Brian Cahn/ZUMA Wire/AL; 53 (LO), Gopher Hole Museum; 54 (UP), Atomazul/AD; 54 (CTR LE), Colaimages/AL; 54 (CTR RT), "Shrek Forever After" © 2010 DreamWorks Animation LLC. All Rights Reserved/PictureLux/The Hollywood Archive/AL; 54 (LO LE), Andjela/AD; 54 (LO RT), stockphoto mania/AD; 55 (UP LE), Dinodia Photos/AL; 55 (CTR), Jeff Bukowski/SS; 55 (CTR RT), Xavier Desmier/Gamma-Rapho/GI; 56, AP Photo/Takhini Hot Pools/Cover Images; 56 (inset), Milena Georgeault/Reuters/AL; 57, davidhoffmann photography/SS; 58 (UP), Citizen of the Planet/AL; 58 (LO), Bill Keough/AFP/GI; 59 (UP), Cow Chip Committee; 59 (LO), Just Another Photographer/SS; 61 (UP), Alexander Shalamov/Dreamstime; 61 (CTR LE), Yingna Cai/SS; 61 (CTR RT), Damien Verrier/SS; 61 (LO), Photononstop/AL; 62 (UP), Bruce Archibald; 62 (LO LE), FLHC24/AL; 62 (LO RT), dottedyeti/AD; 63 (UP), AP Photo/Seth Wenig; 63 (CTR), Catmando/AD; 63 (LO), Olga Mulugeta/Dreamstime; 64 (UP LE), Thomas Marent/MP; 64 (CTR RT), Alexandre Meneghini/Reuters/AL; 64 (LO), Fenolio/Science Source; 65 (UP LE), Todd Pusser/NPL; 65 (UP RT), Joseph Beck/iStock/GI; 65 (LO LE), Gregory Guida/Biosphoto/MP; 65 (LO RT), Jeffrey Greenberg/Universal Images Group/GI; 66 (UP), Bob Kaufman/Alaska.org; 66 (LO), Design Pics Inc/AL; 67 (UP), National Geographic Image Collection; 67 (LO), Jon Sarriugarte; 68 (UP), Inspired By Maps/SS; 68 (LO), Rudolf Novak/GI; 69 (UP), CassielMx/iStock/GI; 69 (LO), Danita Delimont Stock/AWL Images; 70 (UP), Gregory Guida/Biosphoto/MP; 70 (LO), trekandphoto/AD; 71 (UP), Matthew Micah Wright/GI; 71 (LO), Oliver Klimek/AD; **CHAPTER 3:** 72 (UP), SCStock/iStock/GI; 72 (CTR), kikkerdirk/AD; 72 (LO LE), Arthur Morris/GI; 72 (LO RT), Karol Kozlowski/AWL Images; 73 (UP LE), Yaikel Dorta/SS; 73 (UP CTR), Andreas Kay; 73 (LO LE), Babak Tafreshi/Science Source; 73 (RT), Richard Powers; 74 (UP), Gustavo Frazao/AD; 74 (LO), Martin Lindsay/AL; 75 (UP), Diego O. Galeano/SS; 75 (LO), Tony Camacho/Science Source; 76 (UP), Yaikel Dorta/SS; 76 (CTR), Anderson Spinelli/iStock/GI; 76 (LO), Stossi Mammot/AD; 77 (UP), jorge ivan vasquez cuartas/iStock/GI; 77 (CTR), Ricardo Ribas/AL; 77 (LO), baibaz/AD; 78 (UP LE), Rafael/AD; 78 (UP RT), Felipe Bittioli; 78 (LO), Richard Powers; 79 (UP), SCStock/iStock/GI; 79 (LO), Lukas Blazek/Dreamstime; 80-81, Olga_Gavrilova/iStock/GI; 81 (LE), ImageBROKER/AWL Images; 81 (RT), Karol Kozlowski/AWL Images; 82 (LE), Natura Vive; 82 (CTR), Natura Vive; 82 (LO), Diego Grandi/SS; 83 (UP), Walter Bibikow/AWL Images; 83 (LO), Huilo Huilo/Solent News & Photo Agency; 84, worldclassphoto/SS; 84 (inset), Tristan Tan/SS; 85, Doma Collective; 85 (inset), Doma Collective; 86 (UP), Pawel Toczynski/The Image Bank/GI; 86 (LO), Babak Tafreshi/Science Source; 87 (UP), Ksenia Ragozina/SS; 87 (LO), Jonathan Chancasana/SS; 88 (UP), Martin Zabala/Xinhua/AL; 88 (LO), Mazzel1986/Dreamstime; 89 (UP), Phillip/AD; 89 (LO), Pictures Ltd./Corbis/GI; 90 (UP), Pete Oxford/MP; 90 (CTR), Claudio Contreras/NPL; 90 (LO), Albert Beukhof/AL; 91 (UP LE), imageBROKER/AL; 91 (UP RT), Andreas Kay; 91 (CTR), Pete Oxford/MP; 91 (LO), Francisco Gomez; 92 (UP), lamyai/AD; 92 (CTR), dudlajzov/AD; 92 (LO), Olga Lyubkin/AD; 93 (UP LE), photomelon/AD; 93 (UP RT), Pixel-Shot/AD; 93 (CTR RT), Kristians Berents/Wirestock/AD; 93 (LO LE), Sergio Moraes/Reuters/AL; 93 (LO CTR), Oscar Garces/iStock/GI; 93 (LO RT), Marcos Brindicci/Reuters/AL; 94 (UP), USO/iStock/GI; 94 (LO), Arthur Morris/Corbis/GI; 95 (UP LE), Steve Gettle/Minden Pictures; 95 (UP RT), Calin Hertioga/Moment; 95 (LO), Joel Sartore/National Geographic Creative; 96-97, Jens Otte/iStock/GI; 97 (UP), Karol Kozlowski/AWL Images; 97 (LO), Jens Otte/iStock/GI; 98 (UP), renelo/iStock/GI; 98 (LO), Interfoto/AWL Images; 99 (UP), ephotocorp/AL; 99 (LO), Roberto/AD; 100 (UP), Aleksandar Tomic/AL; 100 (LO), Rodrigo Soldon; 101 (UP), snaptitude/AD; 101 (LO), Yesica Fisch/AP/SS; 102 (UP), Luis Echeverri Urrea/SS; 102 (LO), Media Drum World/AL; 103 (UP), gcoles/iStock/GI; 103 (LO), kikkerdirk/AD; 104 (UP LE), Nigel Pavitt/AWL Images; 104 (UP RT), Coulanges/SS; 104 (CTR), Nature in Stock/AL; 104 (LO), Bence Mate/NPL; 105 (UP LE), Kseniia Mnasina/SS; 105 (UP RT), Konrad Wothe/NPL; 105 (LO), Amazon-Images/AL; 106 (UP), Felipe Bittioli; 106 (LO), gcoles/iStock/GI; 107 (UP), Doma Collective; 107 (LO), Martin Zabala/Xinhua/AL; **CHAPTER 4:** 108 (UP), Jarretera/AD; 108 (CTR), olympus E5/AD; 108 (LO LE), Cameron Smith/GI; 108 (LO RT), LMspencer/SS; 109 (UP), Colin Underhill/AL; 109 (LO LE), Gennaro Di Rosa/SS; 109 (LO CTR), Reinhard Holzl/ImageBroker/GI; 109 (RT), Carl de Souza/AFP/GI; 110, Tony French/AL; 111 (UP), cristianbalate/AD; 111 (LO), sam74100/iStock/GI; 112 (UP), Leonardo Papera/AWL Images; 112 (LO), Marko Ignjatovic/iStock/GI; 113 (UP LE), Westend61 GmbH/AL; 113 (UP RT), Reinhard Holzl/ImageBroker/GI; 113 (LO), sjhaytov/iStock/GI; 114 (UP), Science Centre AHHAA; 114 (LO), Carl de Souza/AFP/GI; 115 (UP), Jarretera/AD; 115 (LO), Nikolay N. Antonov/AD; 116 (UP), Gennaro Di Rosa/SS; 116 (LO), Tim Moran Thewainhousehotmail C/SS; 117 (UP), Franziska Kraufmann/picture alliance/GI; 117 (LO), NOTIMEX/Foto/Carlos BaezCBC/SPO/Newscom; 118 (UP LE), dirk94025/AD; 118 (CTR RT), Mariusz Cieszewski/Ministry of Foreign Affairs of the Republic of Poland; 118 (LO), AA World Travel Library/AL; 119 (UP), Kiev.Victor/SS; 119 (CTR), Massimo Borchi/4Corners; 119 (LO), emperorcosar/AD; 120 (UP), Design Pics Inc/AL; 120 (LO), fhm/Moment/GI; 121, Karl Hausammann/AL; 122 (UP), © Matej Kren/Jim Monk/AL; 122 (LO), Patryk Kosmider/SS; 123 (UP), S.O.E/SS; 123 (CTR), Xinhua News Agency/GI; 123 (LO), Dirk Waem/Pool/Photonews/GI; 124 (UP), Konstantin Belovtov/SS; 124 (CTR LE), Ben Birchall/PA Wire/GI; 124 (LO RT), Doug Pearson/AWL Images; 125 (UP LE), Andrew Lloyd/Loop Images/GI; 125 (CTR RT), Matt Cardy/Stringer/GI; 125 (LO), Cristina Candel/© Culture Trip; 126 (UP), Dwra/SS; 126 (LO), LMspencer/SS; 127 (UP), Nigel Bowles/AL; 127 (LO), Jean Kobben/AD; 128 (LE), New Africa/AD; 128 (RT), Jody/AD; 129 (UP), S.O.E/AD; 129 (CTR LE), Pale.photography/AD; 129 (CTR RT), Tomaz/AD; 129 (LO LE), Adrian/AD; 129 (LO RT), Piotr Krzeslak/AD; 130 (UP), Neverse/Dreamstime; 130 (LO), Stringer/AFP/GI; 131, Leon Neal/Staff/GI; 132, venemama/AD; 132-133, chanchai duangdoosan/iStock/GI; 133, Menno Schaefer/AD; 134 (UP), blickwinkel/AL; 134

NATIONAL GEOGRAPHIC and Yellow Border Design are trademarks of the National Geographic Society, used under license.

Since 1888, the National Geographic Society has funded more than 14,000 research, conservation, education, and storytelling projects around the world. National Geographic Partners distributes a portion of the funds it receives from your purchase to National Geographic Society to support programs including the conservation of animals and their habitats. To learn more, visit natgeo.com/info.

For more information, visit nationalgeographic.com, call 1-877-873-6846, or write to the following address:

National Geographic Partners, LLC
1145 17th Street NW
Washington, DC 20036-4688 U.S.A.

For librarians and teachers: nationalgeographic.com/books/librarians-and-educators

More for kids from National Geographic: natgeokids.com

National Geographic Kids magazine inspires children to explore their world with fun yet educational articles on animals, science, nature, and more. Using fresh storytelling and amazing photography, *Nat Geo Kids* shows kids ages 6 to 14 the fascinating truth about the world—and why they should care. **natgeo.com/subscribe**

For rights or permissions inquiries, please contact National Geographic Books Subsidiary Rights: bookrights@natgeo.com

Hardcover ISBN: 978-1-4263-7453-1
Reinforced library binding ISBN: 978-1-4263-7595-8

The publisher would like to thank the book team: Claire Lister and Kathryn Williams, project editors; Julide Dengel, senior designer; Lori Epstein, photo manager; Sarah Smithies, photo researcher; Kate Ford, designer; Anna Claybourne, Richard Mead, Georgina Brown, and Sara Stanford, contributing writers; Alix Inchausti, senior production editor; Lauren Sciortino and David Marvin, associate designers; and the packaging team at Dynamo Limited.

Printed in South Korea
23/SPSK/1